JACOB'S LADDER:
KABBALISTIC ALLEGORY IN RUSSIAN LITERATURE

BORDERLINES:
RUSSIAN AND EAST EUROPEAN —
JEWISH STUDIES

Editorial board:

Mikhail Krutikov (University of Michigan)

Harriet Murav (University of Illinois, Urbana-Champaign), Series Editor

Alice Nakhimovsky (Colgate University)

David Shneer (University of Denver)

Anna Shternshis (University of Toronto)

ACADEMIC
STUDIES
PRESS

JACOB'S LADDER:
Kabbalistic Allegory in Russian Literature

Marina Aptekman

BOSTON
2011

Library of Congress Cataloging-in-Publication Data:
A catalog record for this book is available from the Library of Congress.

Copyright © 2011 Academic Studies Press
All rights reserved

ISBN 978-1-61811-821-9

Book design by Ivan Grave
On the cover: "Ladder to Heaven." Illustration from *Utriusque Cosmi,* by R. Fludd, 1619

Published by Academic Studies Press in 2011
28 Montfern Avenue
Brighton, MA 02135, USA
press@academicstudiespress.com
www.academicstudiespress.com

O, please, reveal to me that wondrous ladder that descends from the heights of Heaven to our miserable Earth, that ladder that only the Wise can climb — but they, those who would learn the Divine Truth, they will ascend higher than the stars and higher than the planets. O, please, God, let me be one of those chosen.

Ivan Lopukhin. The Spiritual Knight

Table of Contents

Introduction:
Kabbalah Then and Now: a Historical Perspective   11

A Quest for Moral Perfection:
Kabbalistic Allegory in Eighteenth-Century
Masonic Literature   39

Knowledge Hidden in Letters:
Alchemic Kabbalah and Russian Romantic
Literature   106

In the Beginning Was the Word:
Magical Kabbalah, the Occult Revival,
and the Linguistic Mysticism of the Silver Age   153

Modernism and Kabbalah:
Linguistic Mysticism in the Literary Doctrine
of the Russian Silver Age   188

Conclusion   226

Selected Bibliography   229

Index   243

Acknowledgements

This book is a result of ten years of research and reading in various libraries and archival collections, and I am thankful for everyone who helped me on this long way with guidance, feedback and encouragement. Moshe Idel and Noam Zion introduced me to the boundless world of Kabbalah long ago at the Shalom Hartman Institute of Jerusalem. Mikhail Vaiskopf and Helen Tolstaya have been always great friends and wonderful teachers. For years I have been enjoying our discussions on Kabbalah, Russian Freemasonry, Judaism and Russian literature. Without them this book would never be envisioned. My professors at Brown University Alexander Levitsky, Svetlana Evdokimova and Robert Mathiesen helped me with the first drafts of this manuscript with their generous insight, erudition and intellectual rigor. I am deeply grateful to Jane Taubman and Bernice Rosenthal who read the first variant of this manuscript and provided me with many helpful comments. I was also fortunate to enjoy a perpetual support of Abbott Gleason who inspired me at the moments of frustration and hesitation and provided me indispensable psychological boost. Without his encouragement this book might have never been finished. Thanks to all those who provided feedback to my articles and conference presentations on various subjects and topics in link to this book, in particular Roman Timenchik,

Michael Wachtel, Lena Silard, Ilya Serman, Anthony Cross and Mark Al'tshuller. Andrei Serkov and Maria Endel have shared with me their deep knowledge of Russian Freemasonic archives as well as their own principal work on the subject. I am grateful to Nancy Pollak for her enthusiastic support and intellectual stimulation, to Julia Hersey-Meitov for her kind help with poetic translations, and to my editor Marilyn Miller for her patience with my endless rewritings and multiple questions. My special thanks go to everyone at the Academic Studies Press: Igor Nemirovsky, the series editors Mikhail Krutikov and Harriet Murav, and to my anonymous reviewers for extremely stimulating and practical guidelines and a constant belief in the future of this project.

The work on this book was sustained by the generous support of the Department of Slavic Languages of Brown University, Hillel Foundation of Brown University, American Councils for International Education, and the Provost Office of Hobart and William Smith Colleges.

I devote this manuscript to my parents, Lina and David, and my husband Valery, whose constant emotional assistance helped me survive through all these years of completing this manuscript.

INTRODUCTION
Kabbalah Then and Now: a Historical Perspective

Jewish mystical thought, widely known as Kabbalah, remains one of the most grossly misunderstood parts of Judaism. In traditional Judaism, Kabbalah refers to a set of esoteric teachings meant to define the inner meaning of both the Hebrew Bible and traditional Rabbinic literature, as well as to explain the significance of Jewish religious observances. Kabbalistic philosophy has long been the subject of speculative studies, which stemmed either from simple ignorance or from a general confusion between the original Jewish philosophical teaching and its later magical adaptations. Consequently, during the last few centuries, outside the margins of the Jewish religious establishments, Kabbalah has been associated merely with occultism and perceived as a type of Jewish magic.

In recent years, though, people's response to Kabbalah has been changing. Jewish mysticism, for generations practiced only in yeshivas by a few Orthodox Jews, suddenly has turned into a trendy New Age practice, thus becoming an integral part of popular culture. Madonna has published kabbalistic stories for children. Demi Moore publicly witnesses her interest in Jewish mysticism. A fancy retreat center in upstate New York invites everyone to "experience the mystical texts of Kabbalah in your own body while encountering a Tai-Chi-based movement conditioning to embody the Divine spirit and reconstruct the Divine essence that underlies all being, in your soul."[1] *Vogue* advertises the new "kabbalistic perfume" called *Tree of Life*; and the author of this manuscript has been recently asked to write a short essay on the importance of kabbalistic practices in fitness for a Russian glamour magazine. However, such interest, although it looks puzzling at first, is certainly not new. During the last thousand years, Gentiles have turned to Kabbalah on multiple occasions and for multiple causes. For centuries — beginning in the early 1200s and arguably continuing until the present day — Kabbalah has functioned as a crossroads of European culture and Jewish mysticism.

The relations between kabbalistic teaching and European philosophy in the West have been already comprehensively acknowledged in academic criticism. From Francis Yates' classical tome *Giordano Bruno and the Hermetic Tradition* to the recently published *The Impact of the Kabbalah in the Seventeenth Century: the Life and Thought of Francis Mercury van Helmont (1614–1698)* by Allison Coudert, the influence of Kabbalah on non-Jewish intellectuals has been extensively studied and analyzed. By contrast, the influence of Kabbalah on Russian philosophy and literature is among the issues that still await a serious scholarly study. There are several reasons for this state of affairs. Russian-born scholars hesitate to include this subject in the scope of their research due to the fact that in the course of the twentieth century it mostly appeared to attract those pseudo-scholars who wished to combat the "almighty Judeo-Masonic conspiracy." Indeed, too often, upon spotting a new publication on the role of Kabbalah in Russian culture in a Moscow or St. Petersburg bookstore, a scholar encounters yet another fresh declaration that "the eighteenth-century Russian masons turned to the black magic of ancient Zionists because of their Masonic interest in the mystical and the supernatural," and that "these writers have influenced the rise of the Russian *intelligentsia* which, in its turn, led Russia to the Revolution and the Zionist rule of Yeltsin and Chubais."[2] In terms of Western research, most scholars of Jewish mysticism consider Kabbalah a strictly Judaic phenomenon. Accordingly, they are typically not interested in discussing its influence on either Russian thought or Russian literature. Slavic scholars, by contrast, are not broadly familiar with Jewish mysticism and, therefore, do not feel comfortable touching upon such an obscure subject, especially since the Russian published sources available to the Western reader remain quite limited and are often politically biased. As a result, serious research into this topic is still lacking.

Yet the question of the role of Kabbalah in Russian literary tradition is quite important. Kabbalistic symbolism has been broadly used and encoded in Russian belles lettres of certain periods. Understanding it is crucial in helping the reader not only to decipher many important metaphors and images in literary works that now seem peculiar and enigmatic, but also in helping change the scholarly perspective of the role of mystical and magical Jewish imagery in Russian literature. Such an understanding also proves that the majority of so-called "kabbalistic" concepts used in such anti-Semitic essays as Pavel Florensky's *Israel in Past, Present, and Future* or Vasilii Rozanov's *Ekhad or Thirteen Wounds of Yushchinsky* did not originated in Jewish philosophy but in Russian literary imagery based on the largely mythological stereotypes. These stereotypes created a particular interpretation of Kabbalah that has predominated in Russian anti-Semitic works up to the present time, as amply demonstrated by numerous pamphlets distributed by the National-Patriotic political camp. This book analyzes the process of the formation and gradual development of these stereotypes and their appeal to targeted audiences.

Until recently, most research discussed the use of kabbalistic motifs in Russian literature without distinguishing them from other occult elements that intrigued Russian intellectuals. However, lately there has been a rise of interest in the study of Kabbalah in Russian thought. Russian scholars Konstantin Burmistrov and Maria Endel have recently produced a number of articles on the place of Kabbalah in the doctrine of Russian Freemasonry. Burmistrov has also discussed the influence of Kabbalah on early twentieth-century Russian philosophy. American scholar Judith Kornblatt has analyzed the influence of Kabbalah on the writings of Vladimir Soloviev. Nikolai Bogomolov has briefly touched on the issue of occult kabbalistic symbolism in the poetry of Russian Silver Age, and Israeli scholar Mikhail Vaiskopf has discussed the question of kabbalistic allegory in Russian Romanticism.[3] Still, in comparison with other topics, this theme remains under-investigated; and, moreover, none of these studies either argue for the presence of the specific genre of a "kabbalistic text" in Russian literature or name those literary devices that construct such a text. Even in recent literary studies, such as Mikhail Vaiskopf's book, Kabbalah has not been analyzed as a particular type of mystical poetics. Instead, authors have concentrated primarily on historical and religious or philosophical questions, rather than offering a detailed close literary analysis of the imagery and narrative forms that characterize the development of the kabbalistic narrative in Russian literary works. The existing scholarship on the influence of Kabbalah on Russian literature is still limited to the discussion of the role of kabbalistic symbolism in disjointed literary works that belong to various historical eras or literary schools.

While scholars have successfully presented the historical and cultural background that shaped the interest of Russian thinkers in Kabbalah during particular periods, they have aspired neither to provide a complete analysis of the evolution of the perception of Kabbalah in Russian consciousness, nor to show the reflection of this evolution in Russian literature. By contrast, this volume follows the evolution of kabbalistic symbolism in Russian intellectual culture as reflected in Russian literature from the end of the eighteenth century to the beginning of the twentieth. The most important sources for this manuscript are found in the archival collections of Widener Library at Harvard University, the New York Public Library, private possessions, and major Moscow and St. Petersburg archives (the Russian State Library, the Russian National Library, and the Russian State Archives of Literature and Art).

Historical research has been combined with a detailed analysis of literary criticism on Russian and Western Romanticism and Modernism, Russian eighteenth-century literature, and Russian Freemasonry. This volume explores Jewish and Christian mystical philosophy and esotericism, cultural history and the history of ideas, Western historical periods and literary movements, and Russian media. However, the main focus of this book is the close study of literary works presented in their broad cultural and historical context. This investigation covers the reflection of kabbalistic allegory in Russian poetry and prose over the course of two centuries, with special attention to Russian pre-Romantic literary works of the last decades of the eighteenth century, Romanticism, and the Silver Age. This coverage includes the most famous authors of these periods as well as the virtually unknown or forgotten.

Recently, a new trend in Kabbalah scholarship has developed, which is oriented towards studying kabbalistic texts as a poetic narrative rather than just theosophical or mystical-experiential literature.[4] While this book intends to look at texts originally written as literary, not theosophical, pieces, the majority of these texts followed specific literary codes and tropes that originated from authentic theosophical kabbalistic texts. The methodological goal of this study is to identify and interpret those specific linguistic and metaphoric devices that formed particular "kabbalistic" allegorical "codes" in Russian literature, which over the time began to be used as typical stereotypes for any writer who adhered to the use of kabbalistic allegory in either poetry or fiction. Thus, rather than simply studying the influence of kabbalistic thought on various Russian writers, this work argues for the existence of a tradition of kabbalistic narrative in Russian literature and shows the development of this tradition from the late eighteenth to the early twentieth century.

This argument encompasses not only issues involving the written text, but also those cultural factors that played a significant role in the interpretive process of kabbalistic symbolism in Russian literary works. Further, this study advances an analysis of the mystical poetics created by Kabbalah through a structuralist and culturally-semiotic reading that on the one hand, can ignite interest in the mystical and poetic endeavors of those Russian authors who have been influenced by Kabbalah, and on the other hand, will show the major elements characteristic of this "kabbalistic" narrative. Thus, from a wide body of literary works, only the texts that most clearly reflect the typical literary interpretation of Kabbalah during certain particular periods have been chosen. A detailed study of cultural semiotics (i.e., various cultural codes) that corresponded to the particular interpretation and use of specific models of "kabbalistic allegory" further advances the literary analysis. The theoretical conclusions presented in this study are based on closely studied literary material as well as secondary sources such as memoirs, newspaper articles, and non-literary works that, when presented together, help to deconstruct established clichés and argue for the development of a specific genre in Russian literature that can be understood only through the prism of a broad cultural appreciation and interpretation of Kabbalah as theosophy and poetics.

The close reading of a range of texts serves as the basis for an analysis of the practical application of three central kabbalistic allegories to Russian letters: the allegory of divine emanations (*sefirot*), the allegory of Wisdom (*Hokhmah*), and that of primordial Adam (*Adam Kadmon*). The book consists of five chapters. The first chapter offers the classification of diverse eighteenth-century Russian kabbalistic texts and sources, the vast majority of which remain unpublished. It then discusses the role of three central kabbalistic allegories in the Freemasonic literature of the second half of the eighteenth century. The chapter establishes the origins of these images, discusses their interpretation in Russian Masonic non-literary texts, and shows their transformation in major eighteenth-century literary works. This part of the book helps to fully illuminate the important place that kabbalistic allegory occupied in Russian pre-Romantic literature and enables a better understanding of the first stage of the dissemination of kabbalistic images in Russian literary circles, which would later provide a base for the further development of kabbalistic symbolism. Unlike the works of Burmistrov and Endel, which primarily concentrate on the study of kabbalistic imagery in eighteenth-century non-literary texts, this chapter aims to focus on the role of kabbalistic imagery in Russian literary pre-Romantic consciousness.

The second chapter discusses the mutation of kabbalistic imagery in the works of Russian romantic writers. It argues that in the early nineteenth century the Russian understanding of kabbalistic teaching underwent a significant transformation. In eighteenth-century Masonic archives, the quantity of magically oriented materials is considerably less than the number of materials on ethical and mystical themes. Russian philosophical poetry of that period, written mostly under the influence of Masonic ideology, thus shows less interest in magical Kabbalah than in the ethical mystical allegories of Adam Kadmon, Wisdom, and *sefirot*. Occult and alchemical texts, although widespread among eighteenth-century

Freemasons, had no significant influence on Russian eighteenth-century literature and achieved popularity among literary circles only between 1810 and 1820. In the second decade of the nineteenth century, Russian intellectuals began to perceive Kabbalah as a magical science rather than a mystical philosophy. They brought forward the concept of kabbalistic "scientific mysticism," which is often referred to as *kabbalistika* rather than *Kabbalah* in Russian literature of this period. The chapter analyzes the development of this approach, which gradually reduced the meaning of Kabbalah to simple numerological magic in the works of the younger generation of Russian romantic writers.

In the 1840s, Romantic "scientific" mysticism began to fall out of favor and was progressively replaced by materialistic positivism. By the mid-nineteenth century, the interest in kabbalistic scientific magic gradually lost its place in Russian literature. The third and fourth chapters analyze the role of this new interpretation of Kabbalah in the poetic works of Russian authors of the Silver Age. The close literary analysis of these works serves as an example of the practical embodiment of modernist theory: that magical kabbalistic symbolism can be used as a tool in an attempt to reconstruct the world prior to Adam's fall — the era when language was powerful enough to create rather than describe reality. The two prior Russian interpretations of kabbalistic allegories of Wisdom, Adam Kadmon, and *sefirot* — the magical and the mystical, fuse together in the literature of Silver Age in an attempt to construct a new artistic philosophy. These chapters also briefly touch upon the role that the romantic and modernist interpretation of kabbalistic symbolism played in the formation of the "kabbalistic" aspect of the Judeo-Masonic myth that represented Kabbalah as a secret Judeo-Masonic magical teaching. A detailed analysis of the Judeo-Masonic mythology is beyond the scope of this study. However, this work aspires to significantly change the scholarly perspective of the roots of "kabbalistic" stereotypes in twentieth-century anti-Semitic propaganda by proving that the interpretation of the kabbalistic imagery in anti-Semitic political works that formed around 1905–1917 mirrors and elaborates on those particular cultural semiotics of Kabbalah that originated in Russian romantic literary circles and became widespread in the literary milieus of the early twentieth century.

The development of kabbalistic allegory in the Russian literary tradition cannot be fully comprehended without first analyzing its evolution within European philosophy. Kabbalah arrived from the West; therefore, it is necessary to trace the phases in the gradual formation of the body of texts that eventually reached Russia in the middle of the eighteenth century. As already noted, during the last thousand years Gentiles have turned to Kabbalah on numerous occasions and for numerous reasons. Whereas some were interested in its theoretical mysticism, others considered Kabbalah an occult doctrine and used it as a practical manual for magical purposes. There were scholars who tried to find in kabbalistic teaching the traces of lost primordial knowledge, and those who believed that its postulates would reform established religious traditions. However, as K. Burmistrov pointed out, no single Christian kabbalist tradition existed; therefore, when discussing such phenomena as Christian Kabbalah, we should rather refer to a certain type of comprehension of Jewish mystical teaching in non-Jewish consciousness.[5] For many Christian apprentices of Kabbalah, their interest in kabbalistic doctrine went hand in hand with that of other non-dogmatic religious teachings. As a result, the scholar has to be extremely accurate while discussing and tracing kabbalistic images in Christian thought, since many of them have parallels in Gnosticism or Neo-Platonism.

The body of kabbalistic literature is very large and the aim of this work is not by any means to shed new light on the development of Kabbalah in the West. Yet a brief summary of its development will introduce the reader to the background necessary for a later focus on Russian literary works. During the last century, secular scholarship has applied various approaches to the study of Kabbalah, from classical works by Gershom Scholem to more recent studies by Yehuda Liebes and Moshe Idel. While the classical tradition, started by Scholem, has illuminated kabbalistic texts mostly from historical, theosophical, or mystical-experiential perspectives, the newer research, represented, for example, by Michael Fishbane or Nathan

Wolsky, has contributed to the study of kabbalistic narrative as a literary text, concentrating on its mystical poetics.[6]

In order to examine kabbalistic narrative, it is important to name and identify those particular poetic images that originated in Jewish kabbalistic tradition as philosophical allegories but simultaneously can be also clearly regarded as literary metaphors. Those images form a special type of mystical poetics that is essential for our understanding of the place that Kabbalah occupied in the Russian literary imagination. It is also important to summarize and briefly analyze the particular narrative structure that was characteristic of the most essential kabbalistic work, the *Zohar*, since this structure was widely used and interpreted in Russian literary works that were influenced by kabbalistic mysticism. Two major aspects in theosophical Jewish Kabbalah also require explanation, as they later evolved into two separate Christian traditions, the mystical and the occult, which in some historical periods either merged with or detached from each other. The understanding of the constituents of each of these two traditions prior to the beginning of the modern period will assist in tracing the later development of kabbalistic hermeneutics in eighteenth-century Europe, and consequently in the modern Russian literary tradition.

A detailed analysis of Jewish mystical literature remains outside the boundaries of this research; therefore we will concentrate here on only few texts that belong to this tradition. The first is the early Jewish mystical text, *Sefer Yetzirah* (*The Book of Creation*), which is devoted to speculation concerning God's creation of the world and its present structure.[7] *Sefer Yetzirah* describes the universe as being created through numerological and linguistic principles and introduces the concept of ten primal numbers, known as *Sefirot*, which, in combination with the twenty-two letters of the Hebrew alphabet, represent the plan of Creation, of all higher and lower things, or "the body of the universe." According to *Sefer Yetzirah*, the first emanation from the spirit of God was the *ruach* (spirit or air) that produced fire, which, in its turn, generated water.[8] As the numbers from two to ten are derived from the number one, so the ten *Sefirot* are derived from one, the spirit of God. God, however, is both the beginning and end of the *Sefirot*, "their end being in their beginning and their beginning in their end, even as the flame is connected with the ashes."⁹ Hence the *Sefirot* must not be conceived as emanations in the ordinary sense of the word, but rather as modifications of the divine spirit.

According to *Sefer Yetzirah*, the twenty-two letters of the alphabet produced the material world, for they are the formative powers of all existence and development. By means of these elements the actual creation of the world took place, and the ten *Sefirot*, which before this had only an ideal existence, became realities. Both the universe and mankind are viewed in *Sefer Yetzirah* in as products of the combination these mystical letters.¹⁰ The linguistic theories of the author of *Sefer Yetzirah* are the fundamental component of his philosophy. *Sefer Yetzirah* introduces the idea that later would become essential for Kabbalah: the idea that God created heaven and earth by means of divine alphabet.

The *creative methods* (i.e., various magical and mystical formulas based on various letters and numbers) discussed in the *Sefer Yetzirah* served as the basis for a new type of "linguistic mysticism." This new type of mysticism was founded on the belief that a mystic could establish personal contact with the divine realm through the specific principles of numerical and linguistic speculation. The first such method, called *gematria*, meant discovering the numerical meaning of the word and establishing a connection with words of the same numerical meaning. The second method, in which letters of a word were used as abbreviations for whole sentences, was named *notarikon*. The third one, *tmura*, dealt with combinations and replacements of words in a sentence according to the principles above. These principles formed that particular role that *Sefer Yetzirah* played in the later literary mystical tradition–it was the first text that defined Creation as a linguistic and semiotic process, which has been recently described by Elliot Wolfson as "a nexus of language, imagination, and world-making that is indicative of poetic orientation to being in the world."¹¹ As Wolfson observes, for the kabbalist, as for the poet, "language, the multivalent vocalizations of the unspeakable name, informs us about the duplicitous nature of truth . . . ; all that exists is a symbolic articulation of the . . . name, the word that is not a sign but a showing that manifests in the façade of reality in its inexhaustible linguistic potentiality."[12]

The majority of scholars define the developments in Kabbalah between the twelfth and the sixteenth century as "early Kabbalah."[13] During this time kabbalistic mysticism separated into two major trends: the ecstatic and the theosophical (also known as theurgical).[14] The theosophical trend concentrated mainly on the study of mystical commentary on the ancient texts that enabled knowledge of and intimate contact with God. The ecstatic Kabbalah focused on the practical applications of kabbalistic symbolism to mystical meditations that could help the mystic achieve contact with the divine realm, and on descriptions of that mystical experience. The techniques that were used in those meditations included letter-numbers combinations, the visualization of *sefirot* as vessels filled with liquid of various colors, and concentration on the words of the commandments.[15]

The goals of both the ecstatic and the theurgical mystics were the same: to reach mystical experience by understanding the true meaning of the Torah and to reveal the divine secrets of being. But for an ecstatic Kabbalist the combinations of divine names revealed the path to these secrets, while the adepts of theurgical Kabbalah concentrated on the mystical importance of Jewish religious duties and the whole Torah as the "face of God." Theurgists and theosophers regarded Jewish religious duties as mystical codes that contained ciphered divine secrets. To understand those secrets, one should not only know and practice these duties, especially the prayers, but also observe and practice them with mystical "intention," or *kavana*. Therefore, moral purity and the virtuous life were an essential part of the theurgist's mystical practices.

The development of kabbalistic thought in the thirteenth century was marked by the appearance of the most influential book in the history of Kabbalah in Europe, the book of the *Zohar* (*The Divine Light*). The *Zohar* is the first text that not only contains particular imagery that is reflected in later texts, but also is notable for its particular plot structure. The book consists of the "classical" zoharic story, a mystical allegorical "travelogue" that soon would become a cliché literary frame widely used in Christian kabbalistic texts

Introduction

first in the West and then in Russia. The original story describes the wanderings of famous Rabbi Shimon Ben Yohai in Palestine. During his wanderings, Ben Yohai meets various people and involves himself in philosophical discussions. The composition is filled with numerous interpretations of the Bible, especially Genesis and The Song of Songs, and stresses the importance of a mystical approach to religion. It has multiple fairy-tale features as well, including miraculous donkey drivers, wizards, and wandering desert hermits. The motif of travel is deeply linked to the development of the plot; and the anonymity of most characters signifies their role as "everymen," engaged in a mystical quest in search of spiritual wisdom. It is also important to stress that this is a "mystical" rather than a usual travelogue, since the motif of an earthly journey in the *Zohar* is directly linked with the "heavenly" travels that the human soul experiences during spiritual meditation. This meditation, based usually on prayer and often experienced through visualizing the divine realm through *sefirot*, permits the adept to visit other worlds, receive various visions, and pronounce prophecies. The *Zohar* regards this meditation as a spiritual transformation, similar to death; and the spiritual path of the meditating adept often parallel those of the dead.[16]

According to the text of the *Zohar*, God manifests himself in divine light (in Hebrew *Zohar*), the flow of which is an emanation of the creative energy that actually forged the Creation. The *Zohar* describes this emanation as ten impulses of the divine light, which can be regarded as ten stages of Creation or ten steps by which the divine light comes to earth. The *Zohar* presents *sefirot* as vessels through which the divine energy, *ein-sof*, emanates from the divine realm into the human world. Through this process of emanation, each *sefirah* successfully reveals to humans a particular aspect of divine nature. The *Zohar* characterizes the first *sefirah* as the divine glory (*Keter*, i.e., the origin of Creation), and *Hokhmah* as the second *sefirah* and the first step in the Creation. The other *sefirot* are *Binah* (understanding), *Din* (judgment) *Hesed* (mercy), *Tiferet* (beauty), *Hod* (majesty), *Nezah* (victory), *Yesod* (foundation), and *Malkhut* (kingdom). Together they compose a symbolic figure, known as the "tree of life," that rests on three pillars. The central pillar forms the spine through which the divine dew flows down from the higher realm through the middle world and into the lower spheres, represented as a womb. This metaphor later becomes one of the key allegories of kabbalistic symbolism not only in Jewish but also in Christian Kabbalah and later in kabbalistic alchemy.[17] The highest *sefirah*, *Keter*, plays the role of the divine seed, placed in the divine womb, the *sefirah* of *Hokhmah*, which flows out of *Hokhmah* into the third *sefirah* of *Bihan*, the heavenly mother, and then down into the sea of nothingness. The third *sefirah* thus becomes the river that flows out of its source and is subsequently divided on its way into different streams, until all its tributaries flow into the great sea of the last *sefirah Malkhut*, known also as *Shekhinah*.[18]

The image of *Hokhmah*, or Divine Wisdom, is among the most important in the system of *Zohar*. It is also essential for the understanding of Russian kabbalistic literary texts. In Hebrew in the famous line "in the beginning God created Heaven and Earth," the words *in the beginning* (*bereshit*) suggest a possible double reading, since the word *reshit* comes from the word *rosh*, which means "head."[19] This duality resulted in the belief among some thinkers that the Creation is actually a result of the divine idea of the Deity, his actual "thought" or "wisdom" (in Hebrew, *Hokhmah*). Rabbi Azriel of Gerona writes in his *Explanation of the Ten Sefirot*: "The second *sefirah* is called Wisdom (*Hokhmah*). It is the brain of the Deity, the inner thought, the hidden things, which belong to our Lord, our God. It is the beginning of conceptualization and stands for the angelic power."[20] It is important to note, though, that in Russian mystical works the image of Wisdom (Sophia) is closer to the Jewish *Shekhinah* than to *Hokhmah*, even in those moments when then actual term *Hokhmah* is used. *Shekhinah*, the lowest and the only earthly *sefirah*, is detached from the others by Adam's sin and lost in the material world. Governed by her remembrance of the time when she was united with other *sefirot*, she is constantly searching for the ways to return to her divine "sisters." It is also worth mentioning here that in Kabbalah Creation is seen not as a linear but as a cyclical process, since in this process the divine energy makes a circle and returns to the Godhead. Therefore the Creation is endless and is regarded as an infinite process of *ein-sof* (no-end), just as the essence of God is an infinite *ein-sof*.

Regarded as the conception of Creation, *Hokhmah* is always associated with love and sexual energy. The pictures found in kabbalistic texts portray *sefirot* as the result of mystical intercourse in which a ray of the divine light is rendered as a seed placed by *Hokhmah* in the womb of the divine mother, symbolized by the *sefirah* of *Keter*. Therefore, kabbalistic literature sees *Hokhmah* as the *sefirah* that symbolizes divine love. This love is a bond between God and his creatures, and is physical rather than platonic. As Scholem notes, "The organic symbolism equates the primordial point with the seed sown in the womb of 'the supernal mother,' who is Binah. The womb is brought to fruition through the fertilization of the semen and gives birth to the children who are the emanations."[21] Kabbalah interprets male-female sexual relations as an allegorical representation of the creative "sexual" relation between the *sefirot* and, as a result, reinforces a traditional Jewish focus on marital relations. By contrast with many other esoteric systems, sex in Kabbalah is seen as giving life, not death. For example, one way of uniting with *Shekhinah* is for a male Jew to have intercourse with his wife on the Sabbath.

One of the *Zohar*'s most important idea is that man can affect the cosmic processes by his deeds and thoughts. This idea had great influence on ecstatic Kabbalah, in which prayer was regarded as a meditation that helped man to unite with the divine. An ecstatic kabbalist influenced by the *Zohar* looked at prayer as a tool that would help him to send upwards the impulses which "help to promote greater harmony in the *Sefirotic* realm, and to succeed in bringing down the resulting flow of divine grace and blessing."[22]

The theosophical branch of kabbalistic mysticism that stressed the moral qualities of a mystic over all others became predominant in later, Lurianic Kabbalah, named after the spiritual leader of the school, Rabbi Isaac Luria.[23] In his teaching Luria concentrated not on the idea of the role of divine names in creating the world, but on the place that God and Man both occupied in the process of creation. In his theological system, Luria followed early Kabbalah in its interpretation of *ein-sof*. He asserted that creation took place when God "contracted" his infinite light in order to allow for a "conceptual space" [inside himself] to give birth to the *sefirot* and eventually to the world. Luria called this process *tsimzum* in Hebrew, a word that might be translated as either "condensation" or "withdrawal."[24]

Luria's doctrine primarily concentrated on the allegory of primordial Adam, in Hebrew *Adam Kadmon*, which became the cornerstone of the Lurianic kabbalistic tradition.[25] As with the symbolism of *Hokhmah*, the allegory of Adam Kadmon derives from the duality that exists in the first chapters of the Bible, and, in particular, from two different versions of the story of the creation of man. In Genesis 1:11, man is created as the first of the creatures; in Genesis 2:4, he is created last.[26] This duality resulted in the kabbalistic interpretation of the creation of man, according to which the first man was created not as the last but as the first of all creatures. This first man was called Adam Kadmon, and differed greatly from human beings as we now know them, resembling not so much a material man as a "crystal vessel" full of divine light. In the early Kabbalah the figure of Adam Kadmon served as one of the allegorical representations of the *Tree of Sefirot*, where each *sefirah* represented one part of Adam's body.

The concept of Adam Kadmon can be seen as a natural development of the idea that man has been made in the image of God, and therefore his structure is divine. Luria's theosophy, however, gave a totally new reading to this image. According to Luria's teaching, prior to the moment of the biblical fall the first material man, Adam HaRishon (the first man) and his spiritual ego, Adam Kadmon (the primordial man), had been united as one. God and man had existed in close harmony, and man knew all the secrets of the divine world. The fall of Adam changed this order. The evil forces from the underground world, *qlippoth*, ascended into the world of *sefirot*, and, under pressure, the "crystal vessel" broke into a million pieces, each containing a spark of the divine light. Adam Kadmon was destroyed, and material man, Adam Rishon, lost his eternal life and great knowledge. The exile from Paradise is regarded in Kabbalah as an allegorical exile from *Hokhmah*, i.e., from the Godhead, and thus from unity with God as well.

According to Luria, given that the soul of Adam was the original human soul that contained all the souls of mankind, at the moment of birth each human receives a small piece of the crystal vessel of Adam Kadmon with one spark of the divine light inside. As the major task of a mystic is to reunite himself with God, therefore, the primary aim of man is to rekindle this spark in order to bring oneself back to the source of the divine light and to spiritual reunification with *Hokhmah*. This process of spiritual restoration, called *tikkun* (restoration or mending) in Hebrew, can be achieved by observing moral and religious laws.[27]

The above concepts, adopted by Christian mystics and eventually transplanted onto Russian soil, constituted the basis for the interpretation of kabbalistic allegory in the Russian literary imagination. The onset of Christian kabbalistic tradition is rooted in Renaissance theology.[28] Most Renaissance Christian scholars regarded the study of ancient Jewish wisdom as one step towards the union between the Jews and the Christians, universal religion, and an inauguration of the golden age; consequently, they viewed their study of Kabbalah and Hebrew as primary instruments for deciphering the mysteries of divine creation, signaling the approaching redemption. In Christian kabalistic tradition the central idea of Kabbalah was the idea of the power of the "divine names," united with the belief that all the secrets of divine and earthly beings could be decoded and revealed by manipulation of the names of God as various letters of the Hebrew alphabet. Natural magic (*magia naturalis*) was regarded as a less potent level of Kabbalah, which in its entirety was perceived as the quintessence of magic. The practical application of the "divine names" for magical purposes was further developed in such influential works as Johannes Reuchlin's *De Arte Kabbalistica* (*On the Art of Kabbalah*) and Agrippa of Nettesheim's *De Occulta Philosophia* (*On the Occult Philosophy*) that brought forward the idea that numerous anagrams of the divine name could be used to call upon demons and angels.[29] Agrippa attributed to each demon its own *sefirah* and connected these *sefirot* with astrological signs, which he believed could also be used to summon demons.[30]

The occultists no longer regarded Kabbalah to be an integral part of Judaism. Moreover, they stressed that Jews had misinterpreted and misconstrued kabbalistic concepts and were hostile to the true Kabbalah. However, they constantly promoted the idea that their books originated from primordial tradition and provided their adepts with ancient Jewish wisdom. As a result, in the mind of the average person, Kabbalah gradually became broadly associated with the study of magic and demonology.

In the early seventeenth century, however, Christian Kabbalah underwent a number of significant changes. In the majority of Christian kabbalistic books of this period, kabbalistic symbolism began to be extensively fused with alchemic imagery. This can be clearly seen in the writings of such popular hermetic authors of the time as Robert Fludd, John Dee, and Abraham von Franckenberg. This is also the period when the Lurianic allegories (particularly the allegory of Adam Kadmon as a metaphorical representation of the Tree of Life) begin to be applied to Christian kabbalistic works. This image is certainly evident in John Dee's book *Monas Hieroglyphica (Hieroglyphic Monad)*.[31] Dee's books express, for the first time, the belief that the synthesis of magic, Kabbalah, and alchemy would produce a new philosophy, the "scientific mysticism" which would bring a new dawn into the world.[32] For Dee and Fludd, as well as for the next wave of Christian kabbalists represented by Jacob Boehme, Van Helmont, Von Franckenberg, and Von Rosenroth, this "scientific mysticism" meant the union of magic, religion, and science that its adherents found in alchemy.

While alchemy and alchemists had existed in Europe since the early Middle Ages, the seventeenth century witnessed a new interpretation of alchemic studies. A medieval alchemist was interested in his own pursuit of either universal knowledge or gold, and did not make any connection between his individualized study and the structure of the world. The new type of alchemy, which originated in the early Renaissance but became widespread only in the early seventeenth century, had a different goal. Its apostles, from Dee and Fludd to Paracelsus, broached the idea that alchemy could help man to recover the knowledge lost with Adam's fall. Thus, the seventeenth-century alchemist acted more for religious and mystical purposes than his medieval predecessors. His primary goal was to create a new religious philosophy that would endow

Introduction

human beings with the same mystical attributes they had enjoyed at the dawn of their existence.

This new alchemic tradition, in contrast to medieval alchemy, was deeply linked with Christian kabbalistic ideas, yet it also surprisingly reflected Lurianic Kabbalah, especially in its primary idea that mystical practices can "mend" the broken world and transform humanity into its primordial state. The Renaissance idea that Kabbalah was the divine knowledge that Adam lost after the fall, combined with Luria's concept of *tikkun* as the universal restoration capable of returning mankind to its utopian primordial state, comprised a major part of seventeenth-century alchemic mysticism. Accordingly, Kabbalah became deeply integrated into alchemic study as a central ingredient of the new mystical alchemy, and practitioners of this generation can truly be called "kabbalistic alchemists." However, the Jewish Lurianic concept of Adam Kadmon and *tikkun* is merely a mystical allegory. By contrast, the mystical alchemists regarded Kabbalah not as an abstract philosophy but rather as a science that dealt, much like Pythagorean mathematics, with letters and numbers.

During this period Hebrew words became widely incorporated into alchemic practices. For example, alchemic manuscripts of this period always called an alchemic oven *atanor*, a term that originated from the Hebrew word *Hatanur* (oven).[33] The use of Hebrew had a particular importance for both the writers of "magical" kabbalistic manuscripts and their intended target readership. The majority of authentic Jewish kabbalistic texts were written not only in Hebrew but also, and largely, in Aramaic. However, most sixteenth-century Christian kabbalists were convinced that Hebrew was the divine language of creation and that it possessed a creative force, hidden in letters and sounds often incomprehensible to regular mortals. They were certain that once people really understood the letters in this creative way, they would gain a "living understanding" of the Scriptures, and as soon as they obtained this divine knowledge, the religious peace and unity of the world would swiftly follow. Thus they regarded Hebrew as the "natural language," valued above other languages. This attitude towards Hebrew, established during the Renaissance, continued in the later Christian kabbalistic tradition.[34]

Hebrew was also important for Christian kabbalists because of the belief that Kabbalah contained fragments of ancient wisdom that passed from generation to generation pure and uncorrupted, expressed in the most ancient of all languages, the language of the divine creation. As a result, alchemic texts of the mid-1600s were filled with various Hebrew names for God, Hebrew letters, and pseudo-Hebrew words that were often meaningless gibberish.[35] Such beliefs further advanced an understanding of Kabbalah as linguistic mysticism, which would later make it appealing for the poetic imagination of those authors who were eager to find an esoteric theory to prove that letters and sounds were indeed intimately connected with reality.

In the perception of seventeenth-century Protestant mystics, the allegory of Adam Kadmon developed alongside the famous baroque theory that man (microcosm) is in fact a projection of the macrocosm, i.e., the universe. The internal spiritual world of man is a precise replica of the external universe; whereas man reflects the universe, the universe reflects man. Although this concept dates to the Gnostic theories of the first centuries CE, it was revived and popularized in the seventeenth century. The Jews never considered Kabbalah a science, and alchemy, although practiced among some Jews, was quite marginal to Jewish mystical tradition. By contrast, in the view of alchemic writers like Fludd and Paracelsus, Kabbalah was a manual of mathematical, alchemic, and linguistic formulas that could help them to acquire lost primordial knowledge and to restore the broken world.

The ideas born among kabbalistic alchemists of seventeenth century, primarily in Germany and Bohemia, formed the basis of the ideology of the order of Rosicrucians that soon became widely influential in Europe.[36] The kabbalistic allegories used by the author of the most famous Rosicrucian manifesto, *A Chemical Wedding*, display a deep similarity to the allegories present in the teachings of Luria.[37] The central message of the story is deeply rooted in the belief in complete mystical transformation when "the return of the world to the times of Adam will bring back the lost Light and Wisdom which surrounded Adam before his fall."[38] Attributed to the spiritual father of Rosicrusianism, Johann Valentin Andreae, this book serves as a fine example of the transformation of classical zoharic narrative into Christian mystical allegory. Similarly to the *Zohar*, the *Wedding* is structured as a mystical travelogue. Its narrative plot is divided into seven sections, each describing one day of the protagonist's travel to a mysterious "wedding," and allegorically representing the seven days of Creation. Just as in the *Zohar*, the narrative of the *Wedding* takes place "on the road" and is woven around the travel experience of the main character, Christian Rosenkreutz. The story incorporates mystical and fairy-tale elements that include wandering in deserted enchanted places and meeting mysterious strangers; and it constantly generates either rejoicing and delight or fear and terror in the reader, who is engaged in a sense of a mysterious expectation. By contrast with classical zoharic narrative, which has only a sparse literary frame and is mostly woven around the philosophical and theosophical sermons of the various protagonists, the *Wedding* is characterized by a first-person narration, which provides the text with a very well-structured plot and a strong personal emotional voice. Yet, in spite of the ostensible personal voice of the narrator, the mystical sub-context of the *Wedding* derives not from the narrator's personality or from abstract theosophy but from well-defined mystical and alchemical symbolism that evidently reflects upon a particular hermetic allegorical tradition that represents Rosicrucian esotericism and fuses alchemic, kabbalistic, and Christian mystical allegory.

While both the *Zohar* and the *Chemical Wedding* use the form of a literary text as a vehicle for a meditative work, the *Zohar* provides the reader with abstract hermeneutics constantly open for further interpretation. By contrast, any attempt of the reader to find his own path through the symbols of the *Wedding* fails miserably. Andreae's text is not a source for philosophical exegesis, and neither it is a fully literary text. Rather it is a mystical manifesto provided in a allegorical form that uses already established symbolism, understood only by those adepts who are familiar with the allegorical, hermetic, and alchemic codes that the author uses. The *Wedding* clearly combines Christian and Jewish imagery, yet at the same time it interprets Jewish kabbalistic concepts as alchemic and hermetic symbols rather than theosophical ideas.

The similarities and the differences between the abstract theosophical images of Kabbalah and its concrete alchemic interpretation in the *Chemical Wedding* can be easily seen through a number of small details. At the beginning of the story the protagonist is meditating while enjoying his Easter meal, which immediately points to the Christian nature of the mysteries that he is about to encounter. The meal, however, surprisingly includes such Jewish ritual foods as unleavened bread and Passover lamb. At the peak of his meditation he sees an angelic woman, dressed in azure, white, and gold, who gives him a list containing the mysteries of creation. When questioned as to her origin, the woman answers that she is Wisdom (*Hokhmah*), the envoy of the Father of Light. The woman then hands the protagonist a letter that invites the character to a mysterious wedding. The image of a wedding undoubtedly refers to the idea of spiritual marriage, a union of the divine spirit, the human soul, and the material body. This image was quite popular in Lurianic symbolism, where it was regarded as the achievement of a spiritual bond (*devekut*) between a meditating adept and either God or Divine Wisdom, and is often compared to a sexual union.[39] In the *Wedding*, however, the Royal Chemical Wedding certainly bears not only spiritual but also alchemic meaning. The narrator defines the sacred marriage by the alchemic term *conjunctio* (known also as Great Work), a term used to describe the final chemical mutation of the elements in the retort in the process of making gold. Even the colors, white, azure, and gold, contain encrypted alchemical meanings, each linked to a particular stage in an alchemic transmutation of metals.

Such details are abundant in the story, and their presence characterizes a very important shift that took place in Christian kabbalistic texts in the seventeenth century. The interpretation of the mystery of creation in alchemical Christian kabbalistic literature slowly but steadily changed into a parable for the creation of artificial life, in which the stress fell on the magical side of the story rather than the mystical one. By the middle of the seventeenth century this interpretation had become quite predominant. Yet, although the essence of the Christian kabbalistic allegory of the period gradually shifted from its original kabbalistic meaning, the majority

Introduction

of Christian works kept using the same "mystical travelogue" narrative form, as well as basic kabbalistic symbolism that they now infused with alchemical imagery. Along with the *Chemical Wedding*, another mystical travelogue would later play an important role in the development of Russian 'kabbalistic' narrative: Abraham von Franckenberg's manuscript *Raphael, Oder Artzt-Engel* (*Raphael: The Doctor-Angel*), published in 1676.

The primary goal of a Christian seventeenth-century kabbalistic mystic and alchemist was to emphasize the unity of science and religion by showing how the mysteries of Bible exactly paralleled those of the Kabbalah. Seventeenth-century interpretation of Kabbalah also elaborated on the relations between Kabbalah and Christ's divinity and drew a parallel between the kabbalistic doctrine of Adam Kadmon and the concept of Jesus as primordial man in Christian theology. The Lurianic idea that the kabbalist must prepare his limbs for the indwelling of the divine spirit, or *Shekhinah*, is interpreted along the lines of the so-called "inner Christ" or "Christ within" that has to be revealed in each person's soul. [40]

In the late seventeenth century, however, a small circle of English mystics, known as "Cambridge Neo-Platonics," began to express a strong interest in theosophical Kabbalah. The members of the circle, including John Partridge (1644–1714) and Ralph Cudworth (1617–1688) sought contacts with scholarly Jews in England and Holland and studied authentic sources largely unavailable to the majority of Christian kabbalists.[41] This circle, in its turn, influenced a few German mystics whose writings, although they had been largely influenced by seventeenth-century alchemic mysticism, combined the alchemic interpretation of Kabbalah with theosophical studies. This interpretation was characteristic of late-seventeenth-century Christian Kabbalah and is best represented by the famous treatise *Misterium Magnum*, written by the famous German theologian Jacob Boehme (1575-1624) and the kabbalistic compendium, *Kabbalah Denudata*, composed by theologian Knorr Von Rosenroth.[42] Boehme's and von Rosenroth's treatises further developed the parallel between the kabbalistic doctrine of Adam Kadmon and the concept of Jesus as primordial man in Christian theology. This parallel concurrently evolved in the writings of Dutch philosopher Francis Mercury van Helmont (1614–1698), and subsequently by the eighteenth-century Christian kabbalists Martines de Pasqually and his disciple Louis-Claude de Saint-Martin.[43] These writings shaped a particular secular mystical literary tradition that in a little less than a century would establish itself in Russia, thus creating a foundation for Russian literary interpretation of kabbalistic allegory and kabbalistic narrative.

This book aims to present the reader with a clear answer to the questions of when, how, and why Kabbalah has been used in Russian literary texts from pre-Romanticism to Modernism, and what particular role it played in the larger context of Russian literary tradition. An understanding of this liaison will enable the reader to clarify many enigmatic images in Russian literary works of the last two centuries. It will also help to expose the roots of a particular cultural falsification that played an important role in the anti-Semitic mythology of the twentieth century. This volume is not a study of the history of kabbalistic thought in Russia. Rather, it is a study of Russian literature as a product of a particular Russian cultural mentality, contrasted with Kabbalah as the product of a parallel Jewish and pseudo-Jewish Western mentality, and of those particular cultural clashes born as a result of the social and cultural encounters of all three. Thus, this project is a unique attempt to demonstrate the evolution of kabbalistic symbolism in Russian literature by explaining and presenting its origins and stages of development, which will expand and challenge relevant studies in the field of Jewish–Russian cultural connections.

NOTES

1. Monthly Newsletter, Temple Shomrei-ha-Dat, Elmira, NY (Summer 2009), 3.

2. V. Ostretsov, *Masonstvo, kul'tura i russkaia istoriia* (Moscow: Nash Sovremennik, 1999), 79.

3. See, for example, K. Burmistrov and M. Endel, "Kabbalah in Russian Masonry: Some Preliminary Observations," in *Kabbalah: Journal for the Study of Jewish Mystical Texts*, ed. D. Abrams and A. Elqayam (Culver

City, CA: Cherub Press, 1999): 4; Olav Hammer, "Christian Orthodoxy and Jewish Kabbalah: Russian Mystics in Search for Perennial Wisdom," in *Polemical Encounters: Esoteric Discourse and its Others*, ed. H. Kocku von Stuckrad (Leiden: Brill, 2007); Judith Kornblatt, "Russian Religious Thought and the Jewish Kabbala," in *The Occult in Russian and Soviet Culture*, ed. B. Glatzer Rosenthal (Ithaca: Cornell University Press, 1997); Mikhail Vaiskopf, *Pokryvalo Moiseia: Evreiskaia tema v epokhu romantizma* (Moscow: Gesharim, 2008). An Israeli graduate student, Uri Daigen, is currently working on a PhD thesis on the influence of Kabbalah on Russian mystical philosophy of the Silver Age.

4. See, for example, Elliot Wolfson, *Along the Path: Studies in Kabbalistic Myth, Symbolism, and Hermeneutics* (Albany: State University of New York Press, 1995); Nathan Wolsky, "Mystical Poetics: Narrative, Time, and Exegesis in the Zohar," *Prooftexts*, no. 28 (2008): 101–28.

5. K. Burmistrov, "The Interpretation of Kabbalah in Early Twentieth-Century Russian Philosophy," *East European Jewish Affairs* 37, no. 2 (August 2007): 157–87.

6. Elliot, *Along the Path*; Wolsky, "Mystical Poetics," 101–28.

7. Gershom Scholem, *Kabbalah* (New York: Meridian Books, 1978), 59.

8. Ibid., 109.

9. M. Idel, *Kabbalah: New Perspectives* (New Haven: Yale University Press, 1998), 129.

10. For more on *Sefer Yetsirah* see Gershom Scholem, *Major Trends in Jewish Mysticism* (New York: Schocken, 1995). The first sentence of *Sefer Yetsirah* reads: "Twenty-two letters: God drew them, hewed them, combined them, weighed them, interchanged them, and through them produced the whole creation and everything that is destined to come into being." Scholem, *Major Trends*, 86.

11. Wolfson quotes another early text, *Maayan Hokhmah*, that proposes ideas similar to those in *Sefer Yetsirah*: "combining the letters of the divine name, you will learn to understand all human languages, the speech of birds and animals, and even the talk of the palm leaves." *Maayan Hokhmah* regards the creation as a vocalization of the letter *alef*, the first letter of the Jewish alphabet, which is also the first principle, "the first movement," that initiated creation.

12. Elliot Wolfson, *Language, Eros, Being: Kabbalistic Hermeneutics and Poetic Imagination* (New York: Fordham University, 2005), 25–26.

13. See, for example, Joseph Dan, *The Early Kabbalah* (New York: Paulist Press, 1986); Scholem, *Major Trends*.

14. The division of Kabbalah into these two trends was first suggested in Scholem, *Major Trends*.

15. As Idel notes, "The medieval ecstatic Kabbalist hyperactivated his mind by concentrating with great intensity upon the combinations of letters, their ongoing permutations, vocalizations, chants, breathing exercises, and head and hand movements. He was chiefly interested in one human facility, the intellectual, which had to be saved by freeing it from the body. Although several details of the ecstatic techniques were connected with the body, the latter was considered to be an obstacle rather than a means for attaining the mystical goal." Idel, *Kabbalah: New Perspectives*, 267.

16. For example, one part of the book, called *Heikhalot*, describes the seven houses of divine light, which usually are revealed to a righteous deceased but can be also shown to a spiritually purified meditating mystic. Ibid., 110. For more on the spiritual exegesis in the *Zohar* see Y. Liebes, *Studies in the Zohar* (Albany: State University of New York Press, 1993); D. A. Green and L. S. Lieber, *Scriptural Exegesis: The Shapes of Culture and Religious Imagination* (Oxford: Oxford University Press, 2009); Michael Fishbane, *The Kiss of God: Spiritual and Mystical Death in Judaism* (Seattle: University of Washington Press, 1993).

17. Alexander Roob says that in the cosmology of Gnosticism, the sea monster, Leviathan, forms the outermost circle of the world of creation, which is inaccessible to the experience of the senses, and shuts it off from the divine world of light and love. The Kabbalah also places a veil between God and Creation. Jacob Boehme called the world below this veil "lower waters", and in Blake's mythology man has been travelling the sea of time and space since the Flood. Alexander Roob, *Alchemy and Mysticism* (London: Taschen, 2001), 116.

18. Chaim Vital, a famous kabbalist of the sixteenth century, interpreted the first lines of Bible as follows: "The world was created by a divine seed, thrown into the boundless waters of the lower world." Chaim Vital, *Hechal Adam Kadmon* (Jerusalem: Hebrew University Press, 1973), 12.

19. This image might have its roots in the statement from Proverbs 8 and Job 28 that proclaims that "in Wisdom God created Heaven and Earth." In many circles the interpretation of these texts led to the assumption that Wisdom was an expression of the divine power that created nature and mankind. Some parts of this assumption can be seen in the

Introduction

apocryphal *Book of Enoch* in which God commands his Wisdom to create man.

20. Azriel of Gerona, in *The Early Kabbalah*, ed. Joseph Dan, 94.

21. Scholem, *Kabbalah*, 112.

22. Louis Jacobs, *Jewish Mystical Testimonies* (New York: Schocken Books, 1976), 180.

23. Luria spent his youth in Egypt where he met such famous kabbalists as Samuel ibn Fodelia, and became interested in Kabbalah. In 1570 he moved to Safed with his family. Soon he became the principal disciple of the spiritual leader of the scholars of Kabbalah in Safed, Moshe Cordovero. After Cordovero's death in 1570, Luria began to impart his own kabbalistic system to a number of Cordovero's disciples. The system soon became very popular, not only among the scholars of Safed, but also in Jewish circles in Europe.

24. In the words of Rabbi Moses Hayyim Luzzato, a follower of Luria, "the first stage in God's Creation of the world is 'withdrawal,' when God created [inside himself] an empty space in which eventually were produced all the *sefirotic* realms." Jacobs, *Jewish Mystical Testimonies*, 180–81.

25. For the difference between the earlier and later Jewish kabbalistic traditions see Jacobs, *Jewish Mystical Testimonies*, 180–81; Scholem, *Major Trends*.

26. In Genesis 1:11 ". . . God said: 'Let the earth sprout vegetation, seed-bearing plants, and fruit trees of every kind.'" Then in 1:24: "God made wild beasts of every kind and cattle . . . and said: 'let us make a man in our image, after our likeness. They shall rule . . . the whole earth.' And God created man in His image, in the image of God He created him." In Genesis, 2:4: " When the Lord made earth and heaven—when no shrub of the field was not yet on the earth and no grasses . . . had yet sprouted, the Lord formed man [*Adam*] from the dust [*Adama*] of the earth. He blew into his nostrils the breath of life, and man became a living being." *The Torah* (Philadelphia: The Jewish Publication of America Press, 1962).

27. Scholem, *Major Trends*, 195.

28. Even some Jews supported these ideas. One of the Christian Florentines, for example, noted that during his journey to Constantinople he met a famous rabbi who told him that "if the Messiah for whom they had waited does not come, all Jews will convert to Christianity." David

Ruderman, ed. *Essential Papers on Jewish Culture in Renaissance and Baroque Italy* (New York: New York University Press, 1992), 311.

29. Fore more on Agrippa of Nettesheim, see *Die Cabbala des Heinrich Kornelius Agrippa von Nettesheim* (Stuttgart, 1855); M. G. M. Van der Poel, *Cornelius Agrippa, the Humanist Theologian and His Declamations* (Leiden: Brill Academic Publishing, 1997). For more on Reuchlin see E. Rummel, *The Case Against Johann Reuchlin: Social and Religious Controversy in Sixteenth-Century Germany* (Toronto: University of Toronto Press, 2002).

30. The tradition brought forward by Agrippa constituted a particular "occult" branch of Christian kabbalistic texts that combined kabbalistic ideas with astrology, alchemy, and magic and used them primarily for "practical" magical purposes. A good example of such a text, *Liber Claviculae Salomonis* (*Sefer Mafteah Shlomo*), was actually a composite of parts written originally partially in Greek and partially in Latin in the late fourteenth century and later mistakenly attributed to the Jewish kabbalistic tradition. *Liber Claviculae Salomonis* dealt mostly with various recipes for creating pentacles, magical amulets, and incantations that bestowed magical power on these objects. Another example is *Ehayat ha Haim*, known also as *Picatrix*, which was written by an anonymous author in Arabic around 1600.

31. See Francis Yates, *The Rosicrucian Enlightenment*, London: Routledge, 1986

32. Ibid., 81.

33. See B. Gerrit, "Hayyim Vital's 'Practical Kabbalah and Alchemy': A Seventeenth-Century Book of Secrets," *The Journal of Jewish Thought and Philosophy* 4 (1994), 55–112; Idel, "The Origin of Alchemy According to Zosimos and a Hebrew Parallel," *Revue des Etudes Juives* 145, nos.1–2 (1986): 117–24.

34. For example, in his work *The Alphabet of Nature*, late seventeenth-century Christian kabbalist Van Helmont describes each letter of the Hebrew alphabet in terms of its shape and sound and the significance these aspects have for the intrinsic meaning of the letter. Similar views can be seen in other seventeen-century Christian kabbalists, such as Knorr von Rosenroth and Abraham von Franckenberg.

35. For Helmont's view of Hebrew language see Allison Coudert, *The Impact of the Kabbalah in the Seventeenth Century: the Life and Thought of Francis Mercury van Helmont (1614–1698)* (Leiden: Brill, 1999), 63.

36. In Burmistrov's words: "Rosicrucian manifestos insistently call for the unity of magic, alchemy, and Kabbalah as one religious ideological

synthesis that required a religious approach to all numerological and mathematical studies." K. Burmistrov, "Zametki o kabbalisticheskoi alkhimii," in *Solnechnoe spletenie*, nos. 12–13, electronic text available at http://www.plexus.org.il/texts/burmist_zametky.htm, last accessed on August 21, 2008.

37. For more on the history of the Rosicrucians see Yates, *The Rosicrucian Enlightenment*, 401 and passim; Christopher McIntosh, *The Rosicrucians: The History, Mythology, and Rituals of an Esoteric Order* (York Beach, ME: S. Weiser, 1998); idem, *The Rose Cross and the Age of Reason: Eighteenth-Century Rosicrucianism in Central Europe and Its Relationship to the Enlightenment* (Leiden: Brill, 1997).

38. Yates, *The Rosicrucian Enlightenment*, 113.

39. Coudert, *Impact of the Kabbalah*, 146.

40. Ibid.

41. Burmistrov, "Khristianskaia kabbala."

42. Unlike popular pseudo-Jewish occult kabbalistic writings, *Kabbalah Denudata* provided a large collection of authentic Jewish materials, including the essays *Pardes Rimonim (Pomegranate Garden)* by Cordovero, *Shaar'e Orah (The Gates of Light)* by Joseph Gikatilla, and large parts of the *Zohar*, paired with excellent commentary. Rosenroth published two other volumes under the title *Kabbala Denudata* (Frankfort-am-Main, 1684), containing the *Sha'ar ha-Shamayim* of Abraham Cohen de Herrera and several of the writings of Isaac Luria.

43. For more on von Helmont, see Coudert, *Impact of the Kabbalah*.

A Quest For Moral Perfection
Kabbalistic Allegory in Eighteenth-Century Masonic Literature

Kabbalah and the Rise of Modern Russian Mysticism: Social Prerequisites

The rise of the popularity of Kabbalah in Christian Europe in the sixteenth and seventeenth centuries was linked to the utopian and messianic beliefs of those disillusioned Europeans who anticipated the apocalyptic failure of the contemporary world and envisaged the return of the Golden Age. The mystical reception of Kabbalah was primarily stimulated by the attempt of European thinkers to confirm and evolve the religious and philosophical doctrines with which they were already familiar, such as Christianity and Neo-Platonism. Simultaneously, the occult interpretation of Kabbalah led to the formation of quasi-kabbalistic stereotypes that played a significant role in the later misrepresentation of Kabbalah among most Europeans. By contrast with Western Europe, kabbalistic teaching did not play a significant role in Russian thinking prior to the mid-1700s. When kabbalistic mysticism finally reached Russia, Russians used and largely copied those narrative forms and the literary images that originated in Europe. At the same time, however, Russian authors infused this narrative structure and imagery with new meaning that although sometimes derived from European literature, was original and new in many ways.

The three decades encompassing the 1780s to the 1810s comprised the literary era known as Russian pre-Romanticism, which largely reflected the imagery and ideas borrowed from Masonic mysticism. While most of the authors analyzed in this chapter have undeservedly fallen into certain oblivion in the years since their deaths, they played a significant role in the creation of the tradition of Russian philosophical poetry. Those Russian poets who were influenced by Masonic mystical ideology willingly and widely utilized non-traditional kabbalistic mystical symbolism in their writings, partly because of the literary situation of the last decades of the eighteenth century, when Russian poetry, still at an early stage of its development, was strongly characterized by the search for new literary forms and new poetic language. Secular theosophical literature, a genre that had long existed in the West, had not yet been introduced into the Russian literary tradition. Those Russian authors who were interested in pursuing mystical ideas certainly remained Orthodox Christians in their beliefs. However, under the influence of the "secular," Masonic form of mysticism that came from the West, they attempted to express their philosophical beliefs through the use of "Western" non-traditional mystical imagery. Surprisingly, kabbalistic imagery and that particular type of "mystical," "kabbalistic" travelogue presented in previous chapter adapted itself very well to Russian literary soil; and, although this kabbalistic "subtext" of eighteenth-century Masonic poetry has been either largely neglected or strongly misrepresented (as in politically-biased anti-Semitic works), the broad use of "kabbalistic" imagery and literary forms in late eighteen-century Russian works can actually be regarded as a courageous poetic experiment, which is extremely important for the understanding of that generation of Russian authors who first applied their theosophical knowledge to individual literary texts. The models borrowed from Jewish sources, although altered and adapted by Western theosophical literature, merged in these texts with Russia's own religious and cultural tradition, thus creating a new type of "secular" mystical poetics opposed to already established Orthodox religious "poetic" devices, thus constructing a foundation for future Russian metaphysical literature.

The first reflection of kabbalistic ideas in Russian literature appears approximately in the 1780s. The kabbalistic imagery encoded in Russian literary texts of that time can be fully apprehended only if it is analyzed in light of Russian Masonic symbolism; therefore, it is important to summarize briefly the development of Russian Masonic mysticism and the role that Kabbalah played in it. Archival materials bearing on Masonic ideology are scarce, often encrypted, and primarily unpublished, which creates objective difficulties for scholars. Nevertheless, the Russian Masonic archives available to researchers contain vast collections of materials devoted to Kabbalah and its Masonic interpretation; and these materials provide extremely valuable insight into the allegorical imagery of Russian eighteenth-century mystical literature.

In the Russian tradition of the study of the history of Russian Freemasonry there is a large gap that divides the old prerevolutionary school and the new post-Soviet school that has developed largely since the late 1990s. The "classical" nineteenth-century approach, exemplified most explicitly by A. Pypin, M. Longinov, and G. Vernadsky, concentrated on the ethical and moral aspects of Russian eighteenth-century Masonic ideology and overshadowed Masonic mystical ideology, first, because their positivistic views, largely characteristic of the second half of the nineteenth century, prevented them from taking mystical ideology seriously, and second, because they completely lacked knowledge of either Western esotericism or Jewish mysticicm. Later, in the Soviet period, the scholarly study of any mystical ideology was strictly forbidden. Western scholars that analyzed the Russian Freemasonry, primarily S. Baehr and D. Smith, followed mostly the same approach as their prerevolutionary Russian predecessors, deliberately avoiding the investigation of mystical and particularly Jewish mystical subjects. By contrast, in the works of young post-Soviet scholars, especially Konstantin Burmistrov and Maria Endel, the role of Kabbalah in the philosophical system of Russian Freemasons occupies the central role. Burmistrov and Endel have conducted a vast archival search and discovered a large number of writings and documents that prove that throughout the whole of the eighteenth-century, Russian Masons used Kabbalah and applied it to their own philosophical theories. Mainly, Burmistrov's and Endel's approach to the study of Kabbalah in Russian Masonic doctrine is historical rather than literary. Yet those Russian eighteenth-century poetic works that have been influenced by Masonic mysticism broadly employ kabbalistic allegory as a literary device, manifested in a specific system of allegorical images and in a specific genre, best defined as a "mystical travelogue" that largely copies the narrative of "zoharic" allegorical travelogue through the use of the same form and elements of kabbalistic allegorical imagery similar to those used in the West. A close look at the role played by the allegorical concepts of Adam Kadmon and Love-Wisdom in the literary embodiment of the mystical and philosophical system of eighteenth-century Russian Freemasonry brings forward an innovative argument that these concepts constitute the core of the particular type of literature that can be defined as Russia's first metaphysical poetry. By contrast, such allegories are absent from eighteenth-century philosophical poetry that was not written under Masonic mystical influence, such as the works of Lomonosov or Derzhavin. Therefore, the literary study of kabbalistic allegory in eighteenth-century Russian philosophical poetry is necessary not only to help to decode numerous images that remain enigmatic for most scholars and readers of eighteenth-century Russian literature, but also, and more importantly, to comprehend the cultural semiotic context that primarily contributed to the formation of Russian metaphysical poetics.

Therefore, the central stress of this chapter is placed on the close reading of the literary texts rather than on the study of the eighteenth-century Russian Masonic philosophy; in particular, it concentrates on the work of three authors, all very different yet all profoundly influenced by Russian Masonic mysticism: Fyodor Kliucharev, Mikhail Kheraskov, and Semyon Bobrov. Each of these authors represents a different type of writer. Mikhail Kheraskov, regarded as the most important Russian poet by Catherine the Great, hails from the tradition of Russian Classicism. Semyon Bobrov, well-respected by his contemporaries as an author of pre-Romantic works of the very late eighteenth century, exemplifies the poetry of the younger generation of eighteenth-century writers; and Fyodor Kliucharev, whose poetic works were written primarily for Masonic occasions and were little known outside the Masonic circles, represents a typical "court" Masonic poetry. However, all of these three broadly employ kabbalistic symbolism and narrative form in their texts.

The approach of this study derives primarily from Yury Lotman's semiotic theory that anything linked with meaning in fact belongs to culture. According to Lotman, every period's literary and ideological consciousness and aesthetics have a systemic quality of cognitive, ethical, and aesthetic values. In this case, the Masonic interpretation of kabbalistic concepts produced what Lotman would term a *semiosphere*, a particular "semiotic space," the boundaries of which defined the devices used by all Masonic poets, thus making each of them, regardless of their own literary style and the literary school they belonged to, an explicit example of the manifestation of the role of kabbalistic allegory in early Russian literature.

Earlier scholars of Russian masonry, like G. Vernadsky and M. Longinov, described the birth of modern Russian mysticism as a part of Masonic philosophy that was in some ways a reaction to the Enlightenment thought of Voltaire that dominated Russian intellectual life throughout the period.[1] The belief in the power of reason that Voltaire proposed characterized Russian masonry during its early stage of development. The early Russian lodges, constructed according to the rational English Masonic system, were created to unite various people who considered themselves the apostles of a new, non-religious morality. To Christian mysticism, they opposed what they called "natural mysticism," similar to the doctrine expounded in Voltaire's deistic philosophy. Yet the new morality that Voltaire's philosophy required was impossible for a simple person to adhere to. The only solution in such a situation was the union of all those who called themselves "people of the new moral code," and this organization had to be an exclusive, secret society. Thus, the religion of the rationalistic Masons was directly linked with the moral order created by Voltaire's teachings.[2]

Rationalistic Freemasonry reached its peak in the early 1770s.[3] The morality of this English-oriented Russian masonry was not deeply connected with mystical theories or mystical practices, although simultaneously a specific mystical subculture was starting to develop in Russia, with a definite set of stereotypes and symbols and an element of mystery.[4] It was also at this time that the first knowledge of Kabbalah entered Russia. One of most famous Masons of the age of Catherine the Great, senator and writer Ivan Elagin (1725-1793), was the first key figure in the dissemination of kabbalitic ideas in Russian Masonic thought. A Voltaire enthusiast at first, Elagin broke away from rational Freemasonry and created his own kind of mysticism, often called rationalistic mysticism, wholly adapted to the principles of religious morality. At this time he became interested in kabbalistic teachings, and immersed himself in reading the Old and the New Testaments and the writings of the Church Fathers. He also started studying Greek and Hebrew. Natural religion and a moral code based on the principles of reason were the two keystones of Elagin's masonry. In the 1770s lodges of the Masonic union led by Elagin became the centers of this new "religion of reason."

The early "English" Masonic lodges in Russia were connected through St. Petersburg Germans with Prussia and especially with the Berlin lodge *The Three Globes*.[5] Its members comprised some devoted theosophists who studied Christian Kabbalah, magic, and alchemy. The archives of *The Three Globes* contain a number of pseudo-kabbalistic writings of the sixteenth and seventeenth centuries that were popular among German mystics. Among these were the writings of John Dee, Christian Knorr von Rosenroth, Raimond Lull, Robert Fludd, and Hermann Fichtuld, which became available to Russians through personal contacts with European visitors.

The mystical interests of Russian Freemasons of this period reflect the similar interests of their European partners: both were primarily interested in practical, alchemical "Kabbalah."[6] This interest in Kabbalah as a magical science related to alchemy is apparent in virtually all the texts that circulated among Russian Freemasons in the 1760s and early 1770s, as, for example, in an anonymous translation of Hermann Fichtuld's *Cabala Mystica Naturae* from Elagin's private collection: "Kabbalah is a natural philosophy devoted to the true comprehension of celestial spirits and elements with the help of the divine light. The greatest part in this doctrine is the theory of letters, since letters are inhabited by spirits and every letter is the home of a particular spirit."[7] The same alchemical approach to Kabbalah can be seen in another manuscript of the same period that explains how to create an amulet that would help its owner to find the philosopher's stone: "The base of the amulet should be made of crystal on which you should engrave the name *Elohim* so that the letters that form the name make a complete circle, and then inscribe a *tetragram*."[8] Elagin's example shows that even rationalistic Freemasons took an interest in esoteric and alchemical subjects. Similar to seventeenth-century mystical thinkers, Elagin's circle perceived Kabbalah as a "scientific" magic, that is, magic based on mathematical logic and the "rational" rather than supernatural powers; thus, its use did not oppose the rational beliefs of its adepts but went hand in hand with them. Thus, while two principal trends in Russian Freemasonry of the late eighteenth century are usually identified in criticism as rational and mystical, these trends were strongly interrelated.

Physician Stanislaus Pines Eli, a baptized Bohemian Jew who arrived in St. Petersburg in either 1776 or 1787, played an extremely important role as a source of the quasi-kabbalistic knowledge popular among the members of early Russian lodges. Elagin mentions him as "Eli, a person well-educated in the great science of magic, Jewish language, and Kabbalah."[9] Elagin claimed that Eli helped him to understand "the books of Fludd and Fichtuld, Egyptian myths and hermetic secrets, and above all, the kabbalistic mysteries hidden in the writings of Moses."[10] He also reported that Eli was the author of a Masonic work titled *Bratskie uveshchaniia k nekotorym bratiiam svobodnym kamenshchikam* (*Fraternal Admonitions to Some Bretheren Freemasons*). Elagin understood and interpreted this book in the same way as other hermetic manuscripts, which contained, according to his belief, the "great secret knowledge." In Pypin's opinion, this book was a typical example of "Rosicrucian nonsense, with its false depth and alchemical inventions." He notes that, without any serious understanding of esoteric systems, Elagin finally "was lost in them as in the deep woods."[11] Indeed, Eli himself regarded Kabbalah much as did the scholars of the Renaissance, not distinguishing between Kabbalah and other esoteric studies.

Elagin's most important composition, called *Explanations of the Mysterious Meaning of the Creation of the Universe in Holy Scripture*, *which is a key for understanding of the Book of Truth and Errors*, is written as a personal diary and cannot be considered a literary text.[12] However, it represents an extensive commentary on the key themes of kabbalistic doctrine, such as God and Creation, the elements, and the divine names, which later find their way into Masonic literary works. As K. Burmistrov correctly noted, "on the basis of Holy Scripture — using the kabbalistic concepts *Ein-Sof*, emanation of the *Sefirot*, Adam Kadmon, four worlds-*Olamot*, as well as the hermeneutical techniques of *gematria, notarikon*, and *temurah* — Elagin developed a kabbalistic version of the Masonic cosmogony."[13] It is likely that the composition is a decoding of the kabbalistic subtext of the famous mystical work *Des erreurs et de la vérité* (1775) by French mystic Louis-Claude de Saint-Martin, whose books, largely influenced by seventeenth-century Christian Kabbalah, were very popular among Russian Masons. Elagin's non-Christian interpretation of the New Testament presents, for the first time, an image that would become widely popular in later Masonic writings and widespread in Russian eighteenth-century literary texts influenced by Masonic ideology: he regards Jesus Christ as the perennial primordial man, Adam Kadmon — and thus also as a Mason, one of the "hieroglyphs of perennial Jews." Elagin's example shows not only how strong the interest in Kabbalah was among educated Russians of the mid-eighteenth century, but also how this interest altered their traditional Christain beliefs: a phenomenon that is instrumental in understanding the peculiarities of the social and religious views of Russian Freemasons, and in decoding many of those images in Russian literary works of the second half of the eighteenth century that up to now have seemed largely vague and incomprehensible.

The Crisis of Freemasonry and the Emergence of the Masonic Circle of Nikolai Novikov

In the late 1760s rational masonry faced a serious crisis. The majority of Elagin's lodges were nothing more than agreeable social clubs that flourished as "excellent places to dine and enjoy good company."[14] Without an understanding of the true mystical meaning of what happened in the lodge, the secrets that usually drew a new adept to masonry soon lost their significance and the rituals became boring, bizarre, and even comical.[15]

Those intellectuals who looked for spirituality rather than for a social club, including Elagin himself, thus turned their attention to a parallel Masonic union established in Russia by Baron Johannes George von Reuchlin (1729–1791), an expatriate German who adhered to the Swedish-Prussian Masonic system that worked according to the "mystical" system of Johann Wilhelm Ellenberger, known also as Johann Wilhelm von Zinnendorf.[16] The Swedish-Prussian system, a fabricated variant of the orginal Swedish Rite, was created by von Zinnendorf in 1770 and observed by the Grand Lodge of Freemasons of Germany. By contrast with the Grand Lodge of England, the Swedish-Prussian system was characterized by a stronger interest in mystical subjects than the English Freemasonry and by a strong emphasis on the Christian nature of all Masonic activities practiced by its members. In 1771 Baron von Reuchlin opened the first Swedish-Prussian lodge, Apollo, in Petersburg. From the beginning, von Reuchlin sought to merge with the Elagin lodges. Eventually Elagin, who had become disillusioned with the "English" system, accepted von Reuchlin's offer to merge, and soon von Reuchlin became his spiritual teacher and mentor. However, this union seriously disappointed some members of both Elagin and von Reuchlin's lodges, who were dissatisfied with both superficial "English" masonry and with the political interests of the members of the Swedish system. Among the disappointed was scholarly publisher and journalist Nikolai Novikov (1744–1818). In a famous dialogue between Novikov and von Reuchel, the former, distracted by his vain search for mystical truths in the lodges he had attended, asked the latter to help him distinguish true masonry from the false. Von Reuchlin replied: "true masonry pursues no political goals but only serves those of morality and spiritual enlightenment, and leads a person through the study of oneself to the moral atonement through Christian faith and religion."[17]

Unable to find such a Masonic lodge in Russia, Novikov and his colleagues created their own circle. This new Masonic institution, widely known as the Order of Russian Rosicrucians, gathered around Novikov, and therefore was later often referred to simply as "Novikov's circle."[18] The Order was strongly tied with the German Order of God and the Rosy Cross that emerged in Germany in the 1750s. The rise of Freemasonic organizations in Europe in the early eighteenth century had led to an explosion of Rosicrucian groups in Germany, Austria, and Eastern Europe, and to the creation of the "new" Rosicrucianism that was based on seventeenth-century Rosicrucian teaching, but at the same time was an entirely new organization. The allegories of the Tree of *Sefirot* and Adam Kadmon, and the importance of mystical numbers and letters, played an extremely important role in seventeenth-century Rosicrucian doctrine, and the "new" Rosicrucians borrowed much from their mystical predecessors.[19]

The Order of Russian Rosicrucians originated in 1782 and soon became the most influential Russian Masonic institution. Its influence was so great that after the 1780s two independent trends existed in Russian Freemasonry: traditional Masons and Rosicrucians.[20] Frequently considered to be the first Russian journalist, Novikov aimed at advancing the cultural and educational level of the Russian public. His publishing house, mostly founded by Masons, produced a third of contemporary Russian books and several newspapers.[21] The prominent members of his Masonic circle included philosopher and writer Semyon Gamalea (1743–1822), writer Mikhail Kheraskov (1733–1807) (who also served as a curator of Moscow University), Senator Ivan Lopukhin (1756–1816), Count Nikolai Trubetskoi, and many others. Famous Russian historian Nikolai Karamzin and radical writer Alexander Radishchev were among those influenced by Novikov's Masonic activities.

Novikov's Masonic philosophy was far more widespread than earlier Masonic ideas in Russia, due to Novikov's publishing activities. The Masonic literature of the period between 1760 and 1770 was scanty and insubstantial. Masons did not have either a publishing house or a journal. Novikov's circle, by contrast, created a great body of mystical and Masonic literature. Novikov's publishing house produced a vast number of mystical books and articles in the circle's numerous magazines, such as *Utrennii svet* (*Morning Light*), *Vecherniaia zaria* (*Evening glow*), and *Pokoiashchiisia trudoliubets* (*The Resting Laborer*).²² Such extensive publishing activity meant that Novikov's Masonic circle had a much greater influence on the public than earlier Russian Freemasonry.²³

Novikov himself described his mystical pursuits as a reaction to the leading role of Voltaire's ideology in Russian intellectual circles. However, Novikov's masonry appeared also as opposition to earlier rationalist Masonic ideology. The fears and hopes of Russian intellectuals, combined with their belief in the approaching Golden Age, demanded a sincere quest for moral mystical truths, a much deeper search than the one that had taken place in earlier Russian lodges. As a result, mysticism in general and the mystical side of Kabbalah in particular interested Novikov's Masons more profoundly than had been the case with earlier Russian masonry. One of Novikov's friends and a fellow Mason, Count Pozdeev, wrote in a note to a friend: "Read the Bible but beware of those books that lead you away from those mystical texts that teach you Wisdom and Love of God. Through these texts you will learn the great knowledge of Nature in which the world of piety dwells. They will lead you to the light of the Divine Glory and to the Golden Age that we have lost." ²⁴

Mystical writings, from Rosicrucian texts to the books of Protestant mystics John Pordage and Johann Arndt, became the foundation of Novikov's Masonic ideology. Most of these writings belonged to the Rosicrucian seventeenth-century alchemical and mystical system that developed a mystical version of the biblical myth of the fall of man. Russian Masons inherited the belief in the importance of kabbalistic symbolism from their Rosicrucian predecessors. Several groups of "kabbalistic" texts were instrumental in both Russian Masonic philosophical thought and its reflection in the Russian literature of the late eighteenth century.

The Major Groups of Masonic Kabbalistic Texts

For a long time, Jacob Boehme was given the credit for introducing kabbalistic ideas to Russia through his book *Mysterium Magnum*, which was translated by Semyon Gamalea and became extremely influential among Russian Freemasons.²⁵ Although the role of Boehme's writings in Russian Masonic thought cannot be disputed, many other Masonic manuscripts show the deep interest of Russian eighteenth-century Masons in Kabbalah.[26] These texts can be divided into three basic groups: the original writings of Russian Masons devoted to kabbalistic issues, the translated works of European Christian kabbalists, and translations of authentic Jewish kabbalistic texts. Although the latter are often not quite true to the originals and usually are written in a form of loose translations, commentaries, and interpolations from various textual sources, their presence contradicts the established critical opinion that Russian Masons received their knowledge of Kabbalah from indirect sources only. Russian eighteenth-century Masons were, in fact, quite familiar with a significant number of authentic kabbalistic books. The Moscow State Archives contain at least two translations of the *Sefer Yetzirach* as well as some excerpts from the *Sefer ha Zohar* and a translation of the famous thirteenth-century text *Shaar'e Orah* (*The Gates of Light*) by Joseph Gikatilla, accompanied by multiple quotations from the commentary to this text made by sixteenth-century Polish kabbalist Mattityahu Delakrut.[27] Archival collections also contain various texts by European (mostly German) Christian kabbalists based on works by Pico della Mirandola, Johannes Reuchlin, and Athanasius Kircher. These texts include *The True and Right Kabbalah* by Wilhelm Kriegesman, *The Jewish Kabbalah* by Gaspar Schott, and *A Short Version of Kabbalistic Teaching* by Jacob Brucker. These works contain lengthy commentaries on and quotations from earlier kabbalistic authors as well as substantial quotations from *Sefer ha Zohar*. These works, which have only recently been analyzed and classified, provide a completely new insight into the role of kabbalistic mysticism in Russian eighteenth-century Freemasonic thought.[28]

Novikov and some of the members of his circle shared the interest of the earlier Russian Masons and the German Rosicrucians in occult and hermetic studies. However, the widespread belief that Novikov and his fellows saw no difference between the mystical and magical sides of Kabbalah is questionable.[29] Among the Masonic manuscripts found in Russian archives there is at least one that tries to explain the confusion between the mystical Kabbalah and alchemic pseudo-Kabbalah. This manuscript, *An Exposition of the Kabbalah or the Secret Philosophy of the Hebrews*, was written by Johann Wachter in 1706 and translated anonymously as *Kliuch k tainstvennoi evreiskoi kabbale* in St. Petersburg in 1778. It provided an extensive analysis of authentic Jewish Kabbalah. Wachter claimed that his goal was not that of a defender or an attorney but rather of a true historian; however, he believed that Kabbalah was a teaching devoted to the apprehension of the good and noted that:

> The numerological and alphabetical Kabbalah, so popular in our day, since too many people believe that it can open the hidden door to the greatest secrets, reveals no mysteries and is nothing more than a deception. I have no doubt that Jews who have the reputation of a very artful folk, used this deceptive teaching to lead seekers away from the true Kabbalah that teaches us to perceive the power of the divine light and Wisdom via the paths of Truth and Good.[30]

Wachter's interpretation of Kabbalah directly corresponds to the mystical ideology of Novikov's Masons, in comparison with the earlier Russian Freemasons who associated the term Kabbalah mostly with the practical, literal (*bukvennaia*) side of kabbalistic teaching. This association is clearly seen from Elagin's statement that "Kabbalah teaches us to perceive the mysteries of the divine Creation through the symbols and allegories that are hidden in the hieroglyphs of the Bible. The most important substance of Kabbalah is the ability to give us powers to understand the internal thoughts of God through the alphabetical signs concealed in the letters.[31] By contrast, most of Novikov's Masonic circle despised practical Kabbalah, which they associated with alchemy and magic, and considered the theoretical Kabbalah the only "true Kabbalah" (*istinaia kabbala*). For earlier Russian Masons, morality was connected with rational religious feelings rather than with pure mysticism and, as a result, the moral mysticism of Kabbalah interested them considerably less that the mystical linguistic powers that Kabbalah seemed to offer. For Novikov's Masons, personal mysticism and morality were not opposites but were strongly bound together, each impossible without the other.[32] For Elagin's Masonic generation, Kabbalah mostly provided keys for interpreting the Scriptures and discovering the hidden layer of the biblical texts. Obtaining such keys provided Masons with a feeling of being chosen and unique, through obtaining the secret knowledge that others lacked.

For Novikov's Masons, the foremost idea in Kabbalah was the concept of *tikkun-ha-olam*, that is, Luria's idea of the personal improvement that would eventually lead to the improvement and salvation of the world fallen because of Adam, the restoration of lost Wisdom, and the return to the Golden Age. The exposition of the Masonic interpretation of this idea is seen in a manuscript named *An Oration of the Man of Eziless*, a paraphrase of a part of *Ma'amar Adam de Azilut*, described by Scholem as an anonymous kabbalistic work of the seventeenth century in which "the basic tenets of Lurianic Kabbalah are systematically and originally presented."[33] The Masonic use of the concept of *tikkun* was not the invention of Novikov's circle. It had been already expressed, for example, in the writings of French mystic Louis-Claude de Saint-Martin (1743–1803) and his spiritual mentor, also a Frenchman, Martines de Pasqually (1710–1774), a Christian kabbalist, mystic and Mason. However, Novikov and his followers, who were interested in the social reformation and the moral improvement of society, placed the concept of *tikkun* at the center of their ideology. The members of Novikov's circle were the first to render this concept in Russian philosophy and literature.[34]

Wisdom and Divine Light: Masonic Interpretation of the Concept of Creation in Eighteenth-Century Literary Works

The two most widespread allegories found in Masonic literary texts that derive from the kabbalistic tradition are the images of Love-Wisdom and Primordial Adam. These images were applied to and interpreted in Russian literary texts that were influenced by Masonic ideology. Of the two, the image of the creative power of Wisdom was more central. In the literary ideology of Novikov's Masons, this image was always connected to the myth of the lost primordial age that operated as one of the most important motifs in the literature of Novikov's circle. For Novikov and his fellow

Masons, the restoration of the lost paradise paralleled the recovery of the primordial state of man. According to this form of Masonic doctrine, paradise could be restored only by the unification of man with "higher wisdom" (*premudrost'*).[35] This reading of the image of Wisdom, widespread among Novikov's fellows, marks the major difference between the use of kabbalistic symbolism in earlier Russian Masonic allegory and in Novikov's mystical Freemasonry. Russian Rosicrucians regarded Kabbalah as an encoded text that contained the secret primordial knowledge (Wisdom) that man had to obtain in order to return to the glorious state that prevailed before the fall of Adam. As one Masonic manuscript stated, "when God started to take the primordial wisdom away from people, they had to inscribe whatever knowledge they still had in the form of hieroglyphs or signs. It is the Kabbalah that contains those signs that contain the origin of all earthly and celestial things ever created."[36] In the major Russian Masonic publications, the power of Wisdom always enables the Mason to undergo a spiritual purification and transformation, a process that is largely similar to the Lurianic concept of *tikkun*, and moreover, is often defined and characterized by its original Hebrew term, *tikkun-ha-olam*.[37] While discussing the concept of *tikkun-ha-olam*, Russian Masonic authors usually regarded it as a process of harmonization of the wrecked structure of *sefirot*, in particular, the repair of the broken link between Malchut and Tiferet. For example, one Masonic manuscript says: "We know that Adam's fall separated the last letter "hai" from the name "Iehova," and hence also tore away Malchos from Tefferes."[38]

Most of the authors who were associated with Novikov's Masonic activities still remained pious Orthodox Christians; and therefore, their mystical writings primarily reflect their Orthodox religious beliefs. However, they were also certainly influenced by that particular mystical ideology that was characteristic of Novikov's Masonic circle. As a result, the image of Wisdom in these writings, on the one hand, reflects the Orthodox symbolism of Wisdom, found in the works of Church Fathers and in Orthodox Russian tradition, yet on the other hand, clearly manifests its connection with kabbalistic symbolism. One of the Masonic manuscripts, for example, discusses the connection between Divine Wisdom, primordial Adam, and God: "The kabbalists say that the Kingdom of Wisdom is the infinite Primitive cause, the infinite home of infinite Light [that] emanated the fundamental first Principle, through which come further emanations. It is Adam Kadmon, the primordial Man [Urmensch], the archetypal symbol of Universe — the Microcosm that projects upon Macrocosm."[39]

The same ideas are also repeated in other Masonic publications. For example, an anonymous author in the Masonic magazine *Vecherniaia zaria* in 1782 wrote:

> Before everything there was the eternal intelligent light, the enlightening Reason of Reason. He was there alone and nothing existed prior to Him. He was the primordial point and the point of our beginnings and He will be the endpoint; he was alone but simultaneously He was many united in one, and He contained everything. He is God, and there is a name given to him: Will — Love — Wisdom.[40]

The kabbalistic interpretation of the images of Divine Wisdom and Adam Kadmon lie at the center of the public lectures that Johann Georg Schwartz delivered first at Moscow University and then at his private home in 1782. Schwartz (1751–1784) was one of the most prominent Russian Masons of the eighteenth century. Russian Masons were already aware of the German Rosicrucians by the mid-1770s; however, the Order began to act in Russia only after Schwartz met Johann Christoph van Wollner, the main ideologist of the German order, during a visit to Germany.[41] He received from him an appointment as "the only Supreme Director" of the Rosicrucian Order in the Russian Empire and permission to begin work in Moscow. In Moscow Schwartz was appointed to the position of professor of philosophy, and from that time he maintained ties with Moscow University. He was known to have great authority with students. During his years in Moscow he initiated the establishment of seminars in pedagogy and translation, and the first student society, *Druzheskoe Uchenoe Obschestvo* (The Friendly Learned Society), which soon became a center of intellectual life.[42] Schwartz's preaching had a great influence on his audience. As one of his listeners remembered, "Schwartz's simple word removed blasphemous and heretical books from the hands of many simple wisdom-seekers and replaced these books with the true word of the Holy Bible."[43]

The written version of Schwartz's lectures refers to Kabbalah many times.[44] Schwartz calls Kabbalah "the substantial science through which the kabbalist watches the mysteries of Creation through the eye of Divine Wisdom." He says the three chapters of Genesis are written "in a kabbalistic manner" and believes that "Wisdom was the second emanation of the Divine Light from which the earthly and the heavenly worlds have been made. This light penetrates all things just as our thoughts do and has no end, no beginning, but is reflected forever in the human soul."[45] Schwartz believed that Masonic doctrine was a secret science that originated among the Jewish sectarians who lived in Israel right before the time of Christ, and were known for their pious lives. He was also certain that the teaching about the lost sparks of the Divine Light had been handed down from generation to generation as part of the oral tradition until it was adapted by the Order of the Rosicrucians, and that this spark was the source of the Divine Love-Wisdom.[46] The influence of Schwartz' lectures can be widely observed in Masonic magazines. For example, Schwartz's ideas are echoed in the following lines of an anonymous text printed in *Pokoiashchiisia trudoliubets*: "The true Kabbalah brings us back to that knowledge that Adam possessed before his pitiable fall, for it is told to us: 'in every soul there is a spark of the Divine Light.'"[47]

As in the works of Saint-Martin, Eli, or Boehme, kabbalistic ideas in Schwartz are often on the subtextual level and borrowed from variety of Jewish and non-Jewish sources; however, they show his true interest in real mystical Kabbalah. Although some members of Novikov's circle maintained the alchemical interests of the seventeenth-century Christian kabbalists, and alchemical images were also present in the translated Rosicrucian quasi-kabbalistic writings of Georg von Welling's *Opus Mago-Cabbalisticum et Theosophicum* (1719) or Abraham von Franckenberg's *Rafael, Oder Artzt-Engel*, these images are not strongly emphasized in original Russian writings.[48] Vernadsky notes that German Rosicrucians complained that many of their Russian brothers "like theosophical and mystical books but despise any kind of alchemy."[49]

As previously mentioned, Novikov's enlightening activities resulted in the formation of a strong literary circle of authors whose works were strongly influenced by Masonic symbolism. The kabbalistic interpretation of the allegory of Wisdom presented in Schwartz's lectures and in Masonic journals was further developed in these works. Ivan Lopukhin's *The Spiritual Knight*, for example, is a major Russian Masonic philosophical work that analyzes the allegory of creation in accordance with kabbalistic views. *The Spiritual Knight* is written as a Masonic commentary on creation and the fall of Adam. Lopukhin regards God as a cyclical process similar to *ein-sof*. He describes creation as a product of the divine light which flows in and out of an endless abyss, and stresses that creation results from the emanation of the divine light, which "behaves as a cyclical process that mysteriously pulls himself into himself, then emanates [out of himself] and will thus circulate forever."[50] This book was extremely popular among the members of Novikov's circle. Lopukhin's interpretation of the images of primordial Adam and Love-Wisdom became a foundation for the poetic imagery that was widespread in late eighteenth-century mystical literary works.

This kind of interpretation is evident in a famous Russian Masonic hymn, known mostly as "a Masonic ode," and written by Fyodor Kliucharev (1751–1822), one of the most devoted members of Novikov's circle. Contemporaries often called Kliucharev a "Masonic court poet," meaning that most of Kliucharev's poems were written for special Masonic occasions. As a result, his writing uses typical Masonic imagery, which Kliucharev usually places within the boundaries of a well-established eighteenth-century poetic form, the ode. However, such limitations, although they to some extent characterize Kliucharev as a mediocre poet, offer the opportunity to look at a "typical" Russian Masonic literary text and see how it uses and interprets kabbalistic symbolism:

> You, a true and righteous spirit,
> Reveal to me the laws of Wisdom,
> Come and renew my heart,
> So that my thought can fly back to you
> From my earthly body,
> Please, raise the veil of mystery.

> Wisdom's words have finally come true.
> My spirit is free from its body;
> Raising the cross I became white as snow,
> I am soaring into an unclouded land
> Like a new spirit.[51]

Kliucharev's poem opens with a description of his personal mystical meditative experience:

> The sacred flame enfolds the senses,
> My spirit struggles to ascend
> Onward to the temple concealed from mortal beings.
>
> I shall unlock a tome of Providence and let
> My soul-wings transport me
> To the place, where by the highest destiny, I see
> The shining chamber where the future days,
> The flow of time, the world's ranks
> Are steadfastly arranged by the Almighty God.[52]

Kliucharev describes the transformation from the earthly to the spiritual by the term "Wisdom's council," a force that raises the veil of mystery and enables the adept to see the secrets of the divine realm, represented as "unclouded land." The text is characterized by the frequent use of colors such as blue, white, gold, and scarlet, which certainly reflect Rosicrucian symbolism, like that in the *Chemical Wedding*. At the end of the poem the speaker asks God to send immortal Love-Wisdom to earth again so that the gates to the heaven can be open to mortals. Kliucharev calls Wisdom "the beloved daughter of the deity" and the source of divine light.[53] However, Kliucharev's poetic voice soon changes, and the text suddenly transforms from meditative lyrics into a political statement. Rather than perceiving mystical truths or viewing his own destiny, the speaker utilizes his spiritual revelation to prophesy a great future for the Russian Empire. Liberated from evil passions, "revived by Peter" and "animated by Catherine," Russia awaits such a great destiny that the whole universe is amazed by it. The speaker pronounces that great prosperity will come to his land when it finally "sees the East in the North." The use of the word "East," which in Masonic terminology allegorically stands for a Masonic lodge, suggests that future Russian prosperity is linked with the government's appreciation of the virtues of Freemasonry, since the term "North" in this context certainly means the Northern Russian capital, i.e., St. Petersburg. The author deliberately places mystical imagery into the typical classicist form of a "high" ode, which allows him to combine theosophical and political imagery. This combination is characteristic of most average "mystical" poems of Novikov's Masonic circle and can be defined as a "theosophical ode," a genre likely created entirely under Masonic influence.

Kliucharev stresses the creative role of Wisdom as an envoy of the divine light. He calls Wisdom "the divine love" and describes it as a creative power that has given birth to the world by assigning elements to their places and calling up their "spirits." Along the lines of the allegory of *ein-sof*, he explains God as a flow (*techenie*) of the creative divine light that leads "worlds" from darkness into endless existence:

> When He creates the worlds,
> He emanates His kind Light into them.
> He pronounces [the word] and they flow in order,
> Born, grown, ripened,
> Dead and born again
> Into a new circle of life.[54]

Kliucharev presents a similar interpretation of creation in another poem, entitled "Voploshchenie Messii" ("The Embodiment of the Messiah"). In this poem he depicts the divine world as an "abyss of living light" hidden behind the line that a "mortal cannot cross."

> Faraway, where the immeasurable loop of earthly worlds
> Ends in a line, which even an immortal mind's gaze
> Does not dare to traverse,
> A chasm of light remains still,
> Vast as a sea that no man may cross.
> It's full of life, forever is life-giving,
> It dulls the darkness of a thousand suns.
>
> This light — the threshold of a chamber,
> Abyss of all that is our Father, Almighty, Living God,
> All creatures of the Lord Creator.
> His breath engulfs all; and all he sees
> Through the gloom and darkness, and down to the pit of hell.

> He shines in the good, and blazes in the wicked,
> He flows, He permeates through them all.[55]

Interestingly, Kliucharev notes that this light is not God, but his presage, a substance that serves as the first stage of the divine flow through which he reveals himself to humans. The following stanza reveals to the reader the name of this mysterious substance, the first creation of the divine, Sophia. Such small yet important poetic details as the use of the terms "endless divine flow," and "spheres," and the representation of creation as a flow of divine energy and the depiction of Wisdom as the first stage in creation, show that Kliucharev's ode indeed uses kabbalistic rather than Christian mystical allegory. The speaker also describes the abyss of light that represents Wisdom as an impassable sea (*nepreplavny pont*), which corresponds to the image of *Malkhut*, often confused with *Hokhmah* in Christian kabbalistic texts, as an endless sea.

At the same time there is an evident hint of alchemic terminology in the poem as well — for example, God is defined as "the source of elements" (*istochnik elementov*), and the creation is called "the mixture of all elements" (*smes' elementov vsekh*). The use of such terms supports the argument that most of the images found in Russian eighteenth-century literature still reflect the Christian seventeenth-century kabbalistic tradition that united kabbalistic mysticism with alchemical allegory. However, the alchemic allegorical language in Kliucharev's poems, as in other contemporary works, is substantially less important than theosophical allegory. The moral purification of the speaker and the spiritual result that this purification has on both the speaker and his country is the keystone of the poetic message of the author, while alchemic symbols are used simply as poetic elements, which are considered by the author as de rigueur for a mystical text.

A deeper and more elaborate interepretation of the image of Love-Wisdom is employed in Mikhail Kheraskov's epic *Vladimir Vozrozhdennyi (The Duke Vladimir Reborn)*, considered one of the major literary works of the late eighteenth century. *Vladimir* is interesting not only as an example of the practical application of Masonic "kabbalistic" imagery to a literary work, but also because it is the first Russian work written in the form of a "mystical travelogue," which serves as the first practical application of kabbalistic narrative to Russian literature. The narrative form of the allegorical "philosophical" travelogue is widespread in general in late eighteenth-century literature; however, Kheraskov's travelogue largely differs from such famous works of this genre as Sterne's *Sentimental Journey* or Radishchev's *Journey from Petersburg to Moscow*. Kheraskov's epic is not a true expedition, but an allegorical journey of the soul: the protagonist's voyage is a spiritual quest for moral perfection that largely reflects the narrative structures of both the *Zohar* and the *Chemical Wedding*. The text combines mystical theosophical homilies of various Russian saints with folk fairy-tale elements, such as evil wizards and magical serpents, all depicted in a typical classicist "high" poetic style. The setting takes place mostly in nature and employs images characteristic of a mystical travelogue, such as enchanted forests, dangerous paths, beautiful gardens, deserts, dark caves, mountains, and pure springs with healing water. The springs represent the healing powers of God; caves are hermitages for traveling saints, which protect the protagonist from evil spirits so that he might spend the night listening to mystical sermons; forests stand for obstacles on the way to salvation; while paths are human choices. Finally, a beautiful garden stands for the divine Eden. The travelogue occupies the second half of the epic, with the exposition of a wise old man, Cyrus, who tells the Russian Duke Vladimir (a symbolic figure since Vladimir was known as the baptizer of Russia) that the Holy Spirit has been shown to him as creative divine light that emanates from God. Vladimir is a kind and honest man, yet his soul is "in the slavery of earthly vanity" (*v rabstve suety*). At the end of the poem, the spiritual improvement that Vladimir gains through his mystical illumination enables him to see the divine light and Wisdom, which leads to his rebirth and eventually to his embrace of Christianity.

Zoharic narrative structure is fused in the poem with folk Russian elements, and kabbalistic images go hand in hand with Orthodox Christian imagery, thus creating a particular and quite unique genre that can be called "an allegorical Masonic travelogue." Kheraskov's epic serves as a fine example of the merger of Orthodox faith and kabbalistic allegory in a Russian Masonic text. A short passage from Kheraskov's epic, in which Cyrus explains to Vladimir the mystery of Creation, exemplifies this merger:

> When the sky was not yet wholly covered by stars
> Divine Wisdom illuminated the universe.
> The emanation and the creation of the divine thoughts,
> She brought order and enlightenment into the world.
> She sees all, and animates all,
> And she gives birth to every earthly creature.
> She is the ray of the divine, the greatest light.[56]

At the first glimpse, Kheraskov's interpretation of Wisdom reflects the passage from the biblical text taken from Proverbs 8:22-31.[57] Yet the original biblical passage lacks such clearly kabalistic allegories of Wisdom as an emanation of the divine thoughts, a ray of light, or a sexual force that gives birth to every earthy creature. Such a mixture of kabalistic and biblical symbolism deviates significantly from the canonical Christian Orthodox interpretation of the symbolism of Sophia that dominated in medieval Russia. Just as in Kliucharev's ode, Kheraskov echoes the kabbalistic interpretation of the allegory of *Hokhmah*.[58] In Orthodoxy, although Wisdom is instrumental in the creation of the world, the symbolism of Sophia-Wisdom usually functions as an allegorical embodiment of Christ.[59] While the majority of medieval icons portray Sophia as female, this representation is nothing more than a persona, an allegorical picture. The medieval Sophia is female but not feminine. As Donald M. Fiene argues, "The church's unyielding position . . . was (and is) that only Jesus Christ, the Son of God, is the true Sophia — the divine Wisdom of God — in accordance with 1 Cor. 1:23-31: 'Christ is the power of God and the Wisdom of God.'"[60] Kheraskov's depiction of Wisdom is completely different. First of all, for Kheraskov Wisdom is Godhead, the brain of the Deity and its inner thought that serves as the beginning of conceptualization. Kheraskov presents creation as the first emanation (*istekshee tvorenie*) of divine thought depicted in the form of "a great light, a divine ray." He also stresses the Creation as a sexual act. Orthodox interpretation of Wisdom generally lacks this sexual subtext; however, it is strongly present in the kabbalistic interpretation of

Hokhmah. Kheraskov's interpretation of Wisdom also reflects the Christian kabbalistic confusion between *Hokhmah* and *Shekhinah*, for he evidently regards Wisdom as the divine mediator between the upper and the lower worlds, which "sees and animates everything." Kheraskov calls Wisdom a creative spirit that he compares to a river that flows from its divine source into an endless sea.[61] He states that this spirit, which shines in darkness, emanates from the mouth of God in order to fill the void in the world.

A further reference to the image of Wisdom as a creative force that signifies love is found in another passage from the same epic, which describes the figure of Wisdom, dressed in blue and white and golden-haired, standing next to her sisters Faith and Hope. In Russian folk and religious tradition such a female trinity is usually read as Faith, Hope, and Love (*Vera, Nadezhda, Liubov'*). In the full version of this formula the three sisters are usually accompanied by their mother, Sophia-Wisdom. Kheraskov alters the traditional reading by replacing *Love* with *Wisdom* and thus unites these two images in one.[62] Like in Kliucharev's poem, the colors that represent Wisdom in *Vladimir* most probably reflect seventeenth-century Rosicrucian allegory — the figure of Wisdom, dressed in blue (azure), white, and gold also appears in the *Chemical Wedding*. Kheraskov also connects the image of Wisdom with the secrets of the divine language, Hebrew. He regards Hebrew letters as a "template" which contain divine revelations.[63] He also repeatedly mentions a mysterious divine book sometimes called "the book of destinies" (*kniga promysla*) and sometimes "the book of light" (*kniga sveta*). This book is available only to the enlightened and contains all the mysteries of the world.

Cyrus explains to Vladimir that his mystical commentary presents the duke with the true meaning of the story of creation, which is different from the traditional Orthodox interpretation. Yet his explanation, although it contains many non-traditional theosophical allegories, still remains within the borders of Christian tradition. The eternal salvation of the created world will be brought by Jesus, who, by contrast with Judaism, is regarded by Cyrus as the divine Messiah. Moreover, the author's attitude towards Jews is rather ambivalent, if not anti-Semitic. One of the passages of the epic,

Kabbalistic Allegory in Eighteenth-Century Masonic Literature

based on the supposedly historical meeting of Duke Vladimir with the Wise Men of the Khazars, describes his conversation with an invented literary "King of the Khazars," Kozar'. In his conversation with Vladimir, Kozar' laments that the Jews crucified Christ, "a good man, who did not do any evil," just because "he proclaimed himself Messiah, while [the Jews] knew that the time of the Messiah had not yet arrived."[64] Vladimir responds that it is not for the Jews to decide when it is time for the Messiah to come and leaves Kozar' alone, proclaiming that his people do not need the law of those expelled by God from the whole universe for their sins. Later in the poem, Cyrus complains to Vladimir that Jews have distorted and misinterpreted the authentic mystical scriptures, so that now only "the wise" can recreate their true essence; therefore, it can be argued that Kheraskov clearly regarded kabbalistic symbolism as a doctrine that belonged to the Christian rather than the Jewish tradition.

Although most of the poem describes Vladimir's spiritual revelations, Kheraskov ends the epic with a political rather than a mystical message. Vladimir's moral enlightenment leads him, and eventually his country, to prosperity and mutual happiness. Vladimir is compared to Catherine, whose enlightening activities bring Russia from darkness to light. The author concludes the poem with hope that Catherine's appreciation of "true spiritual enlightenment," evidently represented by Masonic mysticism, would help his country to return to the Golden primordial age.

Theosophical poetic commentary on the mystery of creation is central for the poems of Kheraskov's disciple, Semyon Bobrov (1763 or 1765-1810), who represents the younger and the last generation of eighteenth-century Masonic authors. Bobrov is not an easy poet to read. To the modern reader his images seem vague and confusing. In fact, many of Bobrov's own younger contemporaries considered his poems ponderous, cumbersome, and artificially archaic. However, his poetry serves as a fine example of Russian pre-Romanticism and an explicit example of the literary embodiment of Masonic philosophical symbolism.[65]

Little is known about Bobrov's biography. Born in 1763 into the family of a priest, he entered a theological academy when he was ten years old, and in 1780 entered a gymnasium at Moscow University. He became a student at the university in 1782. Apparently during the years he spent at Moscow University in the early 1780s, Bobrov established his first personal contacts with Novikov's Masonic circle, and began to publish work in Masonic journals. Bobrov was a member of both the Friendly Learned Society and the translators' seminar established by Schwartz; it is highly likely that the Masons helped support him during his residence at the university. George Vernadsky mentions that Bobrov translated or editied at least one of the mystical manuscripts in the Russian Masonic collections.[66] M. Al'tshuller notes that Bobrov's poetic activity started in the journal *Pokoiashchiisia trudoliubets*, which was saturated with Masonic ideas. Bobrov had an excellent knowledge of English, and in 1806 he planned to prepare a translation of poems attributed to the legendary Gaelic warrior-poet Ossian. However, his family circumstances and a serious illness, which might have been the result of his alcoholism, interfered with those plans. He died in 1810, at the age of 45.[67]

Modern Russian scholar V. Sakharov points out that Bobrov infused his poems with a whole encyclopedia of images and themes reflecting the philosophy of Russian Freemasonry.[68] However, Sakharov does not investigate Bobrov's Masonic images and allegories, so many of his suggestions remain unproven. According to Al'tshuller, the personal contact between Bobrov and the Freemasons might have started during the years that Bobrov spent at Moscow University in the early 1780s.[69] Bobrov's most famous Masonic poem, "Razmyshlenie o sozdanii mira, pocherpnutoe iz pervoi glavy bytiia" ("A Meditation on the Creation of the World, drawn from the First Chapter of Genesis") appeared in 1785, two years after Schwartz's lectures at the university and in the same year that Kheraskov's *Vladimir* was published. There is every reason to believe that Bobrov, as a poetic disciple of Kheraskov, had read Kheraskov's poem prior to its publication. Yet Bobrov's poem differs significantly from Kheraskov's work and even more from Kliucharev's. Kliucharev's *Ode* simply employs Masonic mystical symbolism; Kheraskov's epic infuses this symbolism with original imagery and places it in a well-developed literary narrative form. Yet both authors clearly remain within the boundaries of Christian mystical tradition. The images that Bobrov uses in his poem are certainly more radical and do not reflect a traditional Orthodox reading of Genesis, but rather Bobrov's own interpretation of the Bible, largely based on Masonic symbolism. Bobrov writes that meditation brought him to the primordial countries where the light of the Trinity shone all by itself:

> The primordial lands that no reason can grasp
> Where the three beams of light shone alone,
> Mighty and powerful in His holy silence,
> It showered his glorious luster into the endless abyss.[70]

Bobrov then proclaims that Wisdom was born as an emanation of the divine thought when God looked inside himself to see his future creation:

> This is the great God that watches
> All that is yet to be born inside him,
> He draws the images of creatures not yet born
> And thinks about their future motion.[71]

These lines, although again reflect biblical symbolism from Proverbs and the Book of Wisdom that describe divine Wisdom as a living force that "can do all things and renews everything,"[72] directly point to the Lurianic conception of *ein-sof*, in which God is described as a physical living force which "looks" at the space "inside himself" to give birth to the world — a concept missing in the original biblical texts. It is clear that this view of creation differs markedly from the established Christian interpretation. The Christian Bible opens with the lines "in the beginning God created the heavens and the earth," yet there is no indication of the fact the God created the world *inside* himself. Rather, Bobrov's interpretation of creation echoes Luria's concept of *tsimzum*, the notion in the kabbalistic theory of creation that God "contracted" his infinite light in order to allow for a "conceptual space" inside himself in which a finite, seemingly independent world could exist.

Bobrov further develops the motifs of divine light and Creation in the poem "Tvorenie mira" ("The Creation of the World"), which appeared shortly after "The Meditation." In this poem he also links Wisdom with love and articulates love's sexuality by using expressions such as "embryo," and "love pours into the mixture," which bear sexual and alchemical symbolic connotations. The word "mixture" certainly echoes an alchemic mixture, similar to that used for the creation of an artificial human, or homunculus. Love flows (*vtekaet*) into this mixture and gives the "mixture" that creative power necessary for the creation of the world. Evidently love stands in the poem for one of the divine emanations, most probably again for the emanation of the *sefirah* of *Hokhmah*. The creation is depicted as a kabbalistic process, presented in the typically mystical and partially alchemic kabbalistic tradition of the seventeenth century. In this poem Bobrov calls creation "an emanation of the Deity" (*proistechenie blestiashche bozhestva*) and names God "the key of Light" (*sveta kliuch*).[73]

Bobrov marked the text of "The Creation of the World" as "a translation from the French," which suggests that the text may have been influenced by the works of Saint-Martin or even Martines de Pasqually. Saint-Martin's book *Des erreurs et de la vérité* was translated into Russian in 1785, roughly coinciding with the publication of Bobrov's poem. Bobrov's poems "The Creation of the World" and "The Meditation" may or may not have been influenced, directly or indirectly, by the translations of Saint-Martin's or Martines de Pasqually's texts, by original Russian Masonic publications such as *Duke Vladimir Reborn* or *The Spiritual Knight*, or by such oral sources as Schwartz's lectures. There is, however, at least one direct Masonic source of influence which proves that Bobrov indeed used Masonic and Jewish or quasi-Jewish symbolism in these poems. In the same issue of *Pokoiashchiisia trudoliubets* in which Bobrov's poem first appeared, there is a translation of an anonymous text entitled *Ob istorii Moiseevoi, tvorenii mira, i zhizni liudei do potopa* (*On the History of Moses, the Creation of the World, and the Life of people before the Biblical Flood*). The work professed that "Moses has given us the true story of the creation of the world through the oral tradition that was available to those few who learned it from their ancestors."[74] According to this text, the creation of the world was, in fact, the diffusion of a great light, which was the true light of Wisdom, and the primary concentration of this light can still be found in

Kabbalistic Allegory in Eighteenth-Century Masonic Literature

those places where Noah left his ark after the flood.[75] Bobrov was a member of the editing board of the magazine and therefore had certainly helped with and participated in the publication of that issue as he did with all others; therefore, placing two texts on the same topic in the same issue does not appear to be a coincidence. Bobrov had certainly seen the text "On the history of Moses" prior to publication; and his poem seems to be his own interpretation of this particular text, which might deliberately have been placed side by side in the same issue by the editorial board.

These ideas are further developed in the next issue of the same magazine in an article titled "O mire, ego nachale i drevnikh vremenakh" ("On the World, its Beginning and Ancient Times"):

> The most ancient and profound of all stories, which tells us about the early days of the world, is certainly the allegorical fable that narrates the story of Chaos, the disorderly mixture of elements and all earthly things that Love learned to divide so as to make them fertile and flourishing. The Greek writings tell us that the Night gave birth to an egg, and from this egg Love was born, and Love, in her union with Chaos, gave birth to the whole world. And Plato tells us that Wisdom means Love, the material substance in which the embryo of the world is hidden. Therefore, we can see that Jewish kabbalistic Wisdom is the very same Love that the Greeks told us about, for the Greeks called Night and Abyss by their Jewish names, Erev and Tartar. And so we know that the Greeks probably borrowed these terms from the books of Moses and developed them later into their own secret doctrines.[76]

The symbolic idea of "a creative egg" was also very popular in mystical alchemy. Paracelsus noted that "the world is egg-shaped and swells from the swirling center of chaos."[77] Paracelsus regarded the sky as a shell that separateed the world and God's heaven from one another, as the shell does the egg. The yolk represented the lower sphere: the earth and water. The white represented air and fire.[78] Similarly, in *The Creation of the World*, Bobrov described the world as an open egg wrought from Chaos by a creative spirit that warmed it and forced it to open.[79]

Bobrov elaborates on these ideas in his poem "Liubov' ili tsarstvo vseobshchei liubvi" ("Love or the Kingdom of Universal Love"), published in the third issue of *Pokoiashchiisia trudoliubets*:

> Not yet did the worlds go around the sun.
> In the ancient primordial worlds
> These hanging spheres
> Were yet hidden in Chaos.
> Yet, you, Love, were already alive
> You took the power and animated their sprouts
> As a divine spirit, poured into their first shoots.[80]

Al'tshuller identifies the image of "hanging circles" (*visiashchie shary*) with planets. It is far more likely, however, that this image refers to *sefirot*. Again, Bobrov was among the editors of (and one of the primary translators for) *Pokoiashchiisia trudoliubets*, and most of his poems borrowed the terms and images presented in those non-literary texts that appeared in the magazine. The article "On the World, its Beginning and the Ancient Times" describes creation thus: "The world was revealed in ten kinds of emanations, ten images which we called Sefirot: ten primordial circles, ten figures of things."[81] The terminology in "Love or the Kingdom of Universal Love" evidently echoes that of the article. Bobrov also manifests the idea that *Hokhmah* (which he identifies either as Wisdom or as Divine Love), regarded in Kabbalah as the first step in creation, had existed prior to the creation of the other *sefirot*; and while other *sefirot* were still hidden in the chaos, *Hokhmah* began animating them as a creative spirit which had poured its power into their "shoots" (*rostki*).

These examples prove that the allegory of Love-Wisdom and its role in creation in Masonic poetry directly corresponds to the Masonic interpretation of kabbalistic mysticism as it is reflected in the theosophical articles written and/or translated by Russian Rosicrucians. This allegory reflects the Masons' belief that their activities helped them to regain the creative Wisdom possessed by primordial Adam in paradise. The correct interpretation of this allegory in Russian literary works of the last decades of the eighteenth century is impossible without an understanding of the Masonic background that influenced and produced it. However, this allegory, although always depicting similar features, was developed differently by various eighteenth-century authors. For some authors, like Kliucharev, the use of theosophical imagery remained just a poetic cliché, necessary for a particular genre. In Kheraskov's work, "kabbalistic" theosophical allegory received a philosophical and ethical interpretation but was still secondary to commentary on the necessity of moral and social enlightenment in Russia. By contrast, social criticism was completely missing in Bobrov's poems, which were rather personal poetic commentaries on biblical texts that derived from Masonic mystical symbolism and originated in a non-traditional and arguably kabbalistic reading of the story of creation. These poems have much in common with later Russian eighteenth-century theosophical poetry, and are already representative of pre-Romanticism rather than Classicism.

The Primordial Adam:
Masonic Interpretation of the Concepts of Adam Kadmon
and the Universal TIKKUN

The kabbalistic subtext of creative Wisdom in Russian Masonic symbolism is further developed in another key allegory in the moral doctrine of Novikov's circle: the parable of the primordial Adam, which clearly resembles the Lurianic concept of Adam Kadmon. Russian Rosicrucians believed that their primary goal was the restoration of that primordial unity of man and universe that had ended with the Adam's fall; therefore, the Masonic activity of Novikov's circle concentrated not only on self-knowledge, knowledge of nature, and knowledge of God, but also incorporated these activities into a harmonious process of self-improvement. As a result, the image of Adam Kadmon, his fall, and his projected return to the primordial state, was one of the most important ideas in Masonic philosophical ideology. It was directly linked to the Masonic teaching of the future restoration of the original unity of mankind and is central to our understanding of Russian Masonic symbolism of the eighteenth century. Burmistrov argues that although Masonic ideas reflected Christian tradition, the particular image of Adam Kadmon was perceived in accordance with kabbalistic doctrine.[82] However, the Masonic use of this allegory is highly syncretic and includes elements drawn not only from kabbalistic but also from Gnostic, biblical, and apocryphal texts.[83]

A Quest for Moral Perfection

In this system, the Mason is likened to Adam, the one who originally possessed true knowledge but had lost it, and must obtain it anew through a long process of self-improvement that eventually would lead the world to the restoration of primordial harmony and the return of the Golden Age. As with the kabbalistic texts, the allegory of Adam Kadmon in Masonic publications is united with the myth of creation and the image of God as *ein-sof*, a force that reveals itself through the *sefirot*. *Notes on Kabbalah*, a manuscript in the Russian State Library, comments on the nature of the divine creation:

> In order to perform the creative emanations that reflected the nature of the divine, the infinite Primitive Cause, the infinite spirit of infinite light, emanated [from within himself] his very first source from which all subsequent emanations would be made. This source was Adam Kadmon, the primordial man. This first-born was revealed in ten gradations of various emanations and the same number of the corresponding sources of the divine light that we call *sefirot*. The kabbalists say that God declared his secret knowledge to Adam, but Adam because of his fall tore away from his *Sefirah*, i.e. the kingdom of God, and lost his wisdom.[84]

The Christian kabbalistic interpretation of the image of Adam Kadmon is also expressed in translated Rosicrucian texts and in Wachter's book on Kabbalah. It is also apparent in *Hirten-Brief an die wahren und ächten Freimaurer alten Systems* by Christian August Heinrich von Haugwitz, which was quite popular among Novikov's masons and strongly influenced Lopukhin's *The Spiritual Knight*. Translated as *Pastorskoe poslanie k istinnym i spravedlivym svobodnym kamenshchikam drevnei sistemy*, the book was usually known as simply *Pastorskoe poslanie* (*The Pastor's Letter*). Haugwitz says that the fall of Adam resulted in the fall of all nature, since his curse became the world's curse. Thus, the material Adam must be repudiated and a new, spiritual Adam must be born, which will result not only in the purification of the individual but also in the restoration of the primordial world unity.[85]

The image of Adam Kadmon is closely tied with a central allegory of Russian Rosicrucian literature: the teaching of two Adams, one spiritual and internal (*vnutrenni* or *dukhovny* Adam), and the other material and external (*vneshnii* or *vetkhii* Adam). This allegory is seen not only in Jewish but also in Christian tradition. In Christianity the doctrine of two Adams originates in the writings of St. Paul, primarily in his *Epistles to Corinthians*. According to Paul, there is a double form of man's existence; for God created a heavenly Adam in the spiritual world and an earthly one of clay for the material world. The earthly Adam came first into view, although created last. The first Adam was of flesh and blood and therefore subject to death; the second Adam was a spirit whose body was only of a spiritual nature. The concept of the two "Adams" was a key element of apostolic Christianity, yet its interpretation varies significantly from the Jewish mystical reading of the same allegory. For St. Paul, the *First* Adam signifies the material Adam, i.e., the first man, while the second, the *Last* Adam, means the Messiah, Jesus Christ, the chosen one who would resurrect the humanity. As St. Paul says in his First Epistle to Corinthians, "thus it is written, 'The first man Adam became a living being'; the last Adam became a life-giving spirit."[86] By contrast, the understanding of the same doctrine in Russian Masonic tradition echoes the Jewish interpretation of this allegory that makes a clear distinction between the material Adam-haRishon (the *first Adam* in Hebrew) as the *second* Adam and spiritual Adam Kadmon as the *first*, primordial, primal one. By constrast with St. Paul's doctrine, in Jewish mystical tradition Messiah is, on the one hand, the primal Adam, the original man who existed before Creation, his spirit being already present. On the other hand, he is also Adam-haRishon in so far as his bodily appearance followed the Creation, and inasmuch as, according to the flesh, he is of the posterity of Adam. The success of the transformation of the sinful material Adam back into his lost primordial spiritual state, that is to say, his personal *tikkun*, is directly linked to the success of the universal *tikkun-ha-olam*. Most importantly, Russian Masons drew a sharp distinction between Adam Kadmon as primordial Christ and the historical Jesus, reserving the place of the Savoir only for the primordial Christ, Adam Kadmon, and not for the historical Jesus of Nazareth whom they considered merely a copy, "an hieroglyph." As Burmistrov properly stated, this distinction cannot be found anywhere in the earlier Christian esoteric literature that concerned the subject of 'two Adams.'[87]

The *First* Adam in Russian Masonic literature has the features of Adam prior to the fall and is regarded as the universal primordial being in whose image man and the world were created, and whose soul contained all of humanity. The *Second* Adam is the material man, i.e., humanity in its current state. This allegory was encoded in the title of the primarily Masonic magazine, *Evening glow (Vecherniaia zaria)*. The publishers noted that the name of the journal derived from the idea of the first Adam "who shone with the light of Wisdom. The light of our knowledge, alas, is so limited that we can compare it only to the evening twilight."[88] The elaboration of this allegory appeared in many original literary and philosophical works produced by Novikov's circle. Stephen Baehr has even suggested that the name of a popular novel, *Kadm i Garmonia (Cadmus and Harmony)* may contain an anagram of the name Adam Kadmon: KADM i gArMONia.[89] In the majority of Novikov's Masonic publications devoted to the figure of Adam, his life before the fall was depicted as incorporating both Wisdom and divine light — a unity which was lost after his exile from paradise. These publications also mentioned the spark of divine light in the human soul which had to be recovered in order to return to the lost unity with God. For example, an anonymous poem entitled "Chelovek" ("Man") described Adam's mind as the key to truth (*kliuch k istine*) and said that "Adam was the king of shining light," and that "heavenly Wisdom flowed from his mind like water flows from a clear spring."[90] In Kheraskov's *The Duke Vladimir Reborn*, Cyrus explains to Vladimir that,

> He [Vladimir] sees this spark that burns within the soul
> Through which a mortal is born anew.
> This spark of the Divine, this flame of Wisdom
> The fall has turned into the ashes of sin.[91]

Cyrus then explains to Vladimir that the spark he sees in the depths of his soul is the spirit of primordial Adam (*dusha predvechnogo Adama*) and points out that this spark is also a seed from which the Tree of Life grows in paradise (*semia zhiznennogo dreva*). He then comments that both Adam and the Tree are hidden inside Vladimir's own person.[92] In Cyrus's sermon it is apparent how the theosophical, kabbalistic symbols of the Tree of Life, the divine spark, and primordial Adam are interwoven into a traditional commentary on Adam's fall. The fruits of a mysterious Tree of Spheres (*drevo sharov*), apparently referring to the Tree of *Sefirot*, are contrasted with the doomed fruit of the Tree of Knowledge that caused Adam's fall from paradise, since "condemned by a Tree, by a Tree he will be saved." Cyrus also explains to Vladimir that Christ is the new embodiment of primordial Adam, and that rekindling a divine spark in his soul enables an adept to find the "inner Christ" in himself. He says that Christ is a "living body," a lantern of "that divine light that adorned Adam before his fall."[93]

These examples show that the restoration of the spiritual Adam (*dukhovny Adam*) was regarded by the authors of Novikov's circle as a process similar to the *tikkun-ha-olam*.[94] The process of moral self-improvement that would eventually lead a Mason to reunification with Love-Wisdom and his personal salvation was always linked in their ideology with the restoration of universal harmony. This connection derives from the seventeenth-century Christian kabbalistic mystical tradition that reflected the Neo-Platonic idea of the isomorphism of the universe (the macrocosm) and the human (the microcosm, "the small world"). Yet in opposition to the seventeenth-century mystics, Russian Rosicrucians stressed the moral side of this isomorphism. In Masonic teaching, just as in Lurianic Kabbalah and its seventeenth-century Christian interpretation, Adam Kadmon was an archetype for the universal world. Semyon Gamalea, in speeches published in *Magazin svobodno-kamenshchicheskii* (*The Freemason's Gazette*), stated that: "When man is able to suppress his pride and to correct his moral imperfections, the spark of reason will be lit in his heart. From this spark the whole world will be illuminated by the kindly light of Divine Love and Wisdom."[95] The commandments and prayers, which played such a great role in Jewish kabbalistic mysticism and virtually no role at all in the kabbalistic doctrine of the scientifically oriented seventeenth-century mystics, were central in the Russian Rosicrucian interpretation of *tikkun*. The material Adam serves in this interpretation as an allegory for the sinful man who hopes to expiate his sins and return to primordial perfection, where he is able to comprehend God and nature. A Masonic hymn proclaims that "While trying to penetrate into myself / I will be able to perceive God's soul."[96] These views are reflected in Bobrov's "Meditation": he calls Adam "a small replica of the whole world" and "a bond between all earthly and spiritual creatures." Bobrov's representation of Adam Kadmon as a link between heavenly and earthly "countries" also echoes the kabbalistic allegorical depiction of primordial Adam as the Tree of *Sefirot* that serves as a link between the upper *sefirot* resting in heaven and the lower resting on earth:

> For the delight of Angels, God animates the ashes.
> The ashes are breathing! The first-born is alive in Heaven.
> Placed in the center between Heaven and Earth,
> He became a bond between all creatures earthly and celestial.
> He was a small replica of the whole world
> With all its depths and breadths, and heights.[97]

This process of restoration of the spiritual Adam in the material body (*sovlechenie vetkhogo Adama*)[90] was always regarded in Masonic literature as an allegorical death followed by rebirth that again unites kabbalistic theosophical symbolism with imagery taken from the New Testament, especially from St. Paul's Epistles to Corinthians.[98] An anonymous article from a Masonic magazine declared that in death the life of the body would undergo a resurrection and would start a glorious new life: "as our soul approaches the source of the Sun of Truth, it will obtain new wings and will shine in its new state of glory that mortals cannot perceive with their weaker minds."[99] This image is also reflected in Masonic poetry. For example, Bobrov directly links the restoration of the Golden Age with the destruction of the material Adam and the rebirth of spiritual man. In the poem "Sud'ba drevnego mira ili vsemirny potop" ("The Fate of the Ancient World or The Great Flood"), he proclaims that when the sinful earthly-born are consumed by flames, the heavenly-born man will obtain wings and arise to the sky.[100] Bobrov regards the process of rebirth much as do other Masonic writers such as Lopukhin or Kheraskov. For him, rebirth results from the actions of eternal love. In another poem, "Progulka v sumerki ili vechernee nastavlenie Zoramu" ("A Walk in the Twilight or An Evening

Admonition to Zoram"), he explains to his friend Zoram that death is a mere transformation from material to spiritual — a result of the work performed by eternal love.[101] Eternal love (*vsevechnaia liubov'*) again suggests the image of Love-Wisdom, a creative spirit of the Godhead. Bobrov concludes this poem with the idea that through a spiritual bond with Love-Wisdom, a person can be reborn and can return to the origin of the divine light, which Bobrov call by its Hebrew name, *Iegova*.[102]

Spiritual Marriage and Mystical Meditation

Lurianic Kabbalah regarded prayer as mystical meditation, which "leads a person through darkness to God by means of three steps: ecstasy, union, revelation," and which is an essential part of the process of *tikkun*.[103] In the Lurianic tradition the process of meditation is seen as a gradual ascent through all of the *sefirot* to the source of divine energy. A meditative prayer, called the ecstatic meditation, enables a person to communicate with God and to enter the world of divine mysteries. The union with Wisdom serves as the central goal of this meditation. Prayer enables a person to penetrate the *sefirah* of *Hokhmah* and so take the first step toward the mystical union with the Deity.

The literature of Novikov's circle always stressed the importance of meditative prayer in achieving cognizance of truth. The Masonic theory of knowledge required the initiate to pass through three meditative stages. In the first stage an adept was occupied with moral self-correction. In the second stage he had to come to know nature. In the third and final stage, he was able to understand the mysteries of nature and man at a higher level using the spiritual language of the scriptures.[104] This three-stage path was considered the allegory of the return to the time when "the book of nature was opened for humans and the man could comprehend all of its mysteries."[105] Masonic meditations very often involved a spiritual ecstasy that was perceived as individual purification. Masonic writers considered this meditation a process similar to death and resurrection, perceiving it as a transitory death, following by an ascent to the source of light.[106] Masonic authors believed that meditation would not only lead them to a spiritual bond with Wisdom, but would endow them with prophetic vision. For example, Kheraskov described the meditation of the reborn Vladimir in the following way:

> His mind deeply penetrated the higher world
> And in the eye of God his own eyes were opened.
> And having new ears and new eyes,
> He saw heaven wide open before him.
> He saw the centuries yet to come
> And people yet to be born
> And as visible lanterns in the darkness
> The fate of kingdoms was revealed to him. [107]

An anonymous ode in *The Freemason's Gazette* explained that meditation on divine secrets led adepts out of darkness into the temple of Wisdom: "We leave the darkness through prayer, reason, and will / And come to the temple of Wisdom through patience, courage, and work."[108] Similar ideas are prominent in Bobrov's "Meditation on the Creation of the World." At the beginning of the poem, Bobrov states that he is meditating and waiting for a miraculous vision to come: "Oh, primordial eternity, open to me your doors into the lands no mortal mind can see."[109] He tells the reader that in the beginning of the meditation he was suddenly lost in an endless sea. His vision was darkened because of an unknown force, which kept his eyes shut. But finally a prophetic spirit led him out of the sea and revealed to him the mysteries of creation.[110]

Lurianic allegory often compared the meditative ascent to a staircase that leads to the divine throne, known in the Bible as Jacob's ladder.[111] This allegory, which was also common in early Christian Gnosticism,[112] became one of the central allegories of Lurianic kabbalistic mysticism.[113] This allegory was widespread in Russian Masonic writings. Lopukhin believed that universal harmony was a mysterious staircase (*lestvitsa* instead of the common Russian *lestnitsa*), which was a path to knowledge and spiritual enlightenment for any true Mason and mystic.[114] In the poem "Noch'" ("Night") Bobrov described asking the night to reveal the miraculous ladder (*lestvitsu chudesnu*) that descends from heavenly places and elevates wise men above the stars.[115]

Kabbalistic Allegory in Eighteenth-Century Masonic Literature

The epiphany of this meditation is seen in Lurianic Kabbalah and in later kabbalistic symbolism as a spiritual marriage between the Heavenly Groom and Heavenly Bride, i.e. God and *Hokhmah*. Since the first union between God and *Hokhmah* resulted in the Creation of the world at the moment when a divine seed was placed into *Hokhmah* as into a womb, every meditation repeats the act of Creation. This idea is extremely important for Lurianic Kabbalah because it proves not only that God can influence the human world, but also that a human being can have a direct impact on the actions of the Deity. The spiritual marriage, in Western esoteric tradition often called the *Hieros Gamos*, served as a key allegory in the *Chemical Wedding*, and consequently in Rosicrucian theology in general;[116] however, in Rosicrucian texts it evoked a substantially different interpretation. In Russian Rosicrucian works, this allegory approached the original Jewish mystical and moral interpretation, rather than the alchemical reading used by the Germans.[117] It was also often paired with a Christian parable taken from the Gospels (Matt. 22:13) that compares the heavenly kingdom to a wedding feast for a king's son.

In some authors the esoteric image of *Hieros Gamos* simply serves as a poetic device used to highlight an evidently Christian message. The image of the heavenly wedding in Kheraskov's *Vladimir* certainly employs a number of kabbalistic and Masonic terms. Vladimir's quest into the divine realm is structured as ascension "from degree to degree." God is allegorically described as a Tree of Life, and the wedding chamber is called "the house of Wisdom filled with eternal light."[118] However, the central message of the passage describing the wedding is predominantly Christian: the wedding serves as an allegory for resurrected humanity, whereas sinful souls who are not dressed in wedding clothes have no place at the heavenly feast. The groom is Christ and the bride is a human soul.

> A mutual feast is given in the Divine premises.
> A transformed world is invited to this feast
> The groom in a divine crown is sitting on the shining throne
> Together with his bride;
> Sinful souls have no place at the feast
> Everyone should come in bridal clothes.[119]

Other writers are more ambivalent in regard to the balance of esoteric and Christian symbolism in their works: the image of the heavenly bridegroom in Bobrov's poem "Night" is more complicated than the one in Kheraskov's epic:

> Thus at the midnight hour
> A bridegroom comes, wreathed in wondrous light.
> O blissful is he, prepared for a heavenly marriage.
> O how unhappy is the other, who is destined to plunge
> Into cheerless gloom!
> So rise, my soul, do not sleep!
> You will not be sentenced to eternal death.
> Rise — light the holy oil — and watch the halls
> Where your bridegroom, your God and Judge,
> Awaits you.[120]

In evangelical parable the image of the king's son conceals the allegory of God's son, that is, Christ. On the other hand, in Bobrov's poem the image of the "blessed" groom, dressed in "wondrous light" refers more probably to the "source of light," i.e., to God the Father, rather than to Christ. In this context "a bride" is most probably a Masonic adept whose soul has finally regained its primordial light and is now ready for the spiritual marriage. Bobrov commands his own soul to observe moral law in order to become eternal and be able to see the heavenly chamber where her groom, God, is awaiting her.

Liberation from the Passions: The Masonic Interpretation

Most writers of Novikov's circle preached that the destruction of the corporeal Adam began with the liberation of a human being from the passions. This point of view was also standard for rational English masonry. Russian Masonic works unanimously suggest that passions tend to annihilate the divine spark in men.[121] Passions are condemned in many of the Masonic and Protestant mystical texts translated by Novikov and his fellow Masons.[122] However, the evolution of this idea in the majority of the works published by Novikov in the 1780s originated primarily from Schwartz lectures. Schwartz taught that humans were composed of a spirit (*dukh*), a soul (*dusha*), and a body (*telo*). He defined the spirit as the highest aspect of the soul, a spark of the original Adam's soul in man. On the other hand, the emotional soul, or *anima sensitiva*, was ruled by human passions and desires and might eventually lead man away from his mystical goal.[123]

Schwartz comments that his teaching derives from "kabbalistic books," and when he presents the spiritual forces that "are hidden in man," he gives the terms for them in both Russian and Hebrew. According to Schwartz:

> Kabbalistic books teach us that man was made out of the spirit (*sekhel* or *neshama*, known as spiritual reason), soul (*nefesh*) and body. The spirit helps man to be able to conduct an abstract meditation. By contrast, the soul leads him away into the world of earthly emotions and thoughts. *Neshama* is the reflection of the divine mind. *Nefesh* is part of the world of human passions and separates a human being from mystical meditation or pious prayer.[124]

These statements directly reflect one of the central ideas of the *Zohar* and its later interpretation in Lurianic Kabbalah: the concept of the two spiritual forces in man. According to Luria, man has a divine spirit, or *Neshama*, which is what remains of the original Adam's soul, also called the divine spark in man. Man also has a human soul, or *nefesh*.[125] *Neshama* is purely divine and free of sin; by contrast, *nefesh* is closely tied to human emotions and consequently can lead a person to sinful actions. Successful meditation liberates *neshama* from *nefesh* and brings the human soul back to its eternal divine source. Human passions are regarded in this concept as forces that weaken the human soul and drive a person away from this reunification. There is a great deal of similarity between this idea and "the teaching about the two human forces" that is described and explained in detail in Schwartz' lectures. The clearest exposition on this idea in Russian Masonic literature is embodied in Bobrov's epic poem *Drevniaia noch' vselennoi ili stranstvuiushchii slepets* (*The Ancient Night of the Universe or the Blind Wanderer*). Like Kheraskov in *Vladimir*, Bobrov utilizes the genre of mystical "zoharic" travelogue to describe liberation from the passions in the form of an allegorical quest: a journey made by a blind man searching for a doctor who can heal him. The description of material Adam as a blind or a sick man was widespread in Rosicrucian books and Christian Kabbalah. For example, von Franckenberg's *Rafael, Oder Artzt-Engel* narrates the salvation of a sick person by the divine physician-angel Rafael.[126] From the context of the poem it is clear that the blind man is, in fact, Adam, looking for the lost illumination he had possessed prior to his fall.

Bobrov's book clearly belongs to the same tradition. Bobrov, however, not only depicts the allegory of the two spiritual forces in man that appears in Schwartz's teachings, but also uses the Hebrew names found in both Schwartz's lectures and kabbalistic literature. The blind man who is searching for Wisdom is called *Nesham*. The old wise man who restores the blind man's sight is named *Mizrakh* ("East" in Hebrew, which stands for a Masonic lodge[127]); and the person who guides the blind man in his search is called *Zeikhel*, a name which derives from the Hebrew word for reason (*Sekhel*). The countries that Nesham wanders through are also called by their Hebrew names, *Mizraim* (Egypt) and *Yavan* (Greece).[128] The evidence thus suggests that Bobrov's allegory is his personal literary embodiment of kabbalistic ideas, which he most likely acquired from Schwartz and the kabbalistic literature obtained through his Masonic contacts.

In 1792 Catherine, who had always been known for her anti-mystical and anti-Masonic views, scared of French Revolution and largely following the stereotype that blamed French Illuminati for the revolutionary outburst of 1791, ordered the closure of Masonic lodges. To the Empress, Freemasonry always represented "one of the greatest aberrations to which the human race had succumbed." She described it as a strange fad among males only and scorned it as a mixture of religious ritual and childish games. She even wrote anti-Masonic comedy plays. The participation of her son Paul, who always had extremely troubled relations with his imperial mother, in Masonic activities, might have also played a role in Catherine's disgust towards Masonic societies. Other reasons that concerned her about Freemasonry were the secretive nature of its organisation, the powerful standing of its members and the influence that they certainly had at the other Major Courts throughout Europe particularly the Prussian and French Courts. By 1793 the Russian government had largely destroyed the circle of Moscow Rosicrucians. Novikov was imprisoned; others left the cities for exile at their country estates. In spite of official closure, some Masons illegally continued their activities: they were still collecting European mystical works and working on their own mystical writings.[129] Nevertheless, it can be argued that the particular Masonic tradition distinguished by the interpretation of kabbalistic allegories, which was characteristic of the works of Novikov's circle, ceased to exist in early 1790s. When Bobrov's epic poem *Ancient Night of the Universe* appeared in print in 1809, there were very few readers who understood the riddle of the kabbalistic allegorical images encoded in its lines. Romantic poet Viazemsky, in a venomous epigram, commented on Bobrov's epic: "No one doubts that Bibris used the language of God / Since no mortal can understand what he says."[130] A new generation, raised with the new nineteenth-century literary values, had a different interpretation of kabbalistic matters.

The first stage of the dissemination of kabbalistic imagery in Russia utilized the narrative forms of "mystical travelogue" and "spiritual meditation." The eighteenth-century "kabbalistic" narrative — embodied similarly in the West — was structured as "a journey of the soul" and used to comment upon the images of Wisdom, primordial Adam, and human spiritual enlightenment. Within the eighteenth-century Russian Masonic tradition as a whole, knowledge of Kabbalah did not by any means originate from private contacts with Jews. With the possible exception of Schwartz, who spent a few years in the town of Mogilev within the Pale of Settlement, Russian Freemasons had virtually no relations with the Jewish population. Most lodge members belonged to the Russian nobility, and the majority of the lodges existed in the Russian "capitals" of Moscow and St. Petersburg (which had very small Jewish populations); furthermore, Masons refused to accept Jews into their ranks. However, Burmistrov and Endel are correct in claiming that "it is obvious that the interest of Russian Masons in Jewish mysticism was far from superficial."[131] Russian Freemasons used Kabbalah to create a theosophical system that helped them to explain the hierarchical construction of the universe and to communicate with it. Kabbalah provided them with keys for interpreting the Scriptures at the deepest and the most secret level, hidden from those who did not belong to "chosen" Masonic society. Finally, the eighteenth-century Masons believed that Kabbalah helped them to obtain true knowledge about God and man and to facilitate their process of personal and universal improvement. The allegorical images of Love-Wisdom, Adam Kadmon, and *tikkun-ha-olam* served as a philosophical and ideological foundation for the Masonic program of social, religious, and moral reformation in Russia.

While employing the images and the forms already established in Western seventeenth-century kabbalistic tradition, Russian Masons infused them with new mystical meaning while simultaneously downgrading the alchemical interpretation that had been popular in the West. The circle of writers surrounding Novikov established a particular system of images that was born out of the search by mystically-inclined Russian pre-Romantic writers for a new poetic language that would be able to allegorically reflect their theosophical interests. This specific system later provided a base for the further development of kabbalistic allegory in Russian literature. The second stage of this development occurred in the early nineteenth century, as Russian Romantic authors reinterpreted Kabbalah in light of their literary philosophy and grappled with its link to the problem of poetic language as they perceived it.

NOTES

1. George Vernadsky, *Russkoe masonstvo v tsarstvovanie Ekateriny II* (St. Petersburg: Izd-vo im. N. I. Novikova, 1999), 142–45.

2. Some nineteenth-century Russian scholars of Freemasonry blamed Voltaire's influence for the growing cynicism in aristocratic intellectual circles. For example, Alexander Pypin believed that Voltaire's deistic philosophy had shaken an unconscious and primitive faith common among Russian men, and "by throwing people into a desert of spiritual skepticism, contributed to broad social depravity." Vernadsky, *Russkoe masonstvo*, 153. Pypin argued that the extensive popularity of Freemasonry in the late eighteenth century was directly connected with growing fears that Voltaire's philosophy would undermine moral

values and lead society to total depravity. Pypin's views, however, were questioned in later literature. Vernadsky claimed that instances in which Voltaire's ideas became synonymous with moral nihilism were more the exception than the rule.

3. W. Gareth-Jones, *Nikolai Novikov: Enlightener of Russia* (Cambridge: Cambridge University Press, 1984), 128. The first native Russian union of fourteen lodges was founded only in the early 1770s under Ivan Elagin, whose appointment as provincial grand master was signed in London on February 28, 1772 by the Duke of Beaufort. The first English Masonic lodges in Russia served less as organizations with moral or mystical goals than as social opportunities for non-Russian businessmen. It was among foreigners that masonry initially spread in Catherine's Russia, and the lodges were a meeting place for the society of expatriates.

4. Konstantin Burmistrov and Maria Endel, "The Place of Kabbalah in the Doctrine of Russian Freemasons," *Aries* 4, no. 1 (2004): 28–68.

5. For more on this subject see Vernadsky, *Russkoe masonstvo*, 171–72.

6. Pypin, for example, mentions a German mason, Pastor Rose, who lectured in the St. Petersburg lodge *Die Glückliche Eintracht*, which was subordinated to *The Three Globes* in 1760. Pastor Rose told his listeners that he knew kabbalistic formulas and magical words, which would help in the alchemical production of gold. Aleksandr Pypin, *Russkoe masonstvo: XVIII i pervaia chetvert' XIX veka* (Moscow, 1999), 82.

7. RGA, f. 8.op. 216, d. 6, ll. 54–54r.

8. OR RGB, f. 14, op. 1, ll. 51.

9. For more on Eli, see Vernadsky, *Russkoe masonstvo*, 130. See also Andrei Serkov, *Russkoe masonstvo, 1731–2000: Entsiklopedicheskii Slovar'* (Moscow: Rosspen, 2001), 925.

10. Vernadsky, *Russkoe masonstvo*, 186.

11. Pypin, *Russkoe masonstvo*, 91.

12. RSAAA, f. 216, op. 8, d. 6, ll. 41–70.

13. Burmistrov and Endel, "Kabbalah and Russian Freemasons," 52.

14. Gareth-Jones, *Nikolai Novikov*, 129. For more on Elagin see Douglas Smith, *Working the Rough Stone: Freemasonry and Society in Eighteenth-Century Russia* (DeKalb: Northern Illinois University Press, 1999). See also, Burmistrov and Endel, "Kabbalah and Russian Freemasons," 50.

15. Vernadsky, *Russkoe masonstvo*, 61–63.

16. See V. N. Pertsev, "German Freemasonry in the Eighteenth Century," in *Masonstvo v ego proshlom i nastoiashchem*, ed. Sergei Melgunov and Nikolai Sidorov (Moscow: Zadruga, 1914), 1:96–158.

17. Pypin, *Russkoe masonstvo*, 176.

18. For more on the history of the Masonic reform, the formation of Novikov's circle, and the difference between Russian Rosicrusians and their German partners, see Pypin, *Russkoe masonstvo*; Vernadsky, *Russkoe masonstvo*; Mikhail Longinov, *Novikov i moskovskie martinisty* (St. Petersburg, Lan', 2000); Smith, *Working the Rough Stone*; and Gareth-Jones, *Nikolai Novikov*.

19. *The Compass of Wisemen*, by the ideologist of the Order Johann Christoph von Wollner (1732–1800), contained the history of the Order as well as many kabbalistic allegories, although often variously transformed, and multiple references to kabbalistic texts.

20. Serkov, *Istoriia russkogo masonstva v XIX veke* (St. Petersburg: Izd-vo im. N. I. Novikova, 2000), 37; Vernadsky, *Russkoe masonstvo*, 102–4; In-Ho L. Rut, "Moscow Freemasons and the Rosicrucian Order: A Study in Organization and Control," in *The Eighteenth Century in Russia*, ed. John Gerrard (Oxford: Claredon Press, 1973), 198–232.

21. Novikov belonged to the first generation of Russians that benefited from the creation of Moscow University in 1755. He took an active part in the Legislative Assembly of 1767, which sought to produce a new code of laws, and, inspired by this kind of freethinking activity, soon took over editing the *Moscow Gazette* and launched satirical journals patterned after *The Tatler* and *The Spectator*. His attacks on existing social customs prompted jocund retorts from Catherine the Great, who even used her own journal, called *Vsyakaya vsyachina*, to comment on Novikov's articles. A devoted believer in social enlightenment, Novikov used his influence for various noble purposes, such as a large-scale project of promoting Shakespeare to the Russian public.

22. For more on Novikov's publishing activities see Gareth-Jones, *Nikolai Novikov*, 141–48.

23. The influence of Masonic philosophy on educated society at this time may also be related to the connections between the Masons and Grand Duke Paul. Paul was admitted to a Masonic lodge in 1784. His activities became a great inspiration for Russian masonry. Ivan Lopukhin dedicated his major Masonic work, *Dukhovnyi Rytsar'* (*The Spiritual Knight*) to Paul. A famous Masonic hymn proclaimed a great future for Russian masons with Paul's initiation:

> С тобой да воцарятся
> Блаженство, правда, мир,
> Без страха да явятся
> Пред троном нищ и сир.
> Украшенный венцом,
> Ты будешь нам отцом!

> With thee Truth, Peace, and Bliss
> Will reign in our land; without fear
> The poor will approach thy Throne.
> And in Thy great crown
> Thou shall be our Father.

24. OR RGB, f. 13, op. 221.

25. Russias knew of Boehme a century before Novikov's time. This knowledge dates to 1689, when Quirin Kuhlman, a German mystic and a devoted follower of Boehme's mystical ideas, came to Moscow. Although Kuhlman's preaching was considered heretical and he was burned at the stake in October of the same year, the ideas that he taught spread quickly after his death beyond the boundaries of the German colony (*Nemetskaia Sloboda*) of Moscow. Manuscript translations of works by "that Holy Father of ours, Jacob Boehme" began to circulate in Moscow and later in St. Petersburg. However, it was not until the mid-eighteenth century that Boehme's works achieved their dominant position among the mystically oriented part of Russian educated society. For more on Boehme in Russia, see David Zdenek "The Influence of Jacob Boehme on Russian Religious Thought," *Slavic Review* 1 (1962). 43–64. For more on Kuhlman, see James Billington, *The Icon and the Axe: An Interpretative History of Russian Culture* (London: Weidenfeld and Nicolson, 1966.).

26. For additional analysis of kabbalistic texts in the Moscow State Archives, see Burmistrov and Endel "The Place of Kabbalah in the Doctrine of Russian Freemasons," 45–46.

27. OR RGB, f. 14, op. 676, ll. 46–52; ibid., ll. 33–34. One of the noted Masonic translations of *Sefer Yezirah* is published in Konstantin Burmistrov and Maria Endel, "*Sefer Yezirah* v evreiskoi i khristianskoi traditsii," in *Judaica Rossica* (Moscow: Russian State University of Humanities Press, 2002), 2: 49–80. For more on *Shaar'e Orah (The Gates of Light)*, see Scholem, *Kabbalah* (New York: Meridian Books), 409–11.

28. Russian archives, such as the Arseniev Archive or Kaznacheev archive, housed in OR RGB contain dozens of hermetic and esoteric manuscripts

that include a large body of pseudo-alchemical kabbalistic literature, such as *Platonovo kol'tso* (*Plato's Ring*) attributed to Paracelsus, Georg von Welling's *Opus Mago-Cabbalisticum*, and books attributed to Hermes Trismegistus. For more on that, see Pypin's unpublished "Masonic bibliography" in the State Archive of Russian Federation (GRA, f. 1137, op.1, dd. 117–119) or the catalogue of Arseniev's Masonic collection (OR RGB, f. 14), which comprise approximately 2000 manuscripts. See also Konstantin Burmistrov and Maria Endel, "Kabbalah in Russian Freemasonry: Some Preliminary Observations," *Kabbalah: Journal for the Study of Jewish Mystical Texts* 4 (1999): 9–59.

29. See Judith Kornblatt, "Russian Religious Thought and Jewish Kabbalah."

30. OR RNB, f. 3, op. 65–68, d. 110.

31. RGADA, f. 8, op. 216, d. 6, ll. 54–57.

32. See Vernadsky, *Russkoe masonstvo*, 192–93.

33. Scholem, *Kabbalah*, 137.

34. Saint-Martin, Louise-Claude, *O zabluzhdeniiakh i istine* (Moscow: Tip. N. Novikova, 1785).

35. See Stephen Baehr, *The Paradise Myth in the Eighteenth Century: Utopian Patterns in Early Russian Secular Literature and Culture* (Stanford: Stanford University Press, 1992).

36. Burmistrov, "Kabbalisticheskaia ekzegetika i khristianskaia dogmatika: evreiskaia mistika v uchenii russkikh masonov kontsa XVIII veka," *Solnechnoe spletenie* 18–19 (2002): 151.

37. See, for example, OR RGB, f. 14, d. 1655, l.506." For more on the use of the term *tikkun-ha-olam* in the eighteenth-century Russian Masonic publications see Burmistrov, "Kabbalisticheskaia ekzegetika i khristianskaia dogmatika: evreiskaia mistika v uchenii russkikh masonov kontsa XVIII veka," *Solnechnoe spletenie* 18–19 (2002): 151.

38. OR RGB f. 14, d. 993, l. 3–4.

39. OR RGB, f. 14, op. 992, dd. 14–14r.

40. *Vecherniaia zaria* 91, no. 2 (1782): 31.

41. For more on the history of the Rosicrucian Order see Christopher McIntosh, *The Rose Cross and the Age of Reason: Eighteenth-Century Rosicrusianism in Central Europe and its Relation to the Enlightenment* (Leiden: Brill, 1992). For more on the history of Russian Rosicrucians, see Serkov, *Russkoe masonstvo, 1731–2000*, 905; Ia. L. Barskov, *Perepiska*

russkikh masonov XVIII veka, 1700–1792 (Petrograd: Izd. Otdeleniia russkago iazyka i slovesnosti Imperatorskoi Akademii Nauk, 1915), 215–34; Burmistrov and Endel, "Kabbalah and Russian Freemasons," 33.

42. See Smith, *Working the Rough Stone*, 83–84.

43. Vernadsky, *Russkoe masonstvo*, 188. Undoubtedly, Schwartz can be called the spiritual leader of Russian masons in 1780s. He was one of few brothers who composed his own theoretical compositions on masonry and created his own, rather eclectic theosophical system, based on Boehme and other European mystical writers. Schwartz was a native of Transylvania, received his degree at Jena University and spent some time in Asia as an official at the Dutch United East Indian Company. He arrived in Russia after his meeting with the Russian Mason Prince Gagarin (1752–1810), and had settled in Moscow by 1779. Prior to his arrival to Russia, Schwartz spent a few years in the small Belorussian town of Mogilev, which is known for its large Hasidic community. The culture of Belorussian Hasids in the eighteenth century was largely influenced by kabbalistic mysticism; therefore Schwartz's profound interest in and significant knowledge of Jewish Kabbalah may originate from his Jewish contacts in Mogilev. However, since the cultural contacts between Gentiles and Jews were extremely limited in this period, there is no real evidence to prove this suggestion, and it can remain only speculation.

44. OR RNB, f. 3, d. 112, ll. 69.

45. OR RNB, f. 3, d. 112, ll.11 ("Raznye zamechania pokoinogo Schwartza").

46. Burmistrov, "Kabbalisticheskaia ekzegetika," 153.

47. *Pokoiashchiisia trudoliubets* 4 (1785), 94–106, 95.

48. OR RGB, f. 14, d. 1455; ibid., f. 114, d. 41.

49. Vernadsky, *Russkoe masonstvo v tsarstvovanie Ekateriny Vtoroi*, 204.

50. Ivan Lopukhin, *Masonskie trudy* (Moscow: Aleteia, 1997), 35.

51. Quoted in Longinov, Mikhail. *Novikov i moskovskie martinisty.* Moscow: MVD Publishing House, 2000, 416–420

>   Ты, душе истинный и правый,
>   Открой премудрости уставы,
>   Приди и сердце oбнови.
>   Чтоб мысль вослед к тебе летела,
>   Возвысь меня из смертна тела,
>   Завесу таинства поднимь.

> Свершился мудрости совет,
> Уже не в персти дух живет.
> Подъявши крест, стал духом новым.
> Облекшись в снежну белизну,
> Несусь в безоблачну страну.

52. Ibid.

> Объемлет чувства огнь священный.
> Мой дух стремится воспарить
> Во храм от смертных утаенный,
> И книгу промысла открыть.

> Несусь душевными крылами
> В места, где высшими судьбами
> Пресветлый вижу я чертог,
> В котором будущие лета
> Времен течение, чин света
> Расположил великой Бог.

53. Ibid.

54. Ibid.

> Когда миры он сотворяет,
> Свой кроткий свет в них изливает,
> Речет, и в стройности текут;
> Родятся, возрастут, созреют,
> Умрут и в нову жизнь доспеют,
> Воскреснут, вечный круг начнут.

55. F. Klucharev, "Voploshchenie Messii," in *Prinoshenie religii*, ed. M. Vysheslavtsev (St. Petersburg, 1801), 2:21–22.

> Черту последню где имеет
> Неизмеримый круг миров,
> За кою преступать не смеет
> Безсмертный горних взор умов—
> Там бездна света пребывает,
> Как непреплавный понт стоит,
> Полна вся жизни, все живит—
> Тьмы тысящ солнцев помрачает.

> Сей свет—преддверие чертога,
> Пучина всяческих Отца,
> Всесильнаго, живаго Бога,
> Всех тварей Господа, Творца.

> Отсюду Он во всем дыхает,
> Сквозь мрак и тьму в дно ада зрит,
> В благих сияет, в злых палит —
> Сквозь все течет, все проницает.

56. Mikhail Kheraskov, *Vladimir: epicheskaia poema [Vladimir Vozrozhdennyi]*, Moscow, 1785, 93. Kheraskov, who was a curator at Moscow University and an active participant in Novikov's Masonic activities, undoubtedly listened to Schwartz's lectures.

> Еще небесна твердь звездами не сияла,
> Премудрость Божия вселенну озаряла ...
> Из мыслей Божиих истекшее творенье
> Приемлет чин, порядок, озаренье,
> Все в мире зрит она и все одушевляет,
> Родит, к рождению всю тварь приготовляет.
> Она есть Божий луч, она великий свет.

57. Compare with Proverbs 8:22–31:

> [22] The LORD brought me forth as the first of his works,
>   before his deeds of old;
> [23] I was formed long ages ago,
>   at the very beginning, when the world came to be.
> [24] When there were no watery depths, I was given birth,
>   when there were no springs overflowing with water;
> [25] before the mountains were settled in place,
>   before the hills, I was given birth,
> [26] before he made the world or its fields
>   or any of the dust of the earth.
> [27] I was there when he set the heavens in place,
>   when he marked out the horizon on the face of the deep,
> [28] when he established the clouds above
>   and fixed securely the fountains of the deep,
> [29] when he gave the sea its boundary
>   so the waters would not overstep his command,
>   and when he marked out the foundations of the earth.
> [30] Then I was constantly at his side.
>   I was filled with delight day after day,
>   rejoicing always in his presence,
> [31] rejoicing in his whole world
>   and delighting in mankind.

58. Mikhail Kheraskov, *Vladimir: epicheskaia poema*, 93.

59. For more on the biblical interpretation of the role of Wisdom in the Creation see Sergei Averintsev, "Premudrost' v Vetkhom Zavete", in *Alpha i Omega*, no. 1 (1994): 25–38

60. Donald Fiene, "What is the Appearance of Divine Sophia?" *Slavic Review* 48, no. 3 (Fall 1989): 448. While the medieval Orthodox interpretation of Sophia differs significantly from the Russian Masonic interpretation, the allegorical interpretation of the image of Sophia used by the nineteenth-century Russian Christian philosophers Soloviev and Bulgakov more closely resembles Masonic and kabbalistic allegory than Orthodox Medieval dogma. In fact, this difference in the interpretation of the image of Sophia in official Orthodoxy and in Soloviev's teachings resulted in many attacks on Soloviev's theosophy by the official Church. For more on this, see Kornblatt, "Russian Religious Thought and Jewish Kabbalah." Kornblatt argues for the possibility of Kabbalah's direct influence on the allegory of Sophia as it appears in Soloviev. While analyzing in detail Soloviev's interest in Jewish Kabbalah, Kornblatt argues that this interest arose from Soloviev's personal study of Western and original Jewish sources only, and disclaims any possible connections between Soloviev and the early modern Russian mystical Masonic tradition. She claims that before Soloviev most Russians had, at best, vague notions about Jewish Kabbalah, and while she mentions that "kabbalistic ideas had entered Russian intellectual circles through German Romanticism and the quasi-Kabbalistic writings of Jacob Boehme, [and] somewhat more directly, kabbalistic texts written or edited by Christian Kabbalists had been collected . . . by the Freemason N. I. Novikov", she still assumes that "the masons propagated Kabbalistic terminology and symbolism without distinguishing Kabbalah from other esoteric systems" In fact, while many kabbalistic texts in Freemasonic collections indeed belong to the magical Christian Kabbalah, the same conception of Sophia, later seen in Soloviev, first appears in Russia in the original works of Novikov's circle. Furthermore, some members of Soloviev's family had Masonic ties going as far back as the late eighteenth century and thus had good knowledge of the Masonic interpretation of the image of Sophia.

61. Kheraskov, *Vladimir*, 94.

62. Kheraskov also links his image of Wisdom to Catherine the Great, and, by doing so, completely moves the allegory of Wisdom from the male Christ to a female figure.

63. Kheraskov, *Vladimir*, 93.

64. Ibid., 95.

65. For more on Bobrov see M. Al'tshuller, "Lichnost' poeta v lirike Semena Bobrova," in *Reflections on Russia in The Eighteenth Century*, ed. Joachim Klein, Simon Dixon, and Simon Fraanje (Wien: Böhlau Verlag, 2001); idem, "S. S. Bobrov i Russkaia poeziia kontsa 18–nachala 19 veka," *Russkaia literatura XVIII veka: epokha klassitsizma*, ed. Pavel N. Berkov and Il'ia Z. Serman (Leningrad: Nauka, 1964), 12; Vsevolod Sakharov, *Ieroglify vol'nykh kamenshchikov: masonstvo i russkaia literatura XVIII–nachala XIX veka* (Moscow: Zhiraf, 2000), 83.

66. Vernadsky, *Russkoe masonstvo*, 465.

67. Al'tshuller, "Lichnost' poeta v lirike Semena Bobrova," 24. See also Sakharov, *Ieroglify*, 83. Some philosophical and Masonic sources of Bobrov's poetic motifs are analyzed in Liudmila Zaiontz, "Ot emblemy k metafore: Fenomen S. Bobrova," in *Novye Bezdelki* (Moscow, 1995), 50–77.

68. Sakharov, *Ieroglify*, 83.

69. Al'tshuller, "Lichnost' poeta," 139–41.

70. Semyon Bobrov, *Rassvet Polnochi* (St Peterburg: Tip. Iv. Glazunova, 1804), 1.
  Страны предвечности неведомы умам,
  Где свет, трилучный свет сиял собою сам,
  В безмолвии святом величество скрывал,
  И блеск божественный по бездне разливал.

71. Ibid., 51–52.
  Се тот великий Бог, который созерцает
  Все то чему в себе родиться подобает,
  Се образ их существ несозданных чертит,
  И будущее их движенье умозрит.

72. See, for example, *Book of Wisdom*, 7:22–23.

73. Semyon Bobrov, *Rassvet Polnochi*, 53.

74. *Pokoiashchiisia trudoliubets*, nos. 2–3 (1785): 21.

75. Ibid., no. 2 (1785): 21.

76. Ibid., no. 3 (1785): 257, 262.

77. Quoted in V. L. Rabinovich, *Alkhimiia kak fenomen srednevekovoi kultury* (Moscow: Nauka, 1979), 139.

78. Ibid.

79. Bobrov, *Rassvet Polnochi*, 3:3. See also *Pokoiashchiisia trudoliubets*, no. 3 (1785).

80. Ibid.
>Еще вкруг солнца не вращались
>В предвыспренних странах миры,
>Еще в Хаосе сокрывались
>Сии висящие шары,
>Как ты Любовь, закон прияла,
>И их начатки оживляла,
>Как дух разлившись в их ростках.

81. *Pokoiashchiisia trudoliubets*, no. 3 (1785): 67.

82. See Burmistrov, "Kabbalisticheskaia ekzegetika," 152.

83. See Burmistrov and Endel "Kabbalah and Russian Freemasons," 38.

84. OR RGB, f. 14, d. 992, ll. 14–14ob.

85. Vernadsky, *Russkoe masonstvo*, 209.

86. See Corinthians, 15:45–50.

87. See Burmistrov, Konstantin. "Christian Orthodoxy And Jewish Kabbalah: Russian Mystics In The Search For Perennial Wisdom." *Polemical Encounters: Esoteric Discourse and Its Others*, ed. O. Hammer and C.K.M. Von Stuckrad, 25–55. Leiden: Brill, 2007.

88. *Vecherniaia zaria*, no. 1 (1782): 92.

89. Baehr, The Paradise Myth in the Eighteen th Century: Utopian Patterns in Early Russian Secular Literature and Culture (Palo Alto: Stanford University Press, 1991), 79.

90. *Pokoiashchiisia trudoliubets*, no. 3 (1785): 87.

91. Kheraskov, *Vladimir*, 182.
>Ту искру видит он [Владимир] внутри души возженну,
>Которой смертному должно быть обновленну.
>Сей луч Божественный и разума светило
>Грехопадение в греховность обратило.

92. Ibid., 104.

93. Ibid.

94. See similar views in Burmistrov, "Kabbalisticheskaia ekzegetika," 155.

95. *Magazin svobodno-kamenshchicheskii*, no. 3 (1784): 65.

96. Ibid., no. 1 (1784), 142.

97. Bobrov, *Rassvet Polnochi*, 3:6.

> К восторгу Ангелов Боготворится прах.
> Прах дышит! Первенец любимый в небесах.
> Поставлен был меж стран земных и меж небесных,
> Он стал узлом существ духовных и телесных;
> В нем в мале мир вмещен со всею высотой
> Со всею глубиной, со всею широтой.

98. See, for example, Lopukhin, *Masonskie trudy*, 37. See also Gamalea's speeches in *Magazin svobodno-kamenshchicheskii*, no. 3 (1784): 59. Compare to *Corinthians*, 15:45–50.

99. This allegory is rather popular in Freemasonic symbolism in general, since in the Masonic allegorical mind the entrance of the adept into a lodge was always regarded as a rebirth. In Russian and European lodges the ritual of an initiation often included placing an adept in a coffin or taking off one's clothes to symbolize the removal of one's corporeal shell. For more on this tradition, see McIntosh, *The Rose Cross and the Age of Reason*; and Smith, *Working the Rough Stone*. It was also widespread in Protestant preaching; however in that context it was generally used as an allegory for the conversion from Catholicism to Protestantism.

100. *Pokoiashchiisia trudoliubets*, no. 2–3 (1785).

101. Ibid., 24.

> Меж тем как в пламени истлеет
> земнорожденный человек,
>々неборожденный окрылеет,
> паря на тонких крыльях вверх.

102. Bobrov, *Rassvet Polnochi*, 3: 54.

> Постой, Зорам! Ты ль мнишь что мир так исчезает?
> Не мни, то действует всевечная Любовь,
> Что грубый с мира тлен сим образом спадает.
> Подобно Фениксу, наш мир возникнет вновь.

> Wait, Zoram! Do you think that in death we disappear?
> Do not think so! It is universal Love
> That helps us to shed the rough ashes of the world
> And let it recover from the flames as Phoenix does.

103. This sort of spiritual bond with the deity is widespread in Russian Masonic literature, which borrowed it from the seventeenth-century mystical tradition. In that tradition it was usually identified as *Hieros Gamos*, "the spiritual marriage." For more on this see Yates, *The Rosicrucian Enlightenment*.

104. Scholem, *Major Trends in Jewish Mysticism*, 98. See more on the meaning of meditation in Lurianic Kabbalah and Hasidism in ibid., 95–100.

105. See, for example, OR RGB, f. 14r, d. 250, ll. 93–93r (Besedy iz teoreticheskogo gradusa Solomona vedeniy).

106. Ibid.

107. Kheraskov, *Vladimir*, 105.

> Он в высший мир умом проник глубоко,
> И в оке божием его разверзлось око,
> Имея новый слух и новы очеса,
> Увидел пред собой отверзы небеса.
> Изобразилися ему грядущи веки
> И все назначены родиться человеки.
> Как будто зримые светильники сквозь тьму,
> Судьбы различных царств представились ему.

108. *Magazin svobodno-kamenshchicheskii*, no. 2 (1784), 127.

109. Bobrov, *Rassvet Polnochi*, 3: 4.

110. Ibid., 6.

111. Scholem, *Major Trends in Jewish Mysticism*, 83. The image of Jacob's ladder originates from the story told in Genesis, 28: 12–22: "Jacob left Beer Sheba and set out for Haran. He came upon a certain place and stopped there for the night, and the sun had set . . . . He had a dream; a stairway [ladder] was set on the ground and its top reached to the sky, and angels of God were going up and down on it. And the Lord was standing beside him, and he said: 'I am the Lord, the God of your Father . . . and the ground on which you are standing I will give to you and to your offspring' . . . . Jacob woke from his sleep . . . and said: ". . . that is the gateway to Heaven." This allegory has been the subject of many interpretations in later Jewish philosophical and mystical tradition. This image was well-known in Orthodox mysticism, prior to masonry. See, for example, *Lestvitsa* by St. John of the Ladder, an Orthodox mystical text published in the early 1700s.

112. See Hans Jonas, *The Gnostic Religion: The Message of the Alien God and the Beginnings of Christianity* (Boston: Beacon Press, 1963).

113. Louis Jacobs, *Hasidic Thought* (New York: Behrman House, 1976), 37.

114. Lopukhin, *Masonskie trudy*, 43. This image is also influenced by the Christian kabbalistic book by Jesuit priest Bellarmino, anonymously translated as *Lestvitsa umstvennogo voskhozhdeniia k Bogu po stepeniam sozdannykh veshchei*, and also known as "Lestvitsa mudrykh." OR RGB, f. 14, d. 149. For more on this text see Vernadsky, *Russkoe masonstvo*, 405. This image was also popular in Christian Orthodox mysticism.

115. Bobrov, *Rassvet Polnochi*, 3: 29.

116. *The Chemical Wedding of Christian Rozenkreutz* was translated into Russian by Gamalea in 1796.

117. See Baehr, *The Paradise Myth*; and Smith, *Working the Rough Stone*.

118. Kheraskov, *Vladimir: epicheskaia poema*, 94.

119. Ibid. For an Evangelic reference see Matt, 22: 1–14.

> Во граде Божием устроен общий пир
> На пир сей приглашен преображенный мир.
> Жених в божественной является короне
> С его невестою на лучезарном троне,
> Нечистой места нет душе во граде злачном,
> Она придти должна во одеяньи брачном.

120. Bobrov, *Rassvet Polnochi*, 3:13.

> Се в час полуночи грядет
> Жених, одетый в страшный свет!
> Блажен тот раб, его же срящет
> Одетого в небесный брак.
> Нещастен тот, кого обрящет
> Повержена в унылый мрак.
> Блюди, душа моя смущенна,
> Да сном не будешь отягщенна,
> И вечной смерти осужденна!
> Восстань — вожги елей, и созерцай чертог,
> Где ждет тебя жених — твой Судия — твой Бог.

121. Lopukhin, *Masonskie trudy*, 31. See also Vaiskopf, *Siuzhet Gogolia*, 14.

122. See, for example, the translations of the books by John Pordage or John Mason, OR RGB, f. 14.

123. OR RNB, f. 3, d. 112, l. 11 (Raznye zamechania pokoinogo Schwartza).

124. Ibid., 22. These statements are reflected in other Masonic writers, such as Nikolai Trubetskoi or Semen Gamalea. See Vaiskopf, *Siuzhet Gogolia*, 19.

125. OR RNB, f. 3, d. 112, l. 11.

126. Ibid., f. 14, d. 1455.

127. For example, in Derzhavin's "Felitsa."

128. Semen Bobrov, *Drevniaia noch' vselennoi ili stranstvuiushchii slepets*, 2 vols. (St. Petersburg, 1807–1809). Vaiskopf noted that the transliteration of the name *Zeichel* shows that the name in Bobrov's work most probably originated from a German written source rather than from a Hebrew Ashkenazi source that would transliterate the name as *Seichel*. Vaiskopf, *Pokryvalo Moiseia*,

129. See Vernadsky, *Russkoe masonstvo*, 120–24; Pypin, *Masonstvo v Rossii*, 323–32; Serkov, *Russkoe masonstvo*, 266.

130. *Vestnik Evropy*, no. 11 (1810): 14.

131. Burmistrov and Endel, "Kabbalah and Russian Freemasons," 61.

Kabbalistic Allegory in Eighteenth-Century Masonic Literature

Ladder to Heaven

"In man, various faculties of knowledge — sensory perception, the imagination, reason and deep insight — correspond to the tiered arrangement of the macrocosm. The last ring is the direct comprehension of the divine world in meditation. The ladder extends no further, because God himself cannot be comprehended."

(From R. Fludd, *Utriusque Cosmi*, 1619)

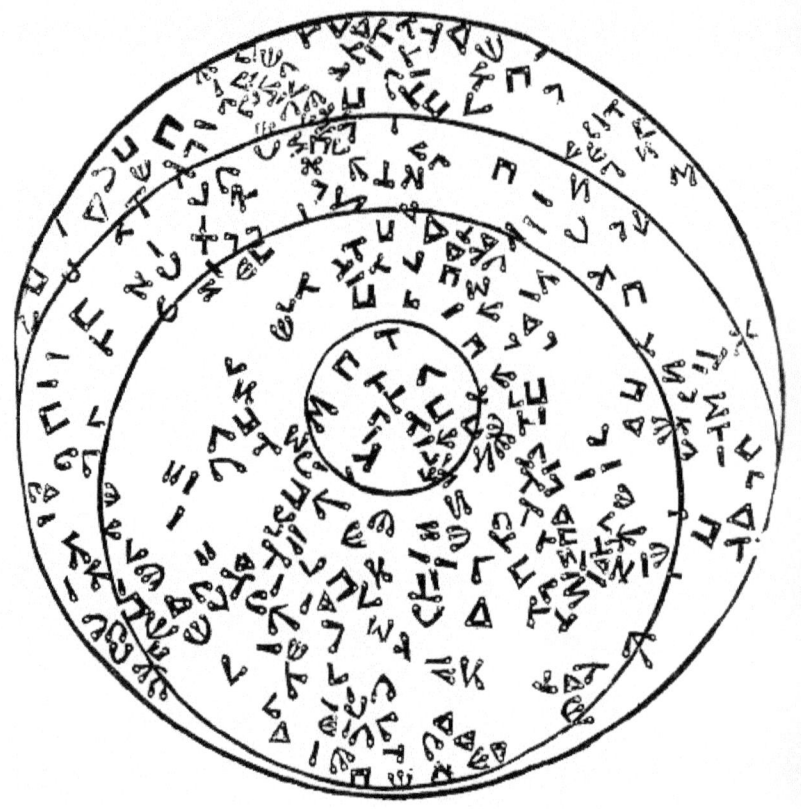

Divine alphabet of Northern Hemisphere

"In the wide space of heaven there are figures and signs with which one can discover the deepest secrets. These brilliant figures are the letters through which the holy and glorious One created Heaven and Earth. According to the Hebrew rabbis the secrets of the alphabet are formed from the figures of the stars and thus are full of heavenly mysteries."

(From Karl von Eckartshausen, *Aufschlusse zur Magie*, 1790)

Kabbalistic Allegory in Eighteenth-Century Masonic Literature

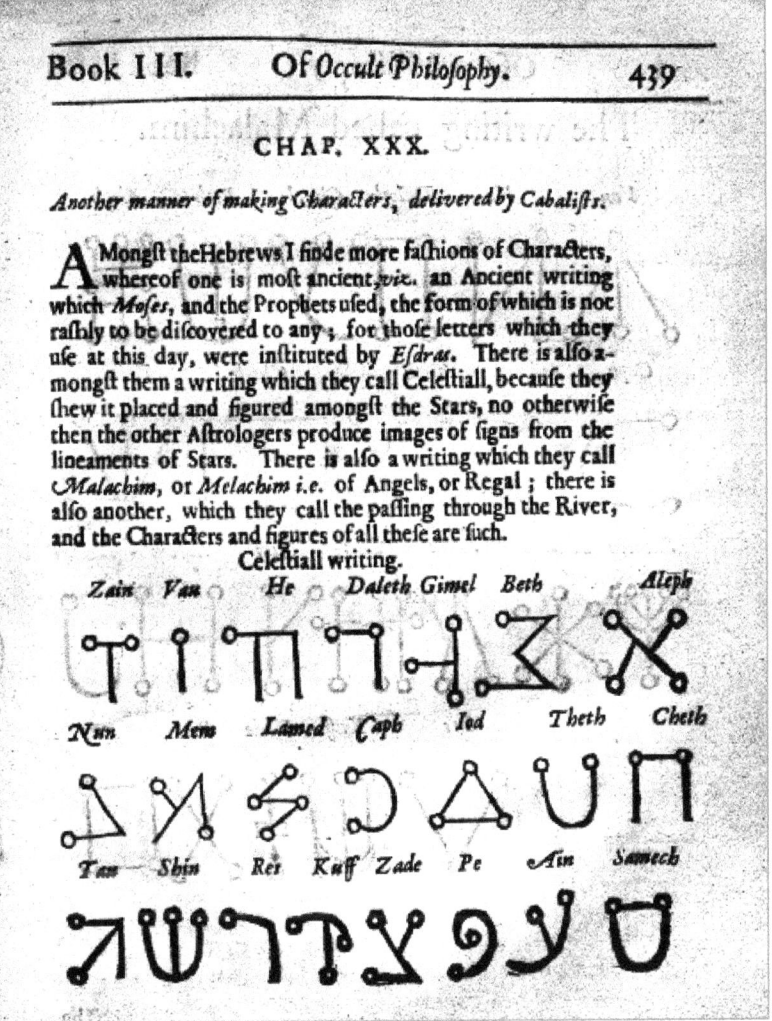

Divine alphabet of Northern Hemisphere

The great chain of being — the unity of material and spiritual matters — is presented in this illustration as a chain rope, drawn from the heaven, that links together Mankind and Nature.

(From A. Kircher, *Magneticum Naturae Regnum*, 1667)

Kabbalistic Allegory in Eighteenth-Century Masonic Literature

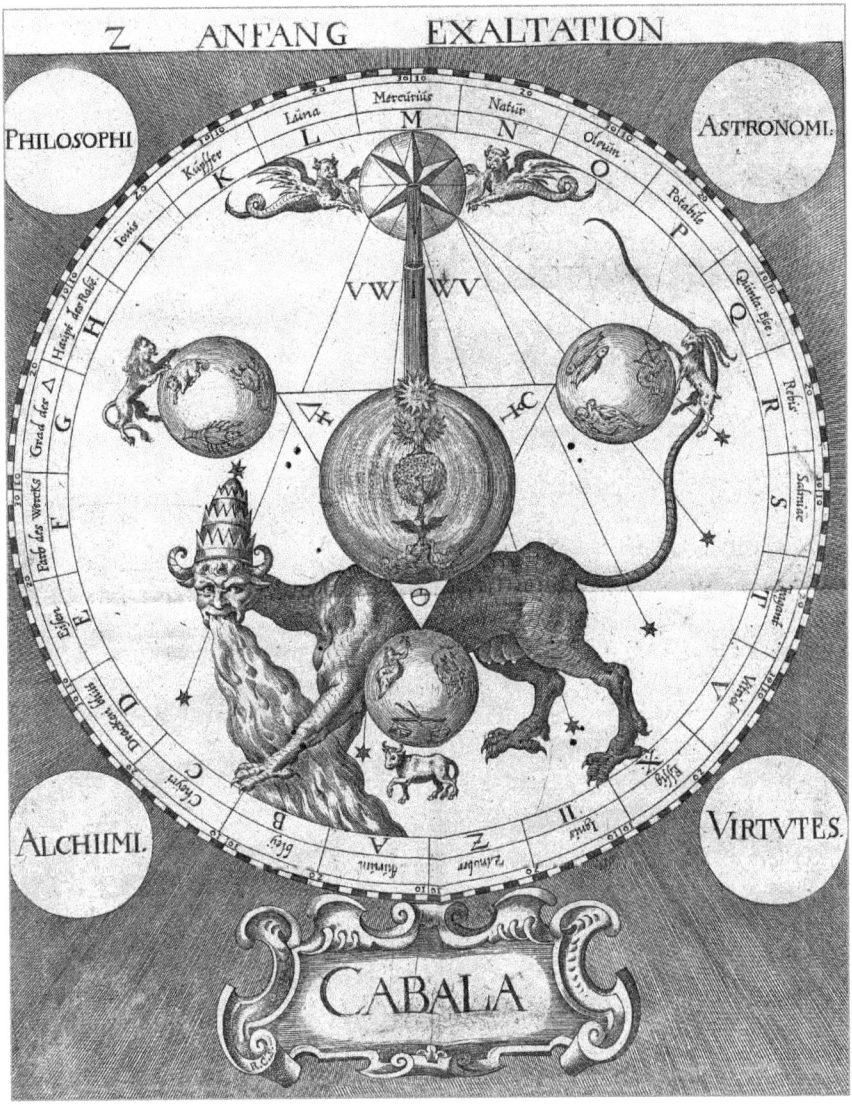

Seventeenth-century Christian Kabbalah, presented as a union of philosophy, alchemy, astronomy and virtues
(From S. Michelspacher, *Cabala*, 1616)

A Quest for Moral Perfection

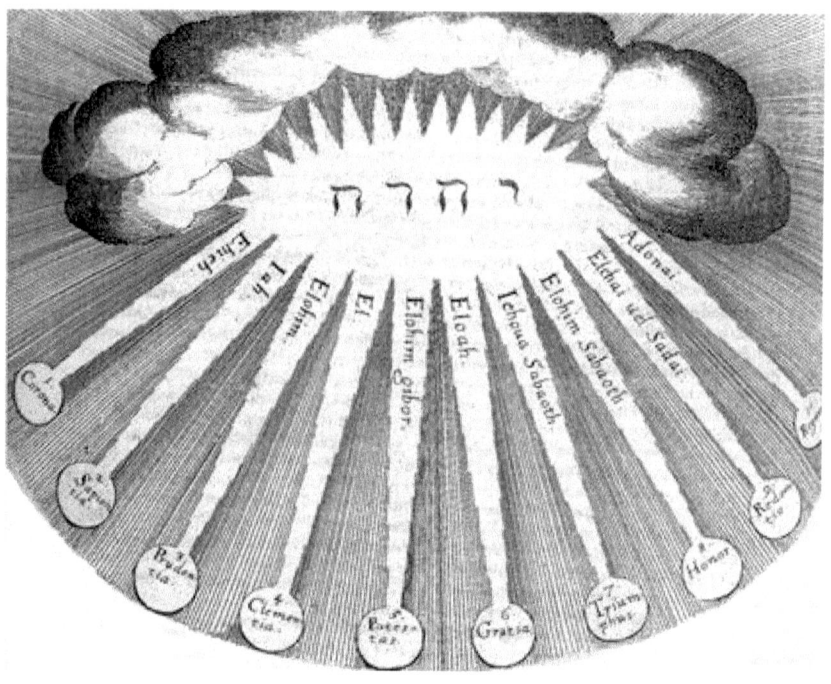

From the great tetragrammaton flow the ten "epithets" of God. These embody various aspects of the Godhead, which in turn correspond to the ten primal numbers of Sefirot

(From R. Fludd, *Philosophia Sacra*, 1626)

Kabbalistic Allegory in Eighteenth-Century Masonic Literature

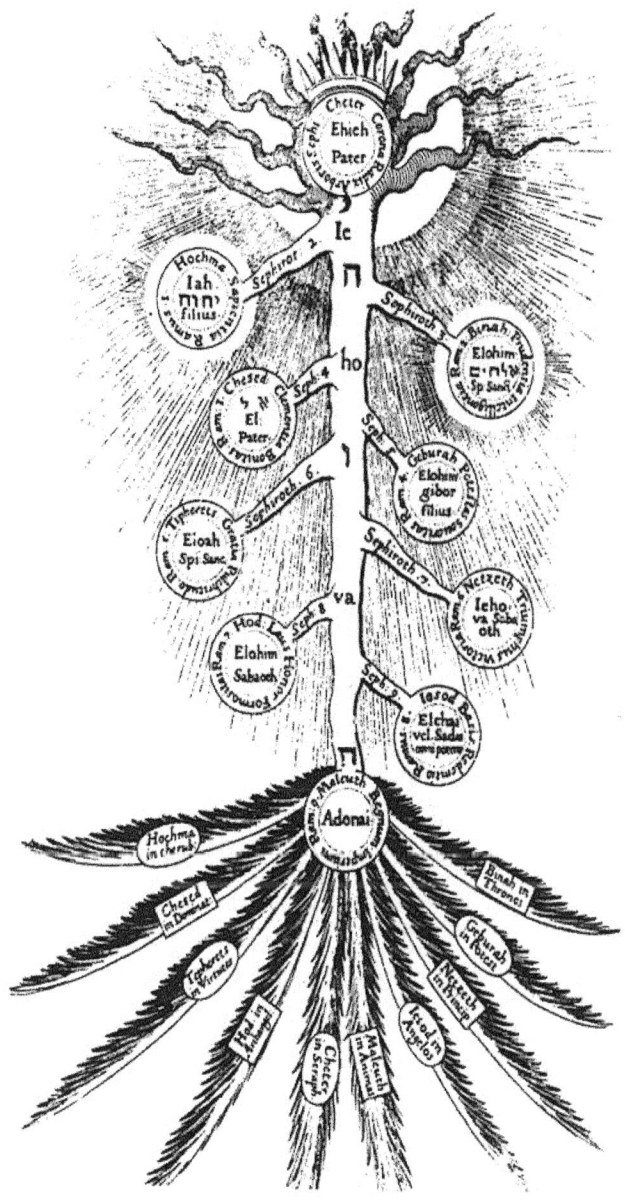

The Tree of Sefirot
(From R. Fludd, *Utriusque Cosmi*, 1621)

A Quest for Moral Perfection

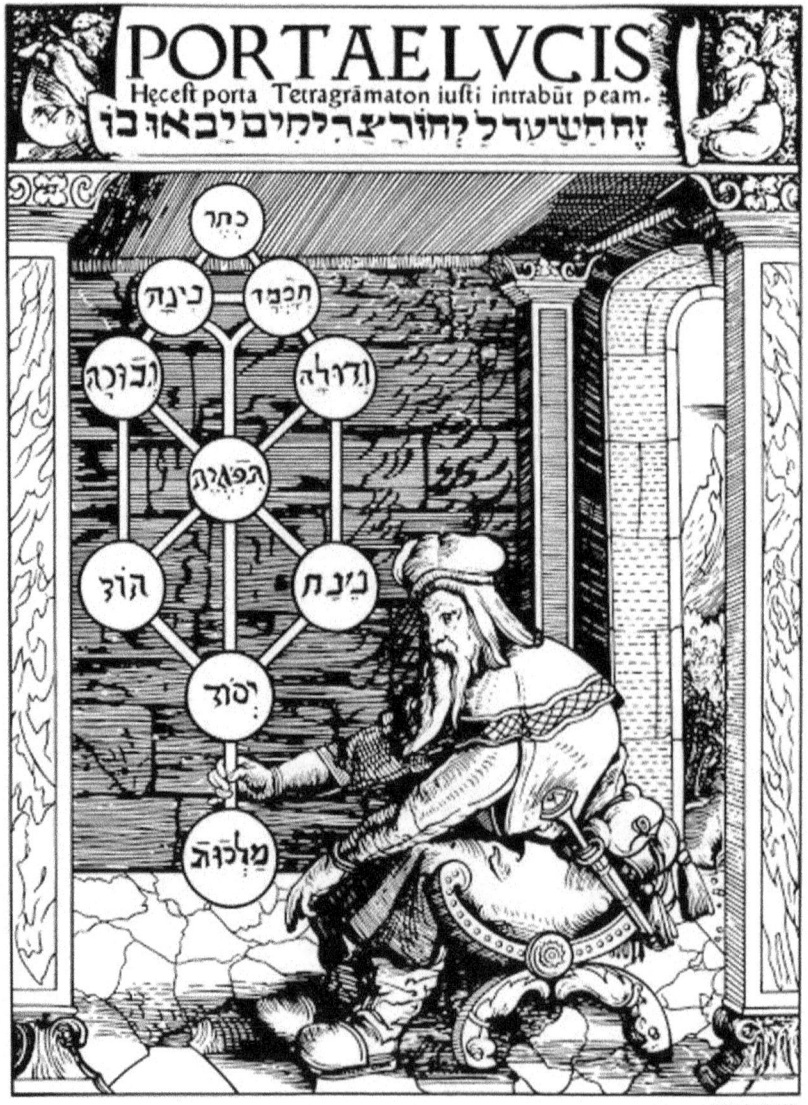

The Sefirothic Tree

**Title picture from *The Gates of Light (Shaar'e Orah)*
by Joseph Gikatilla**

(13th century)

Kabbalistic Allegory in Eighteenth-Century Masonic Literature

The alchemist enters the Divine realm via the seven steps of the Wise that correspond to the seven "earthy" Sefirot. Each step corresponds to a particular stage in the alchemical transmutation.

(From S. Michelspacher, *Cabala*, 1616).

Knowledge Hidden In Letters
Alchemic Kabbalah and Russian Romantic Literature

Mysticism and Freemasonry in Early Nineteenth-Century Russia: Ideological Aspects and Social Background

Catherine's persecution of the Freemasons led to the termination of Novikov's publishing activities and to the cessation of Masonic publications. For more that a decade Freemasonry was absent from the Russian cultural scene, although some small circles of mystics still attempted to function in Moscow and St. Petersburg.[1] This period of disfavor, although destructive for Russian mystics, did not last long. The reign of Alexander I brought Masons back from under ground. In 1803 all Masonic activity was officially legalized and a new wave of mystical sentiments revived in Russian intellectual circles. Suddenly Russian mystical Freemasonry found itself in a completely unfamiliar situation: it was no longer in opposition to the government, but, on the contrary, was supported by the tsar himself.

Even in the 1770s and 1780s, an era marked by great Masonic prosperity, Masonic activity was still essentially opposed to the anti-mystical official ideology of the state. Novikov's attempts to enlighten society through moral mysticism could not succeed due to the constant misunderstanding and resistance of a government that was influenced by the rational materialism of the French Enlightenment and the deistic ideas of Voltaire. Yet by the early nineteenth century, Russian society had begun to demonstrate a crisis of rational thought. Rationalism brought cynicism. Cynicism often resulted in moral nihilism. By 1805 the crisis of the ideology of rational Enlightenment, which had already begun during Paul's reign, had matured so that the society and the government were now ready for religious illumination. As Yakov Gordin recently remarked, the ideology disseminated by the mystical movements and persecuted by the authorities during the eighteenth century suddenly turned into the official ideology of the new authorities in the early nineteenth.[2]

Several developments were central to this crisis. The strong religious and mystical orientation of the new tsar tended away from classical Russian Orthodoxy and toward other religious practices, such as Pietism or mystical Protestantism. The nobility was still haunted by memories of the French Revolution, which they feared to be a direct product of secular enlightenment. The support of the mystically-oriented masonry was, in a way, an ideological defense against the rationally-oriented masonry, in particular, the French Illuminati, who many believed had played a significant role in the French Revolution. The coming of the new century, as well, brought the sorts of powerful millennial fears and expectations that often coincide with the fin de siècle. The new century and the new tsar aroused utopian hopes for and messianic beliefs in the great future of Russian empire. The Napoleonic wars and the leading role that Russia played in the final defeat of Napoleon also caused Russian intellectuals as well as European nobility to regard Russia as a messianic country. The triumphal entry of Russian troops into Paris also helped Russians establish closer contact with Europeans. There were a significant number of Masons among the Russian officers, and these Masons were encouraged to fraternize with their French and German "brothers." Well-known young Masonic writers Nikolai Turgenev (1789–1871) and Alexander Dmitriev-Mamonov (1788–1836) were initiated into a Dresden lodge.[3] These contacts also assisted in reinforcing literary connections between Russians and Europeans, especially French and German Romantic writers.[4] Thus, the reign of Alexander signified a flowering of Russian mystical masonry. As a result, many dormant lodges were revived and new ones were established.[5] Old masons, still attached to the spirit of mysticism, appear to have been particularly active during the first period of Masonic restoration. Mysticism was in vogue in the emperor's immediate circle and had a certain influence on fashionable society.

On the one hand, the new wave of mystical attitudes focused the attention of broader intellectual circles on such authors as Louis-Claude de Saint-Martin or Jacob Boehme. On the other hand, during the early nineteenth century, Russian intellectual circles found themselves under the influence of German Romantic philosophy, which reinforced interest not only in mystical but also in supernatural issues and promoted the growing popularity of the occult among Russian intellectuals. Russian Masonic contacts in Europe also facilitated the broader circulation of occult writings in Russia. Lastly, the new generation's the interest in supernatural matters revived many texts that belonged to the previous Russian Masonic generation. Magical and alchemic texts did not play a significant role in the ideology of Novikov's circle. The quantity of magically oriented materials in Novikov's publications was considerably less than the number of materials on ethical and mystical themes. Nevertheless, some members of the circle were particularly interested in manuscripts devoted to practical magic and alchemy; therefore, Novikov's Masons translated a sizeable number of magical and alchemic manuscripts. These texts, which remained mostly marginal in the eighteenth century, suddenly achieved significant popularity in Russian intellectual circles between 1810 and 1820.[6]

Most adepts of occult theories considered magical Kabbalah an important and influential part of occult discourse. One of the leading figures of Alexandrine masonry, Count Alexander Golitsyn, a senator and founder of the Biblical society in St. Petersburg, called magical Kabbalah "great knowledge given to Christians by Jews."[7] Similar to the Christian kabbalists of the Renaissance, Golitsyn believed that the use of Kabbalah by Christians would encourage Jews to adopt Christianity, and he believed that this religious union would precipitate the return of the Golden Age. He attached importance to the fact that Martines de Pasqually claimed to be simultaneously a Jew and a Christian who "frequently invoked Jewish words and kabbalistic symbols as aids for their spiritual quests" and who revived "the ancient alliance not only in forms

Alchemic Kabbalah and Russian Romantic Literature

but also in its magical powers."[8] As supervisor of heraldic symbols, Golitsyn sought to invest the official iconography of the state with the portentous symbols of occult masonry, magical kabbalistic symbolism, and esoteric pseudo-oriental motifs. Such beliefs were typical for other adepts of Alexandrine masonry as well, and clearly reflect the general messianic convictions of the Alexandrine era.

The reign of Alexander I provided fertile ground for Russian mystical and even occult movements. However, similar movements had begun to flourish in the West even earlier, gradually superseding the ideology of Enlightenment in intellectual circles. At the same time, the occult and alchemic Kabbalah became more popular than the ethical concepts of mystical Kabbalah that had primarily attracted eighteenth-century mystics. This shift was determined by the emergence of the philosophy of Romanticism, which completely changed the role of Kabbalistic symbolism in literature.

Christian kabbalistic literature prior to the eighteenth century included philosophical and ideological texts but never belles lettres. In a break from prior tradition, the authors of Novikov's circle employed the allegories hidden in these texts in literary works. Although strongly influenced by the mystical works of the Baroque in the content of their works, Novikov's authors remained classicists in their attitude towards language and form. The role of language and its magical or mystical powers, so important in Kabbalah, did not play any significant role in eighteenth-century mystical literature, either in Russia or in Europe. German Romanticism became the first literary movement to give kabbalistic symbolism not only thematic but also aesthetic and rhetorical value by turning Kabbalah from a subject into a poetic trope. The causes that led Romantic authors to such an interpretation of kabbalistic doctrine lie in their general conception of poetry, expressed in the literary ideology of German Romanticism.

The Role of Kabbalah in the Poetic Ideology of German Romanticism: The Concept of Transcendental Science

In the eighteenth century, the goal of art and literature was to imitate nature. Classicism regarded the best literary or artistic work as the "ideal copy," the one that most accurately imitated nature. Romantics, on the other hand, asserted that art should not imitate nature but rather shed light upon its dark, hidden spiritual secrets, which were invisible to the everyday eye, in order to open windows of sense into the depths of spiritual life.[9] While classicism regarded the artist as an imitator of the life that God had created, Romantics tried to constitute a second super-nature created by the poet himself. A poet in Romanticism was not, by any means, regarded as God. Yet he was perceived as a prophet, an imitator of God, who did not copy from nature but was inspired by an eternal creative pattern. [10]

The analogy between God and the poet, however, raises an important concern. If literature is regarded as a secondary creation, then "to poetize after this fashion is to recapitulate the original cosmogony."[11] Thus Romantics revived the neo-Platonic idea of language as a divine creative force, or *Logos*. The theory of verbal creation appealed to Romantics for two reasons. First, it supported their belief that the languages of creation and poetry have similar goals: to shed light upon the dark secrets of nature in order to create a new entity. Second, Romantics favored the idea that the language of creation was far from an everyday language: it was poetic, imaginative, and metaphoric, and not always understood by ordinary people. The poetic mastery of the Romantics entailed a struggle with the Word as a linguistic concept; they attempted to include within it a meaning larger than the common message and perceived it as a secret creative code.[12]

The linguistic mysticism of Kabbalah appealed to the Romantics even more than the neo-Platonic theory of *Logos*. From complex occult and neo-Platonic discourses, German Romantics singled out Kabbalah, and especially its linguistic mysticism, as a basis for their poetic ideology. They were the first literary men who saw in Kabbalah not a moral or mystical theory but an aesthetic, semiotic code of creation, which had existed before creation and was used as a matrix for creation. This belief is clear from a note written in 1799 by one of the key figures of German Romanticism, the poet and philosopher Friedrich Schlegel (1767–1845): "The true poetic aesthetic is Kabbalah."[13] Schlegel made the same point in another note, dated 1801, in which he said that "poetry and Kabbalah have similar goals: both try to create a new language: the poetic, metaphoric language of constant change."[14]

Similar ideas can be found in the works of G. P. F. von Hardenberg (Novalis) (1772–1801), who defined Kabbalah as "mystical grammar" and "infinite grammar," with grammar in this context meaning semiotics. Novalis also said that Kabbalah "is a language of mystical signs, which prove to us that there are mystical correspondences between man, universe, and language."[15] Similarly, Schlegel called Kabbalah "mystical grammar, a combinatory art that takes ideas through language out of Chaos."[16]

These definitions echo the ideas of Martines de Pasqually, who in his most famous work, *Traité sur la reintégration des êtres*, called Kabbalah "a science known to us as the grammar of cosmic spheres."[17] However, de Pasqually applied this term to Kabbalah in connection with magic. Schlegel and Novalis, however, made a clear connection between Kabbalah and poetry. The German Romantics were the first to employ the literary interpretation of Kabbalah, described much later by Harold Bloom:

> Beyond its direct portrayal of the mind-in-creation, Kabbalah offers both a model for the processes of poetic influence, and maps for the problematic pathways of interpretation. Kabbalah is the theory of writing which denies the absolute distinction between writing and inspiration, and speaks of writing before writing, and also about speech before speech, a Primal Instruction, preceding all traces of Speech . . . Like poets, Kabbalists richly confused rhetorical substitution with magic, relying upon the basic trope that God had spoken in order to create the World. The *sefirot* are after all ten names of God and together form the great, unutterable Name of God, which itself is a perpetually renewable way of Creation.[18]

This interpretation of kabbalistic doctrine had previously been widely used by mystics or magicians but had never, prior to German Romanticism, been placed at the center of an aesthetic theory. The seventeenth-century Christian alchemic kabbalistic tradition, largely characterized by the utopian ideology of a "new Reformation," combined deep interest in mystical issues with the study of science. Rosicrucian tradition praised Kabbalah so high precisely because it regarded it as "a mystical science" that served as a tool for humans to recover the knowledge they had lost after Adam's fall and dealt, much like Pythagorean mathematics, with letters and numbers. The seventeenth-century alchemist acted more for mystical purposes than for magical ones: his primary goal was to create a new religious philosophy that would endow human beings with the same mystical attributes they had enjoyed at the dawn of their existence.[19] German Romantics largely based their own philosophy on the same idea. Fascinated by the rapid scientific development of their era but simultaneously dissatisfied with rational materialism, they argued for the necessity of establishing a different type of scientific philosophy that would not separate the material and the spiritual but would find a way to unite them to and to "spiritualize" the material world. It was that quest that led Romantics to revive the Christian alchemic interpretation of Kabbalistic philosophy and place it in the center of their own concept of "scientific mysticism."

Scientific mysticism stemmed from the belief that the greatest evil wrought by eighteenth-century science was the detachment of the study of man from that of the universe, and the separation of scientific issues from philosophical and artistic matters. Although scientific mysticism is now an established term broadly used in the criticism devoted to Romanticism,[20] the term "scientifically artistic mysticism" (*nauchno-artisticheskii mistitsizm*) would seem more appropriate, given that the central goal of this mysticism was not only to unite science with mystical philosophy but moreover, to unite science with art. This worldview reflects the idealist utopian thinking of German Romantics, which largely echoed the messianic and utopian beliefs of the seventeenth-century Rosicrucian mystics. Whereas for Romantic theologians and philosophers, the Kabbalah represented the primal religious doctrine of humanity and a bridge between Jewish tradition and Christianity, the literary fraternity saw in it both an esoteric doctrine of the magical and a trope for the mysterious power of language and writing to transcend rationalism and rationalist thought.

The Romantics praised the world of the Renaissance, which regarded art, magic, science, and philosophy as fundamentally harmonious. The scholars of the Renaissance turned to physical or chemical formulas when they tried to find answers to philosophical questions about the mystical essence of the structure of the world and human existence. For such historic figures as Robert Fludd and John Dee, the study of physics, chemistry, or astronomy complemented their magical or philosophical studies.[21] The seventeenth and eighteenth centuries changed this situation by introducing the idea of rational materialism, which was opposed to mysticism and magic, and by divorcing applied science from mystical philosophy. The Romantics believed that rational science, governed by a mechanical picture of the world, was incapable of accommodating such recently discovered phenomena as electricity or magnetism. And, even more importantly, they believed that a mechanical worldview divorced material reality from the human spirit, and thus broke the world in two. The material world was controlled by rigid determinism, and a human being in this world depended strictly on the links of reasons and causes defined by pure material logic. Art, religion, beauty, and the world of human spirit were beyond this logical order.[22]

The idea of the indissoluble union between the material world and the world of spirit became the keystone of German Romanticism, particularly of Friedrich Schelling (1775–1854), according to whom these two worlds should be united in one whole Absolute, and all knowledge should be poeticized and spiritualized. Schelling believed that God ought to be depicted as absolute substance and, inasmuch as the world of man is the replica of the world of nature, both ought to merge in order to return to the source of this divine Absolute. Therefore, the study of man was also the study of nature and vice versa. Schelling's idealism brought back not exactly the old God of revealed religion, but the Absolute — which subsumed all of nature, history, and art in one unified whole.[23]

In order to bring the world back to its lost harmony, Schelling's followers proposed the image of a scientist similar to the scholar of the Middle Ages and Renaissance. For Schelling the ideal scientist was an alchemist: a physicist or a chemist, yet at the same time also a philosopher, often a musician, and usually a poet or an artist. The science of Schelling and the Romantic philosophers was referred to as *Naturphilosophie*: a science of a very special sort that was "used to mean both positive science and metaphysics," a transcendental, "universal" science.[24]

Paracelsus, Agrippa, and other Renaissance alchemists played a significant role in Schelling's philosophy, which gradually achieved a magical and mystical character. Schelling's work was also influenced by Saint-Martin, and probably by Martines de Pasqually as well. Saint-Martin too believed that all sciences, and especially the mathematical sciences, could only approach the boundaries of the kingdom of universal truth and could obtain true power only if they were combined with philosophy, which looks for the spiritual essence of phenomena, and not merely for its material applications.[25]

This belief in transcendental, "universal" science is especially evident in the works of Novalis. Novalis believed not only in the union of art and science but also in the union of all the sciences. In the last year of his life, Novalis composed "a scientific Bible," full of notes on topics such as moral astronomy and musical chemistry. In his book *Die Lehrlinge zu Sais* (*The Apprentices of Sais*) he asserted the following parallel between alchemist and poet: "alchemy is like poetry: it transforms metals from one state to another, just as poetry transforms nature from one state to another, by means of words."[26] Novalis called poetry a transcendental medicine, which used words to heal instead of material elements. The term "magical pharmacy," often used in Paracelsus's works, was understood metaphorically in Novalis's interpretation. Novalis wrote that the "poet is a transcendental physician, and poetry is the true art for the restoration of transcendental health."[27] Thus, the ideal scientist for Schelling and his followers was a scholar, who like the alchemist was able to see the mystical essence of nature that lay behind the material façade, and but at the same time was a poet at heart.

The alchemic interpretation of Kabbalah as a science that fuses mathematical combinations with applied linguistic mysticism and philosophical abstractions certainly appealed to the epistemological beliefs of German Romantics. In 1799 Schlegel scribbled down the following formula: "poetry = absolute science + absolute art = magic = alchemy + Kabbalah."[28] For Schlegel poetry was a synthesis of absolute art and absolute science not unlike the formula of magic as a synthesis of alchemy and Kabbalah. This formula, however, can be viewed both as a mathematical abstraction and as an allegorical spell that defines the relationship of those elements that render the boundaries of poetic "space," and accordingly it resembles the seventeenth-century Rosicrucian idea that the synthesis of magic, Kabbalah, and alchemy would produce a new philosophy, which would in turn bring a new dawn to the world.[29] The difference lies in the fact that the Romantics interpreted the Rosicrucian formula for their own artistic purposes, arguing that "the new philosophy" created by this synthesis would be "the philosophy of poetic writing."

Why did the problem of poetic language suddenly start to play such an important role in the literary philosophy of the early nineteenth century? The answer can be found in the Romantic conception of the Golden Age, regarded by German Romantics as the lost epoch of prehistoric human development, when people had not yet been separated from nature. Undoubtedly, the artistic purposes of the German Romantics were strongly tied to their messianic hopes, stimulated by the approach of the new century.

The concept of the Golden Age in German Romanticism had its source in seventeenth- and eighteenth-century mystical texts. Like the eighteenth-century Masonic and Rosicrucian authors, Romantics considered the Golden Age to be the era before the fall of Adam, when he still possessed divine secret knowledge. Yet one feature differs strongly in the Romantic interpretation of primordial Adam. The Romantics perceived the primordial state of man as a majestic condition in which his speech still possessed divine magical power. They considered this speech a luminous link between man and God that Adam lost when he abandoned the universal harmony.[30] The kabbalistic concept of *tikkun-ha-olam* was as important for Romantics as it was for the eighteenth-century mystical Masons. Novalis's belief in the transcendental "medical recovery" of mankind, achieved by a "spiritual physician," closely corresponds to the allegory of *tikkun* presented in von Franckenberg's *Raphael: the Angelic Physician* or in Bobrov's *The Mysterious Blind*. In contrast with eighteenth-century Masonic mysticism, however, the Romantics interpreted the achievement of *tikkun* as attributable not solely to moral enlightenment, but to art and literature as well. Of all the spiritual knowledge lost by Adam as a result of his fall, the German Romantics were interested primarily in the recovery of the divine language. They believed that obtaining it anew would help to restore lost correspondences between man and nature and would thus bring back the Golden Age.[31]

The Romantics' belief in the inadequacy of rational science to understand such recent discoveries as magnetism also provoked their suggestion that if science finally proved the direct connection between the spiritual and the material, the return to the Golden Age might also be approaching. If so, the aim of the poet should be to help speed up this return in order to establish a new consciousness in which the material and spiritual would finally unite and humanity would return to its lost primordial harmony.[32] The Romantics' belief in the crisis of rational science and their utopian hope for the approach of a new Golden Age played a key role in the transformation of Kabbalah from a religious, ethical teaching into mystical mytho-poetics. In the Romantics' search for a new mythology that would correspond to their religious and aesthetic principles, the linguistic "scientific" mysticism of Kabbalah became a central component.

Kabbalah and the Advancement of the Romantic Concept of Science in Russia: the Emergence of KABBALISTIKA

German Romantic idealism began to penetrate Russia in the first decade of the nineteenth century; however, not until about 1820 did its influence on intellectual circles broaden. Romantic mystical ideology was significantly influenced by the Protestant movement known as Pietism, which in the early 1810s found fertile soil in Russia, in part because Tsar Alexander was particularly interested in mystical Protestant teaching. Pietism was a German mystical movement that stressed the essentiality of an individual's personal mystical experience. It drew its strength from both masonry and mystical Protestantism, and became widespread in Germany at the beginning of the eighteenth century. A number of German Romantic writers were educated by Pietists, including Novalis, while others, like Schelling, found themselves under their direct or indirect influence. Some Pietist ideas, such as the belief in the existence of the universal inner church, were akin to the ideology of the Russian eighteenth-century Freemasons. Therefore, Russian intellectuals, many of whom were in some degree influenced by eighteenth-century Masonic mysticism, responded positively to Pietist mystical preaching.[33] By the 1810s, German Pietists had become well-known among the Russian aristocracy, who saw in those "pious and industrious people"[34] a kind of antidote to both the abstract rationalism of the French Enlightenment and the ideology of the rationalistic masonry, in particular, the Illuminati. The sympathetic reception of Pietism in Russian aristocratic society also reflected Alexander's favorable attitude toward such Protestant organizations as the Bible Society, which was well-received in Russia and was often connected with Masonic organizations. Pietists disseminated their mystical ideas in Russia through the mystical journal *Sionsky vestnik* (*The Messenger of Zion*). This journal, supported by the tsar, was founded by a Mason and disciple of Schwartz, Aleksandr Labzin, and, at the same time, was closely connected to the Bible Society. Pietists' preaching was encouraged by the tsar until the late years of his reign, when the government, concerned about political secret societies, began to worry that the idea of a universal church might endanger the established order. As a result, the wave of mystical Pietism receded in the mid-twenties; however, by then Pietism had already influenced a young generation of Russian writers who had adopted the aesthetic and religious principles of their German Romantic predecessors.

Alexander's reign brought masonry a broader audience, helped to promote mystical ideas in Russia, and encouraged closer relations between Russian and European mystics. The activities of Russian mystical masonry had prepared Russian intellectuals for the ideas of German Romantics, given that the sources for the Russian Rosicrucians and German Romantics often intersected.[35] As N. V. Riasanovsky points out, "many of the same or very similar ideas [from German Romantic philosophy] had already arrived in Russia in the eighteenth century by other routes, [particularly] through Freemasonry and Masonic mysticism."[36] The tradition created by Novikov passed to a new generation of Russian mystics who adopted it, combined it with the knowledge they received from the Pietists, and further developed it. However, Alexander's reforms gradually disassociated secular mysticism from Freemasonry. Once Masonic mysticism found a broad audience and ceased to be linked to an individual's participation in a lodge, it became an independent current related to German Romantic philosophy, which it foreshadowed with its metaphysics and its dialectical struggle of good and evil.[37] As late as the end of 1830s, some Russian literary works continued to show the influence of Rosicrucian kabbalistic allegory. For example, in 1838 the long poem *Mirozdanie* (*The Universe*) by Romantic poet V. Sokolovsky was met with a great acclaim. One of the chapters of the poem, called "Dovremennost'" ("The World before Time"), asserts that God has no end and no beginning. Sokolovsky writes about the creation of multiple worlds (*miry*), and explains that before the creation the worlds, like circles, were hidden in chaos. He continues: "the world before time shone with spiritual Light that emanated from that Love that hid an immortal Word powerful enough to created worlds."[38] M. Vaiskopf believes that Sokolovsky's poem was written under the influence of an unknown mystical or occult source, probably even foreign.[39] The source is likely to have been literary rather than philosophical. Sokolovsky's poem shows a clear influence of the particular imagery and style used in Bobrov's mystical poems "Meditation" and "The Creation of the World." The poem borrows not only Bobrov's images (*miry, predvechnost', istechenie iz liubovi*), but also the poetic rhythm of Bobrov's "Meditation." Evidently already forgotten by most readers by 1838, Bobrov was still an authority for those authors who were searching for mystical images and allegories, and who often mechanically borrowed his imagery without clear knowledge of its true meaning.

The connection between the ideas of the eighteenth-century mystics and the mystical ideology of Russian Romanticism is suggested in the name of the first philosophical Romantic society, the *liubomudry*, which was formed in 1823 in Moscow by Schelling's followers. In English the name *liubomudry* is generally translated as *The Society of the Lovers of Wisdom*. However, it can also be rendered as *The Society of the Adepts of Love-Wisdom*, reflecting the eighteenth-century Masonic concept of Love-Wisdom (*liubomudrie*). Like the Romantics, the *liubomudry* held strong messianic views. Prince Vladimir Odoevsky (1803–1869), the spiritual leader of the society, frequently expressed confidence that the decline of the West was inevitable, and that Russia had a historical mission to save the world.[40] Odoevsky was a rather unique figure for his time. His intererests ranged from physics and chemistry to musical criticism. He combined Romantic artistic tastes with a passionate enthusiasm for scientific development. In the generation of 1820s he became known as "Russian Hoffman," on account of his keen interest in the phantasmagoric and supernatural. Many still consider him the first Russian utopian.

Odoevsky, like other members of the society, shared the utopian idea of the Germans that uniting the arts and sciences would restore the conditions that prevailed during the Golden Age. However, he also had strong ties with eighteenth-century Russian Masonic ideology. Odoevsky never belonged to a particular lodge, yet his viewpoints were unmistakably determined by Masonic ethics. V. Vatsuro has asserted that Odoevsky's views, with their mystical eclecticism, paired with a strong interest in the occult and the belief in the need of social reformation, are probably even more characteristic of Freemasonic ideology than those of Novikov and Schwartz.[41]

In his notes, Odoevsky explicitly outlined his conception of scientific mysticism, explaining that "true science is always a universal study that helps us to reconstruct the biblical Tree of Knowledge, which reflects the absolute essence of the ideal world that Adam possessed before the fall."[42] *Letters from Petersburg: 4338* establishes a direct link with the Rosicrucian and hermetic traditions, although the novel also reveals general similarities with Francis Bacon's *New Atlantis*. Odoevsky portrays a utopian city in which disease has disappeared, transportation is accomplished by air, multi-level houses are built from glass, and greenhouses are lit artificially. This society has been achieved through the creation of the Academy, a governmental body that rules over the world and whose membership includes the most significant scientists, philosophers, poets, and artists. This astonishing society is endangered by an approaching comet; however, even this dreadful disaster cannot ruin the high spirits of its members. A modern scholar Alexander Levitsky notes that the most striking feature of *4338*, apart from the descriptions of advances in technology, is the mention of poets and philosophers as leaders of this technocratic society. Levitsky argues that this is significant not only because of Odoevsky's implicit argument with Plato's banishment of poets from his *Republic*, but also, and far more importantly, because it underscores Odoevsky's understanding of the special role that poets must play in averting the cataclysm from the impact of the comet. He believes that "the Comet turns out to be an anagogic harbinger of the final metamorphosis of the physical Sun into the Spiritual Sun, as well as its union with Matter (Earth)."[43] Levitsky does not draw a parallel between alchemic symbolism and Odoevsky's understanding of the role of poets in the final metamorphosis brought by the comet. However, although the words "scientific mysticism" or "transcendental science" are never mentioned in the novel, the final metamorphosis of the physical sun into the spiritual sun and its union with matter (Earth) are undoubtedly alchemic images. The members of the society do not fear the comet because they see in it an alchemic transmutation of earthy humans into immortal beings. The existing social structure of the city has prepared its members for this transformation; therefore, they do not dread but welcome it.

Odoevsky's depiction of this future utopian government is very close to that of the famous Rosicrucian utopian city Christianopolis, from a work presumably written by the author of *The Chemical Wedding*. Andreae's utopia differs from the famous European utopias of Thomas More or Tomasso Campanella in its unique synthesis of science and Christian ideals as elements of social order. The culture of Christianopolis is based on the Academy, devoted to the study of universal science dominated by four major disciplines: art, music, philosophy, and mathematics. The rulers of the city explain that the central principles of the Academy are those of "mystical numbers and letters." These ideas are clearly reflected in the concept of the Academy in Odoevsky's novel.[44]

Odoevsky read widely in the works of Gnostics and alchemists, Leibniz and Spinoza, Jacob Boehme, and Saint-Martin. However, of particular importance to his early work was Giordano Bruno, whom he saw as a tragic figure caught between faith, magic, and science.[45] Bruno is often considered one the founders of the hermetic-kabbalistic tradition.[46] He was also of particular importance to German Romantic writers, who saw in him an ideal example of the Renaissance scientist. Schelling showed a particular interest in the figure of Bruno, and Novalis devoted several poems to Bruno and his studies. Interest in Bruno's magical studies was quite widespread in Russian Masonic circles. Bruno's principal work on magic, existing in only one copy, was purchased at the end of the eighteenth century by a Russian Freemason, Count Abraham Norov (1795–1869) who brought it to Russia and kept it in his library.[47] Besides Bruno, Odoevsky was also apparently familiar with Martines de Pasqually. During his conversation with Schelling, with whom he had become acquainted in Germany, he pointed out that the name Martinists originally had not described the followers of Saint-Martin but those of Martines de Pasqually, "a well-known mystic and kabbalist." Odoevsky noted that Schelling did not know this fact and that to his surprise the German philosopher's knowledge of Martines de Pasqually's work was very limited.[48]

The "transcendental science" of German Romantics, based on magic, science, and philosophy, became one of the keystones of the ideology of Odoevsky, of *The Society of the Lovers of Wisdom*, and subsequently of Russian metaphysical Romanticism as a whole, and eventually it replaced the moral mysticism of the earlier generation. This new scientifically oriented generation of Romantic mystics played a central role in advancing and developing the Russian concept of *kabbalistika*.

The earlier eighteenth-century Russian mystical works of the pre-Novikov generation often echoed the seventeenth-century interpretation of Kabbalah as a "science" (*nauka*) that studied the principles of the unity of the material and the spiritual aspects of life. It is interesting, however, that in Russian manuscripts, both original and translated, this study is never defined as *Kabbalah* but always as *kabbalistika*. This term appears for the first time in Russian texts in the manuscript translation of Raimond Lull, a monk and scholar who lived in the thirteenth century, yet became famous only in the mid-1600s. Lull was among the first Christians to make contact with Jewish Kabbalists in Spain. He also was among the first scholars to regard Kabbalah as a science rather than a mystical doctrine. Lull's views were reflected in the works of many alchemic kabbalistic and Rosicrucian authors of the mid-1600s, including Robert Fludd, Athanasius Kircher, and others, all of whom subscribed to the idea that one day doctors, kabbalists, and philosophers together would bring the world back to its lost absolute harmony. Half a century before the development of Freemasonry in Russia, between 1698 and 1700, Andrei Belobotsky translated the most important excerpts from Lull's texts. The collection of these translated excerpts was published under the title *Velikaia i predivnaia nauka kabbalisticheskaia* (*The Great and Wonderful Science of Kabbalah*) in which the term *kabbalistika* was introduced in Russia for the first time. This book was very popular in Russia in the late 1700s and early 1800s, and was often referred to by the authors of this period as simply *Raimonda Lulliia Kabbalistika* (*The Kabbalistika of Raimond Lull*). Joseph R. Ritman noted that:

> The art of finding truth, logic, physics, medicine, astrology, and Kabbalah are all intertwined in Lull's great work. In addition to the *Ars Magna*, the Russian followers of Lull appear to have had a particular preference for the Kabbalah in this great philosophical conglomerate. The esteem in which they held the Kabbalah is already evidenced by the expensively and lovingly produced binding of the Russian manuscript from 1725 here shown, the contents of which is announced as a summary of the great science of the Kabbalah. For Lull Platonic philosophy was an essential premise for the Kabbalah. He regarded the Kabbalah as a sort of mystical and cosmological geometry and gave it graphic representation in his *Arbor scientiae* or complete encyclopedia of knowledge.[49]

The preface to the 1801 edition of the book clearly outlined the meaning of the term *kabbalistika* to the readers. It explained *kabbalistika* as "a great and interesting science that aims to unite all existing sciences into one in order to bring mankind back to the lost glorious state through the union of nature, language, and mathematics."[50]

Western sources, including such famous authors as Pico della Mirandola, very often used the Latin adjective *cabbalistica*. However, the noun *kabbalistika* is a Russian innovation not found in any Western European source. It is evident that in Russian literature this term originates from the coordinating Latin adjective. However, the meaning of the noun *kabbalistika* does not simply correspond to Kabbalah. In contrast to Kabbalah, which the majority of eighteenth-century Masons perceived as a moral doctrine, the term *kabbalistika* refers essentially to the linguistic and mathematical aspects of kabbalistic teaching, that is, to the idea of the divine power of letters and numbers. It also adopts from the earlier Jewish and Christian Kabbalah the myth of Adam Kadmon. However, whereas in Jewish mysticism the process of the restoration of the primordial state, *tikkun-ha-olam*, is associated with moral and spiritual purification, in *kabbalistika* this return can be achieved by establishing the proper balance between spiritual and scientific principles. *Kabbalistika* was a mathematical and linguistic philosophy, a "universal science," a union of language and mathematics, theoretically founded on a rational scientific basis as much as on a mystical ideological platform and linked to alchemy. The Masonic manuscripts of the 1770s–1780s were not principally interested in this side of Kabbalah. However, in the first two decades of the nineteenth century, the intellectual and mystically oriented Russians, following their German predecessors, started to show a serious interest in it. As Russian historian A. M. Skabichevsky noted in the late nineteenth century:

> In the 1820s, the young generation, one and all, was carried away by philosophy. However, philosophy was considered as something quite different from our modern interpretation of the word, not a system of ideas or abstract views. It was seen as a mystical universal science able to unite all sciences into one, a secret science, similar to medieval alchemy or kabbalistika. People "entered" the study of philosophy with a sense of mysterious anxiety, hoping to find in it the ability to obtain divine power over nature and raise the curtain of human weakness and ignorance that separated the material world from the hidden world of our spiritual being.[51]

The image of Kabbalah as a universal science appeared not only in Lull but also J. G. Wachter's *An Exposition of the Kabbalah or the Secret Philosophy of the Hebrews*, reprinted in 1807.[52] Wachter's book noted similarities between Kabbalah and the philosophy of Spinoza. He argued that Kabbalah represented a new type of philosophy that would unite the Aristotelian and Platonic world views and construct a "new universal philosophy." Wachter even believed that this "science" should be taught in schools and universities because it "has fewer weaknesses than other philosophies routinely included in curricula."[53] The German original of Wachter's volume was annotated by Leibniz, which definitely enhanced its interest for such Russian intellectuals as Odoevsky, who were interested in mathematics no less than philosophy.[54]

The "scientific" approach to Kabbalah of the early nineteenth century did not completely replace the moral/mystical approach widespread among the eighteenth-century Masons. Rather, the new "scientific" mysticism adopted eighteenth-century images, but filled them with new alchemic and pseudo-scientific meaning. One reason for this shift is that early nineteenth-century Russian intellectuals were significantly more worried about the consequences of rational science for the development of society than both their Masonic predecessors and their German spiritual mentors. Some twenty years divided Novalis and Schlegel from the circle of Vladimir Odoevsky; during these two decades technological advances progressed rapidly. Young Russian intellectuals who understood the necessity of technological development, yet feared rational and materialistic science that abandoned the philosophical implications of scientific discoveries, sought a science that would oppose materialism and "scientific specialization" (*nauchnaia spetsializatsiia*) by combining the study of metaphysics and literature with that of physics and mathematics. *Kabbalistika*, the Romantic interpretation of the alchemic Kabbalah, perfectly fitted their goals.

The Evolution of KABBALISTIKA in Russian Romantic Prose: from "Scientific" Kabbalah to Black Magic

The creative world of Romanticism was inseparable from the world of magic — magical and supernatural matters were essential for Romantic world views. Most of the characters of Russian Romantic works combined the desire to understand the mystical essence of nature and humanity with an interest in magical studies; it is not a coincidence that the protagonist of *Russian Nights* is named Faust. However, quite often in Romantic literature these magical studies were referred to as the study of *kabbalistika*. In a letter to Countess Rostopchina, Odoevsky wrote, "Is it possible to find the origin of the science that we now call *kabbalistika*? We can certainly say that *kabbalistika* originated as a poetical science that is also known to us as *philosophical magic* or *philosophical alchemy*."[55] Odoevsky considered *kabbalistika* a hybrid of magic, philosophy, and mathematics that gave humans the answers to the riddles of nature. Most of the writers of his generation shared this opinion.

A similar interpretation is seen in the short story *Blazhenstvo bezumiia* (*The Bliss of Madness*, 1833) written by Nikolai Polevoi (1796–1846), a highly popular Romantic writer and critic, and the publisher of the literary journal *Moscow Telegraph*. The protagonist of his story, Antioch, who "is seriously devoted to magical and mystical subjects," describes *kabbalistika* as "the world of secret knowledge, of strange and mysterious riddles hidden in nature and the human soul, to which mortals can never find a complete answer." He proclaims that "nature is a secret hieroglyph that can be decoded only by those who possess the secret knowledge and the secret power. *Kabbalistika* is the key to this power and knowledge."[56] Antioch also adheres to the mystical allegory of Adam Kadmon and Sophia:

> Leonid — Antioch used to tell me — you should know that Man is a fallen angel of God, who still bears the seeds of Paradise in his soul. The world is beautiful. Therefore, man is beautiful too, for he is the trace of the divine breath. The storms of earthly passions destroy him; heavenly love purifies him and brings him back to his heavenly bride Wisdom, the sister of Love and Hope and to his glorious primordial state.[57]

The allegory of "a fallen angel of God" in this context suggests that man, according to the narrator, is a fallen heavenly creature; yet the narrator also comments that man is a "trace of divine breath," a metaphor that certainly echoes the image of Adam, who has been created from the divine breath infused into earthy clay. Such a combination allows us to believe that a "fallen angel" in this context is a "divine Adam", i.e. primordial man, and that the power of heavenly Love-Wisdom would be capable of returning him back to Adam Kadmon's primal divine state. The influence of Romantic ideology is also apparent on the character of Antioch, and consequently, on the author. In the narrator's mind, the allegory of Wisdom and Adam Kadmon is connected with the magical kabbalistic powers of numbers and divine names: "the mysterious philosophy of ten *Sefirot*, alchemic formulas, the power of magical letters, the names of angels, the secret numbers, and the Temple of Solomon spoke to him of the capacity for a higher contemplation of Heaven and Earth."[58] It is important to note that the name Antioch in the story is not accidental. It originally belonged to Cyprian of Antioch, a famous pagan sorcerer who eventually became a Christian bishop.[59]

A similar duality in the perception of the concept of Wisdom is also seen in Odoevsky's *Kosmorama* (1837). Sophia is one of the protagonists of the story, a girl in love with the narrator, who saves him from death in a fire at the cost of her own life. Sophia is certainly an allegorical image that stands for divine Wisdom. V. Vatsuro writes that:

> The image of Sophia in the story certainly derives from the mystical literature that Odoevsky had read. Sophia's behavior arises from and is predicted by the ethical and religious ideology of Freemasonry. To see this parallel, we need only to look at the Masonic writings of Ivan Lopukhin. Sophia's behavior is ruled by Love and Faith, and is opposed to Vladimir's rational behavior. Masonic symbolism is also embodied in the ending of the story, in which Sophia dies in a fire, saving Vladimir's life. This act in Odoevsky is interpreted as a spiritual marriage and reflects the Masonic idea that a fiery baptism signifies a spiritual marriage with the Heavenly Bride, Sophia.[60]

The image of Odoevsky's Sophia clearly derives from a Masonic origin. However, the image of the fiery marriage also suggests an alchemic interpretation as well. In alchemy, fiery marriage is a synonym for the alchemic wedding, an allegorical term for the final step in the alchemic transmutation of elements, when all the chemical components in mixture are finally amalgamated. In

Alchemic Kabbalah and Russian Romantic Literature

Lopukhin's writings the spiritual marriage has only moral and mystical connotations — the adept is purified and then reborn. In Odoevsky's *Kosmorama*, just like his *Letters from Petersburg: 4338*, the parable of ultimate human transformation combines moral mysticism with an alchemic allegory.

The principal interpretation of *kabbalistika* as a transcendental universal science continued to play a significant role up to the late 1830s. However, between the 1820s and the 1830s Russian nobility gradually became more interested in magical studies and in kabbalistic numerology than in the ethical precepts advocated by Novikov's generation. This interest, which paralleled the growing approach to Kabbalah as a magical science, was immediately manifested in Russian literature. Romantic literary works of 1830s display numerous fantastic and supernatural themes that for the most part were borrowed from English Gothic writers and from E. T. A. Hoffman (1776–1822), a German Romantic author with a particular affinity for fantasy and horror. Hoffman's writings achieved great popularity in Russia in the 1830s and strongly influenced Russian literature between 1820 and 1840.[61] In 1836, as a part of the collection of Hoffman's stories titled *Die Serapionsbrüder* (*Serapion's Brothers*), Stepanov's press in Moscow published the story *Die Königsbraut* (*The King's Bride*), translated as *Tsarskaia nevesta*. One of the protagonists of the story, Herr Dapsul von Zabelthau, is a passionate devotee of occultism and magic, and a keen scholar of "Kabbalah," which he describes as "a sacred supernatural science, a deep mystery of the universe [that explains] the peculiar nature of the gnomes, salamanders, sylphs, and undines and all other spiritual beings [that inhabit] the deep earth, air, water, and fire."[62] Hoffman's approach to Kabbalah in the story is ambivalent. On the one hand, Hoffman truly believes that magic and supernatural powers exist; on the other hand, he clearly mocks the protagonist's blind faith in them. Knowledge of the "supernatural science" of Kabbalah does not help Herr Dapsul to fight the evil King of Vegetables, a gnome-demon in the form of a giant carrot, who, however, quickly surrenders to the strong anti-demonic powers of bad poetry. Such ambivalence is also characteristic of most Russian literary works of this generation.

This change of interest from mystical to magical subjects manifested by the Russian nobility of the 1830s eventually changed the meaning of the word *kabbalistika*. In the literary works of this decade this term usually denotes not a transcendental science but any practice of the symbolic interpretation of letters, numbers, and words, from gambling at cards to fortune-telling.[63] Several factors may have precipitated this change. To begin with, a similar interpretation of *kabbalistika* was very strong in the fantastic works of Hoffman, and many young Russian Romantics who found the mysticism of Schelling and Schlegel too complicated to follow simply borrowed Hoffman's interpretation, which was easier to comprehend and more straightforward. Interest in kabbalistic numerology was also present in the earlier years of the nineteenth century and was linked to the messianic and apocalyptic sentiments that dominated the minds of Russian intellectuals at the close of the Napoleonic wars. A good example of such beliefs and their reflection in the fascination of kabbalistic numerology for the Masons of the Alexandrine period can be found in Leo Tolstoy's *War and Peace*:

> One of his brother masons had revealed to Pierre the following prophecy relating to Napoleon, and taken from the Apocalypse of St. John.
>
> In the Apocalypse, chapter thirteen, verse seventeen, it is written: "Here is wisdom . . . count the number of the beast, for it is the number of the man, and his number is six hundred three score and six . . ."
>
> If the French alphabet is treated like the Hebrew system of enumeration, by which the first letters represent the units, and the next the tens and so on, the letters have the following value:
>
> a b c d e f g . . .
>
> 1 2 3 4 5 6 7 . . .
>
> Turning out the words l'empereur Napoléon into ciphers on this system, it happens that the sum of these numbers equals 666, and Napoléon is thereby seen to be beast prophesied in the Apocalypse. This prophecy made a great impression on Pierre. He frequently asked himself what would put an end to the power of the beast, that is of Napoléon; and he tried by the same system of turning letters into figures, and reckoning them up to find an answer to this question.[64]

Yet the most significant cause may be linked to the fact that in the last years of Alexander's reign masonry abruptly changed its ideological goals. In the 1820s, a large number of Masonic organizations shifted from mystical studies to social and political issues. For example, by the mid-1820s Astrea lodges began to look more like liberal organizations devoted to social questions than religious societies immersed in mystical arguments. Most Alexandrine Masons of this decade were influenced not only by German but also by English Romanticism, especially by the persona of Lord Byron, who advocated many of the ideas of freedom, conspiracy, and rebellion that played such a prominent role in the Decembrist movement. The allegory of a divine spark that must flare by means of human virtue, which reflected the Masonic belief in the necessity of moral reformation of society, has transformed in the minds of the new generation of Masons into an image of a revolutionary spark that would create a universal uprising. "The flame will burst out from a spark," declared future Decembrist Alexander Odoevsky, a cousin of Prince Vladimir Odoevsky, who never shared his cousin's mystical outlooks.[65] This new type of young Russian Mason rejected mysticism, yet at the same time continued to be interested in esoteric and magical concepts. The majority of Freemasons did not subscribe to a mystical-conspiratorial view of history, but they did not reject the possibility of such explanations. They seem not to have believed literally in thaumaturgy, but they intellectually appreciated the symbolism of alchemy, numerology, *kabbalistika*, and the other occult skills that they were required to learn in Masonic lodges. And the writers among them perceived the literary potential of thaumaturgy, just as they perceived the efficacy of secrecy and conspiratorial methods.[66]

Frightened by the growing political activity of Masonic lodges, in 1822 Alexander I pronounced the official interdiction of masonry in Russia. These drastic measures did not by any means destroy political societies, yet they did contribute to the decline of mystical interests among Russian intellectuals. The tsarist attacks against the Masons resulted mostly from Alexander's fears of the possible subversive role of masonry in Russian society. By contrast, the more general aristocratic interest in magic and the supernatural did not threaten the political life of the state, since the magical interests of the nobility had no political consequences. Therefore, even when the lodges were closed, the government did not work actively to suppress the interest of the elite in supernatural issues. This interest did not decline until the 1840s, and became even stronger after the Decembrist revolt of 1825 was suppressed.

Historians generally speak about the decline of high intellectual activity in Russian society that followed the failure of the Decembrist revolt. During these years the nobility saw occult practices as a way to overcome the depressive feelings in high society that followed the revolt and to find a substitute for the previous intellectual vibrancy that they so strongly missed. As a result, the study of occult sciences, fortune-telling, demonology, magnetism, and spiritualism became extremely popular among the Russian elite. Alexander Pushkin's sister studied palm and card readings. Countess Rostopchina wrote under the penname "Clairvoyant." Pushkin's uncle, the Romatic poet Vasilii Pushkin, wrote that:

> Among the officers of our regiment conversations based on the discussion of various magical and mystical subjects were very popular. Everyone seemed to be interested in magnetism, clairvoyance, and other mysterious phenomena. A few times we even attempted to summon an angel with the help of some kabbalistic incantations.[67]

All these factors contributed to the fact that by the late 1820s numerological magic had primarily replaced other interpretations of *kabbalistika*. *Kabbalistika* was distinguished from regular magic on the basis of the perception that magic was a practice based on an individual's natural magical abilities. By contrast, *kabbalistika* was perceived as "scientific" magic founded on mathematical and linguistic principles. Magic was subjective; *kabbalistika* was objective. It was considered a "science," based, just like as any other science, on rational rather than emotional principles; hence it could be studied and mastered just like physics or mathematics.

Eighteenth-century Russian Freemasonry clearly expressed a positive attitude towards kabbalistic doctrine. This positive attitude was also characteristic of most German Romantics in the first years of the nineteenth century. Russian Romantic writers of the 1830s, however, displayed a certain duality in their attitudes toward Kabbalah. On one hand, most Romantics shared the official opinion of the Orthodox Church that *kabbalistika*, like alchemy or magic, was a heretical, "demonic" practice. On the other hand, some of them simultaneously admired *kabbalistika* because it constituted the foundation of the transcendental science that was essential for Romantic aesthetic ideology. Moreover, the understanding of *kabbalistika* as a science concealed a certain disturbing contradiction. While the magical "science" of *kabbalistika* differed from eighteenth-century materialist science and thus appealed to Russian Romantics, it was also perceived as objective, "rational" magic; and rationalism, in any form, was antithetical to Romantic views. This duality resulted in peculiar consequences: Russian Romantic writers widely illustrated the use of kabbalistic magic but always presented the negative outcome of this use. This attitude toward Kabbalah produced a certain type of a narrative that can be called the "kabbalistic tale," which partially followed the clichés of the original "kabbalistic" mystical travelogue yet largely differed from the eighteenth-century interpretation of this genre. In eighteenth-century Russian literature, kabbalistic symbolism was mostly present in poetry. By contrast, Russian Romantic poetic works, although they widely employ magical imagery, did not demonstrate significant use of kabbalistic imagery. Russian Romanticism incorporated such symbolism into prose, particularly into the specific genre of the "magical" short story. These stories were usually characterized by similar plot structure. They all depicted young intellectuals, eager to learn the secrets of nature, who studied *kabbalistika*. This study proved to be destructive for these apprentices, who exchanged their emotional stability for illusory secrets hidden in "dead letters and lifeless numbers."[68] It led its scholars into a dark world of devils and demons and usually deceived and psychologically destroyed anyone bold enough to enter this world.

Such a tale forms part of Evgenii Baratynsky's short story *Persten'* (*The Ring*, 1832). A metaphysical Romantic, Baratynsky (1800–1844) is better known for his poetry than his prose. In fact, *The Ring* is his only work of fiction. The protagonist of the tale, Antonio, lived several centuries ago in Spain where he "engaged himself in the criminal study of magic taught to him by scholarly Yids."[69] In spite of his fear of the Grand Inquisition, Antonio adhered to his magical pursuits: "He secretly talked with learned Yids and searched endlessly through thick kabbalistic books in order to find answers that would help him to raise the secret curtain that separated him from the secrets of nature."[70] Antonio attempted numerous combinations of magical words and kabbalistic spells, and finally succeeded in summoning a demonic spirit. Antonio accepted the spirit's invitation to follow him into a deep tunnel.

> Antonio followed the spirit, continuing to repeat the kabbalistic formulas in his mind.... Suddenly [he] lost consciousness. When he woke up the next morning, he thought the journey was just a dream. But no! He had changed since the previous night: he saw the world not through the eyes of a human but through those of a demon. He had comprehended the secret of nature. He had acquired Absolute knowledge![71]

This absolute knowledge, however, brought no happiness to Antonio: "he knew everything, past, present, and future; and this knowledge caused him enormous suffering. He had learned the Secret of nature; yet this mysterious secret was as terrifying as it was useless. He felt that everything was in his power yet he did not crave anything."[72]

Persten' exemplifies the shift in the narrative form of the "mystical travelogue" that occurred in the Russian Romantic literature of the period. The mysterious angelic healer, popular in eighteenth-century literature, who enlightens the adept on his travels to the higher truth, has transformed into a demonic spirit that leads his follower on a magical rather than spiritual quest and consequently brings him to destruction. The allegorical natural images, such as forests, mountains, and gardens, disappear almost entirely, giving way to such Romantic clichés as deep dark tunnels, abandoned castles, and underground chambers, which possess no allegorical essence whatsoever, but are simply used to arouse in the reader a sense of the mystery and irrationality of the events narrated. The meditative experience of the "mystical travelogue" is stripped of its spiritual theosophical mood and is converted into a supernatural "demonic" encounter.

The destructive powers of *kabbalistika* are also emphasized in Odoevsky's story *Segeliel* (1833). Segeliel, a satanic physician who "can fill an entire room with letters and numbers," enchants a poor musician whom he instructs in "kabbalistic formulas that reveal to him all the secrets of the world."[73] The musician hopes that this knowledge will help him come to a better understanding of musical harmony. However, the result is quite the opposite. When the protagonist learns everything, he realizes that because of his knowledge he has lost his human emotions. He feels neither love nor excitement any longer, and suffers enormously from his lack of feelings. Odoevsky explains to the reader that the name Segeliel "originates from magical kabbalistic manuscripts: it is one of the spirits created by the imagination of the neo-Platonics and kabbalists."[74] It seems, however, that the name was invented by Odoevsky. Demon Segeliel is not listed either in Jewish or in Christian kabbalistic sources. Mikhail Vaiskopf has suggested that it might derive from a combination of the Hebrew word *Sekhel* (reason) and the suffix "el" that usually characterizes angelic names in Judaism.[75] This would support the point that the story contains a hidden criticism of rational philosophy: it is reason — *ratio* — that serves as an allegorical demonic kabbalist who separates the protagonist from the world of emotions and eventually ruins him.

Another shift in the interpretation of *kabbalistika* occurred during this period as well. In the Romantic works of the 1830s, the link between *kabbalistika* and the study of magical numerology often led to a spurious connection between Kabbalah and gambling. Gambling had been very popular in Russia since the early eighteenth century. However, the connection between Kabbalah and gambling did not exist prior to the late 1820s. By contrast, in later Romantic texts the linkage between gambling and the study of Kabbalah became very widespread. Not only did *kabbalistika* come to be perceived in 1830s as a doctrine connected to gambling, but gambling also came to be regarded as an occult kabbalistic process. A famous phrase from Alexander Pushkin's story *Pikovaia Dama*

(*The Queen of Spades*) supports this linkage. One of the characters confronts another with the provocative question: "So you have a grandmother who can guess three cards in a row and you still have not learned her kabbalistic principles?"[76] The reason for this connection lies in the evident similarity between the numerological understanding of the principles of *kabbalistika* and the principles of such card games as Faro or Schtoss that were popular in Russian high society. Both were based on numerological systems and ruled by pure chance. The lowering of intellectual standards after 1825, which contributed to the increasing interest in supernatural issues, also led to an increased interest in gambling, the only social activity not regarded with suspicion by the government after the Decembrist revolt. Gambling became soon the pastime that replaced political, moral, and intellectual activity in noble society.[77]

Thus, the occult and the numerological principles of card playing, which amused Russian society during this rather stagnant period, merged in the minds of the intellectuals of the 1830s. Sergei Davydov argues that the pervasive sense of the occult in *The Queen of Spades* was essential for Pushkin. He believes that "references to the elixir of life and lapis philosophorum, the secret galvanism, Joseph-Michel Montgolfier's balloon and Mesmer's magnetism, the obscure epigraph from the mystic Emanuel Swedenborg, and the ominous quote from a Fortune-Teller are all indispensable ingredients of Pushkin's arcane brew."[78] Yet all the ingredients of Pushkin's "arcane brew" were characteristic not just of him or of *The Queen of Spades* in particular, but for the whole historical generation represented in Pushkin's story.

By the late 1830s the term *kabbalistika* had come to be predominantly associated in the Russian literary imagination with black magic. Mystical allegories of Kabbalah had been entirely forgotten, and the majority of writers showed no knowledge whatsoever of authentic kabbalistic teaching. In some works of this period *kabbalistika* is understood as fortune-telling. The characters of the novel *Chernaia zhenshchina* (*A Black Woman*, 1834) by Nikolai Grech (1787–1867) comment on a Jewish woman in a following way: "There is an old Jewish bitch here in the village — she reads palms for the officers' wives. Not only does she speak about the future; she knew all about my past. Surely the devil lives under her tongue and speaks to us through her *kabbalistika*."[79] Other stories remark on the magical powers of Jews that enable them to ruin people by luring them into gambling. Most literary works of the period devoted to *kabbalistika* and its adepts reveal strong anti-Semitic views. In all these works Jews are no longer depicted as those who possess the higher truth but as disseminators of black magic. In the novel *Basurmane* (*The Pagans* or *Non-Christians*, 1838), popular historical novelist Ivan Lazhechnikov (1792–1869) employs his knowledge of *kabbalistika*, a "Jewish heresy that answers the riddles of Life and Death," to create a Jewish conspiracy in fifteenth-century Novgorod.[80] In answer to Lazhechnikov, popular dramatist Nestor Kukol'nik imagines a "kabbalistic conspiracy against Orthodox Moscow" in the play *Prince Kholmsky* (1840).[81] Nadezhda Durova, in the novel *Gudishki* (1839), depicts a stable-man, a devoted kabbalist who "has mastered taming horses with his satanic skill."[82]

The image of the scholar of Kabbalah also changed in this period. The later Romantic works completely lack the idea of moral perfectionism that dominated both earlier Romantic and eighteenth-century Masonic writings. A kabbalist had now become simply a magician. He was no longer a humble seeker preoccupied with ethical and mystical problems, but a typical Romantic hero, a Faustian or Byronic figure: selfish, passionate, and willful. With the help of kabbalistic magic, he attempted to summon devils or angels, and to use their power for his own purposes, either to gain money, to win a woman, or to wield power over the world.[83] Concurrently, the interpretation of the images of primordial Adam and material (*vetkhii*) Adam also changed. The material Adam in the prose of 1830s was no longer a Masonic adept in search of moral salvation, but a corrupted Jew. The popular magazine *Russkii invalid* (*Russian Invalid*) published an anonymous allegorical story in 1833 titled "Evreiskoe semeistvo v Peterburge" ("A Jewish Family in St. Petersburg"), which described the Jewish family of Adamski, who lived in a shabby house and wore threadbare clothes while hiding a million rubles in a corner chest. The family was ruled by greed and hatred. Its members "leave the house at night only to wander around like hungry wolves." Their eyes, "like those of spiders," "are flared with devilish hunger."[84] Clearly, such people were vampires or werewolves rather than humans.

At the same time, in most Russian works of the 1830s, the strong anti-Semitic feelings were not particularly linked to Jewish faith. The "demonic Jew" was often a convert. Vladimir Ushakov's story "Gustave Gatzfield" offers a good description of this character: "he is very well-educated, not rich but not too poor, speaks fluent Russian and can sell you the secret of the card game if you pay him well, but never gambles."[85] On the one hand, converted Jews had written the majority of the pseudo-kabbalistic texts found in Russian Masonic archives. Russian Romantic writers, who borrowed their kabbalistic knowledge largely from Masonic literature, evidently noticed this fact and drew their own conclusions: the image of the converted Jew and that of the kabbalist merged in their minds. On the other hand, these works reproduced medieval anti-Semitic beliefs that depicted Jews as heretical, demonic figures by choice. It was not the faith that characterized the demonic nature of Jews but rather their Jewish origin, their "nationality." Such views, however, may or may not reflect the personal anti-Semitism of Russian writers of the first half of the nineteenth century, given that they had been widespread in some German Romantic writings (particularly in Hoffman) and therefore may have been simply adopted as literary stereotypes from German Romanticism.

The description of a kabbalist in Russian Romanticism was typically very general. With a few exceptions, he usually did not have a name or any particular feature. One such exception occurs in the short story "Posetitel' magika" ("A Visitor to a Magician"), published in 1829 by Alexei Perovsky. Perovsky (1787–1836), who wrote under a pen name Antonii Pogorelsky, belonged to the Moscow lodge Felicity (Lozha Blagopoluchia), and was indubitably a Freemason of a new type, a Romantic writer strongly interested in occult, supernatural, and "gothic" themes.[86] The protagonist of the story is neither nameless nor an invented demon, but a historical figure, the famous Christian kabbalist Agrippa von Nettesheim, also known as Cornelius Agrippa. Russian Freemasons were familiar with Agrippa's writings.[87] Pogorelsky's fictional "magician" (*magik*) Agrippa possesses a magical mirror that enables him to communicate with the deceased. One day he is visited by a mysterious stranger who wishes to see his daughter, Miriam, "who died long, long ago." [88] The mysterious visitor turns out to be the Wandering Jew. The words *kabbalah* or *kabbalistika* are not mentioned in the story; however, the principles of the performance of his mirror are mainly based on kabbalistic numerology. Agrippa explains to his guest that to enable the mirror to work "thou should draw circles with thy staff so that every circle will count for ten years since the day when this particular person passed away. And when thou make enough circles, this man will be shown to you in the mirror, and will humbly answer thy question."[89] The emphasis on "every ten years" is not accidental. The number ten plays a central role in practical, "magical" Kabbalah. In kabbalistic numerology it signifies the total number of *sefirot* and, therefore, symbolizes the name of God. Magical circles based on this number were widespread in Christian kabbalistic manuscripts. Agrippa's incantations, chanted during his communication with the deceased Miriam in "a strange ancient language forgotten by mortals," are most probably sung in Hebrew (rather than Aramaic, which was not as well-known as a "Jewish language" among Russian writers as Hebrew was). Fictional Agrippa mentions that while he was singing "it seemed to [him] that [his] visitor was joining [him], as if the language, as obscure as it was, was familiar and known to [his] mysterious guest."[90] Since the mysterious visitor to the magician is the Wandering Jew, it is clear that the ancient language that seemed "well-known" and "familiar" to him is Hebrew. Moreover, the fictional character of magician Cornelius Agrippa that corresponds to the historical figure of Christian kabbalist Agrippa von Nettesheim suggests that Pogorelsky is speaking about kabbalistic magic and not about magic in general.

Among the many gothic stories devoted to black kabbalistic magic, Faddei Bulgarin's story *Kabbalistik* (1834) calls for particular notice. A mediocre but popular writer, Bulgarin (1789–1859) was favored by the government and despised by most of the liberal Russian Romantic writers of Pushkin's circle. The plot of the story *Kabbalistik* is fairly typical. Through a first-person narration, the protagonist describes to the reader how his life was ruined by his interest in mystical cards readings. He laments that he met a Jew who "possessed a great knowledge of ancient *kabbalistika*" that allowed him to "see the distant past just as we see ourselves in the mirror."[91] Of particular interest, however, is the title of the story, *Kabbalistik*, which in the context of the tale should not be translated as "A Scholar of Kabbalah," but rather "A Scholar of Kabbalistika." Bulgarin's story shows us that by the middle of 1830s this Russian invention, the noun *kabbalistika*, had already created a number of morphological forms. *Kabbalistik*, like *fizik* (a scholar of physics) or *khimik* (a scholar of chemistry) was a term not for a scholar of Kabbalah but for a possessor of "the science of Kabbalah," i.e., of Jewish numerological magic.

By the 1830s the magical interpretation of *kabbalistika* had come completely to prevail in the artistic and intellectual world of Russian culture. The image of the kabbalistic Jew created by Russian Romanticism became so widespread and popular that from literature it moved into journalism and, by the end of 1830s, was not considered any longer a literary invention. When in 1838 the popular magazine *Biblioteka dlia chteniia* (*The Library for Reading*) published a lengthy anonymous composition on Polish Jews, its author stressed that "holy *kabbalistika* constitutes the center of Jewish existence," "its adepts do not see the light of a day behind a veil of letters, numbers, and other kabbalistic symbols," and "their minds are seriously damaged by the constant study of *kabbalistika* and Talmud." Even the notion that "due to their egoism, Jews usually love their children and wives" could not save Polish Jews from their reputation as "demonic kabbalistic magicians."[92]

In the early 1840s new, realistic trends started to appear on the Russian literary and intellectual scene. Romantic emphasis on the role of poetic language and interest in mystical and supernatural issues began to give way to Realism, which concentrated on the study of social problems and reestablished the belief in the positive role of rational materialism. By the mid-nineteenth century the belief in universal science slowly but surely lost its place in Russian literature. "Scientific" mysticism began to fall out of favor, being gradually replaced by materialistic positivism. This shift resulted in the sharp decline of interest in kabbalistic and alchemic scientific magic, which, by that time, already had negative rather than positive connotations even inside the Romantic milieu. It would take half a century before these ideas would make their way back into Russian cultural thought and again start to play a significant role in the Russian literary imagination.

NOTES

1. Tatiana Sokolovskaia, "The Revival of Masonry under Alexander I," in *Masonstvo v ego proshlom i nastoiashchem*, ed. Sergei Melgunov and Nikolai Sidorov (Moscow: Zadruga, 1914), 155–58. On Masonic activity in the reign of Paul I, see Serkov, *Istoriia russkogo masonstva XIX veka*, 44–53.

2. Iakov Gordin, *Mistiki i okhraniteli: delo o masonskom zagovore* (St. Petersburg: Pushkinskii fond, 1999), 131.

3. Serkov, *Istoriia Russkogo masonsva XIX veka*, 105. See also, Serkov, *Russkoe masonstvo*, 817, 303.

4. Billington, *Icon and the Axe*, 34.

5. In 1815 four major lodges, Peter's Truth (Petr K Pravde), Palestina, Izida, and Neptun, signed an agreement that marked the creation of the United Grand Lodge of Astrea, named for the Goddess of Justice. This contract marked a new period in Russian Masonic history. From this point on masonry regarded itself as in collaboration with rather than in opposition to the government. The members of Astrea took an oath not to have any secrets from the state or the government and defined their work as the dissemination of morality, faith, virtue, and a total devotion to the tsar and the official institutions of the state. "Some Aspects of Russian Freemasonry during the Reign of Emperor Alexander I," *Transactions of the Quatuor Coronati Lodge* 38 (1925): 6.

6. Ibid.

7. For more on A. N. Golitsyn see Serkov, *Russkoe masonstvo*, 250.

8. OR RNB, f. 332, op. 112, d. 1960, l.13.

9. M. H. Abrams, *The Mirror and the Lamp: Romantic Theory and the Critical Tradition* (New York: Oxford University Press, 1953).

10. Ibid., 276.

11. Ibid.

12. Viktor Zhirmunskii, *Nemetskii romantizm i sovremennaia mistika* (St. Petersburg: Axioma, 1996), 21.

13. A. B. Kilcher, "Die Kabbalah als Trope im ästhetischen Diskurs der Frühromantik," in *Kabbalah und die Literatur der Romantik: Zwischen Magie und Trope*, ed. E. Goodman-Thau and G. Mattenklott (Tübingen: M. Niemeyer, 1999), 167. See also *Die sprache Adams*, ed. A. P. Coudert (Wiesbaden: Harrassowitz Verlag, 1999). On linguistic mysticism and magic in Christian Kabbalah see A. B. Kilcher, *Die Sprachtheorie der Kabbala als ästhetisches Paradigma: Die Konstruktion einer ästhetischen Kabbala seit der Frühen Neuzeit* (Stuttgart: Weimar Metzler, 1998).

14. Kilcher, "Die Kabbalah als Trope," 164.

15. Ibid.

16. Ibid. For more on Novalis, see S. Prokofiev, *Vechnaia individual'nost': Ocherk karmicheskoi biografii Novalisa* (Moscow: Enigma, 2000); E. Silard, *Novalis i Russkaia mysl' nachala XX veka* (St. Petersburg: Izd-vo Ivana Limbaha, 2002).

17. Martines de Pasqually, *Traité de la réintégration des êtres: dans leurs premières propriétés, vertus et puissances spirituelles et divines* (Paris, 1932), 118.

18. Harold Bloom, *Kabbalah and Criticism* (New York: Seabury Press, 1975), 53, 71.

19. See P. Marshall, *The Philosopher's Stone: A Quest for the Secrets of Alchemy* (London: Macmillan, 2000); William Newman and Anthony Grafton, eds., *Secrets of Nature: Astrology and Alchemy in Early Modern Europe* (Cambridge: MIT Press, 2000); Rabinovich, *Alkhimiia*; Raphael Patai, *The Jewish Alchemists: A History and Source Book* (Princeton: Princeton University Press, 1994).

20. See Sarah Pratt, *Russian Metaphysical Romanticism: The Poetry of Tiutchev and Boratynskii* (California: Stanford University Press, 1984); Vadim Vatsuro, "Sofiia: zametki na poliakh 'Kosmoramy' Odoevskogo," *Novoe Literaturnoe Obozreniie* 42 (2000): 1–9.

21. For the magical interests of John Dee and Tycho Brahe see B. Vurm, *Rudolph II and his Prague* (Prague, 1998), 71.

22. Viktor Porus, "Nemetskaia naturfilosofiia i nauka pervoi poloviny XIX veka v poiskakh universal'nogo edinstva," in *Germetizm i magiia: Naturfilosofiia v evropeiskoi kul'ture XIII–XIX vv.* (Moscow, 1997), 489–99. For more on the influence of Schelling's views on Russian artistic life see Pratt, *Russian Metaphysical Romanticism*; Neil Cornwell, *Vladimir Odoevsky and Romantic Poetics: Collected Essays* (Providence, RI: Berghahn Books, 1998).

23. Martin Malia, *Alexander Herzen and the Birth of Russian Socialism: 1812–1855* (Cambridge: Harvard University Press, 1961), 135.

24. Ibid., 93.

25. OR RNB, f. 111, d. 71, ll. 12.

26. Quoted in Kilcher, "Die Kabbalah als Trope," 154.

27. Ibid., 163.

28. Ibid.

29. Ibid.

30. Zhirmunskii, *Nemetskii Romantizm*, 115.

31. To compare this interpretation with the eighteenth-century perception of the concept of a Golden Age, see Baehr, *The Paradise Myth*.

32. Ibid., 116.

33. For more on the history of Pietism in Russia see Aleksandr Pypin, *Religioznye dvizheniia pri Aleksandre I* (St. Petersburg: Akademicheskii proekt, 2000); Sokolovskaia, "The Revival of Masonry under Alexander I."

34. Pypin, *Religioznye dvizheniia*, 115.

35. One such source is undoubtedly Saint-Martin's *Des erreurs et de la vérité*, which avers that "when Man shone with the glorious light of the Divine, the universe was one great whole. The major goal of those who seek light is to unite again the material and the spiritual aspects of the universe and to return the world to its golden primordial state." OR RGB, f. 14, d. 981.

36. Quoted in Neil Cornwell, *V. F. Odoevsky: His Life, Times, and Milieu* (Athens, OH: Ohio University Press, 1986), 195.

37. Ibid., 195.

38.
> Предвечность радостью сияла,
> Духовный свет струился в ней,
> И тьма одеждою своей
> Сей дивный свет не обнимала.
> Он из Любови истекал
> Сей дух и свет неистощимый,
> И в той любви непостижимой
> Глагол бессмертный пребывал.
> Своими мощными словами
> Из хладной тьмы небытия

> Рождал и жизнь и радость я
> И наполнял ее мирами.

V. Sokolovsky, *Mirozdanie* (St. Petersburg, 1837), 7–8. Compare, for example, with Bobrov: "Да любомудрие прострет свой взор орлиный / и возвестит из гроба тел восстанье / и венценосного светильника сиянье". ("Let Love-Wisdom raise its eagle eye and announce the rise of dead from their coffins and the shine of the crowned Light.") Bobrov, *Rassvet Polnochi*, 1:17.

39. Vaiskopf, *Pokryvalo Moiseia*, 109–10.

40. V. Odoevsky, *Russkie Nochi* (St. Petersburg: Sovetskii pisatel', 1968), 219. For more on Odoevsky's philosophical views see Pavel Sakulin, *Iz istorii russkogo idealizma: Kniaz' V. F. Odoevsky: myslitel', pisatel'* (Moscow: Izd. M. i S. Sabashnikovykh, 1913).

41. V. Vatsuro, "Sofiia: Zametki na poliakh 'Kosmoramy' Odoevskogo."

42. OR RNB, f. 111, d. 71, ll. 12–13.

43. A. Levitsky, "V. F. Odoevsky's *The Year 4338*: Utopia or Dystopia," in *The Supernatural in Slavic and Baltic Literature*, ed. A. Mandelker (Columbus, OH: Slavica Publishers, 1988.), 72–82.

44. V. Odoevsky, "Peterburgskie pis'ma," in *Izbrannoe* (Moscow: Khudozhestvennaia literatura, 1988), 79. For an additional description of Christianopolis see Yates, *Rosicrucian Enlightenment*, 270–74. By contrast, the anti-utopian novellas "The Last Suicide" and "The Nameless City" in *Russian Nights* clearly exhibit how the utilitarian materialistic approach to technology will lead society to its destruction. "The Last Suicide" presents a horrific picture of life on an over-populated planet. Odoevsky believed that the problems of this planet derive from mercantile expansion as well as from the fact that its inhabitants have lost their regard for philosophy and poetry. Odoevsky was confident that science developed only for the industrial and economic personal benefit of individuals, coupled with the abandonment of artistic and philosophical values, would eventually destroy society. He clearly shows this in the novella "The Nameless City," which describes the rise and fall of a country on the North American continent, called Benthamia. The economic activities of the Benthamites resemble the rapacious spirit of political economy, which subordinated all spheres of individual existence to commercial profit. Morality has been reduced to the art of balancing accounts, poetry replaced by bookkeeping, and music has given way to the sounds of machinery. The brief period of economic prosperity in Benthamia was soon replaced by total chaos and

the city was completely destroyed. Only the ruins, covered by moss, and hidden in "the deep woods of the North American continent," remind us that the city of Benthamia ever existed. Such negative views demonstrate Odoevsky's strong disapproval of the modern West and especially the United States, where life was allegedly based on Bentham's economic theories of rational and utilitarian egoism.

45. Cornwell, *Vladimir Odoevsky*, 179.

46. See Frances Yates, *Giordano Bruno and the Hermetic Tradition* (New York: Routledge, 1999), 179.

47. For more on Norov, see Serkov, *Russkoe masonstvo: 1731–2000*, 597–98.

48. Vladimir Odoevsky, "Beseda s Shellingom," *Voprosy Filosofii* 5 (1978): 176–80.

49. J. R. Ritman, ed., *500 Years of Gnosis in Europe: Exhibition of Printed Books and Manuscripts from the Gnostic Tradition* (Amsterdam, 1993), 79.

50. OR RGB, f. 4, op. 134, d. 21.

51. A. M. Skabichevsky, "Ocherki razvitiia progressivnykh idei v nashem obschestve," in Vladimir Pustarnakov, ed. *Fridrikh Schelling, — pro et contra: Tvorchestvo Fridrikha Shellinga v otsenke russkikh myslitelei i issledovatelei; antologiia* (St. Petersburg: RHGI, 2001), 335–56.

52. OR RNB, f. 71, op. 52, dd.17, 11.

53. OR RNB, f. 71, op. 52, dd.11

54. Ibid. For the relations between J. G. Wachter and Leibniz, see A. Coudert, *Leibnitz and the Kabbalah* (Cambridge: Harvard University Press, 1995).

55. Quoted in Sakulin, *Iz istorii russkogo idealizma*, 1: 476.

56. N. Polevoi, "Blazhenstvo bezumiia," in *Russkaia goticheskaia proza* (Moscow: Terra, 1999), 17–55, 40.

57. Ibid., 41.

58. Ibid.

59. George Meier, "Sts. Cyprian and Justina," in *The Catholic Encyclopedia* (New York: Robert Appleton Company, 1908), 131.

60. Vatsuro, "Sofiia: zametki na poliakh 'Kosmoramy' Odoevskogo," 169.

61. For more on Kabbalah and Hoffman see D. Kremer, "Kabbalistische Signaturen: Sprachmagie als Spiegel romantischer Imagination bei

Hoffman und Achim von Arnim," in *Kabbalah und die Literatur der Romantik*, 197– ed. 221.

62. E.T.A. Hoffman, "Tsarskaia nevesta," in *Serapionovy Brat'ia*, part 8 (Tip. Stepanova, 1824), 190–321.

63. This definition of *kabbalistika* can be seen in L. G. Leighton, "Numbers and Numerology in 'The Queen of Spades,'" *Canadian Slavonic Papers* 19, no. 4 (1977): 417–43; and idem, "Gematria in the 'The Queen of Spades': A Decembrist Puzzle," *Slavic and East European Journal* 21 (1976): 455–56.

64. Leo Tolstoy, *War and Peace* (New York: Random House, 1995), 621.

65. V. E. Kholshevnikov, *Mysl', vooruzhennaia rifmami* (Izdatel'stvo Leningradskogo Universiteta, 1967), 41.

66. Lauren G. Leighton, *The Esoteric Tradition in Russian Romantic Literature: Decembrism and Freemasonry* (University Park: Pennsylvania State University Press, 1994), 33.

67. Sakulin, *Iz istorii russkogo idealizma*, 1: 379.

68. Evgenii Baratynski, "Persten'," in *Russkaia goticheskaia proza*, 253–66, 254.

69. Ibid., 257.

70. Ibid.

71. Ibid., 256.

72. Ibid.

73. Sakulin, *Iz istorii russkogo idealizma*, 2: 419. See also "Segeliel," in Odoevsky, *Izbrannoe*, 78–97.

74. Odoevsky, *Izbrannoe*, 97.

75. Vaiskopf, *Pokryvalo Moiseia*, 105.

76. A. Pushkin, *The Queen of Spades and Other Stories* (London: Penguin Books, 1978), 16. For a Russian original quotation see "Pikovaia Dama," in *Russkaia goticheskaia proza*, 175–98, 118.

77. Georgii Parchevsky, *Karty i kartezhniki* (St. Petersburg: Pushkinskii Fond, 1998), 24–25.

78. Sergei Davydov, "The Ace in the *Queen of Spades*," *Slavic Review* 58, no. 2 (1999), 309–29.

79. Nikolai Grech, *Chernaia zhenshchina*, part 1 (St. Petersburg, 1838), 115–16.

80. Vaiskopf, 252.

81. Vaiskopf, 267.

82. Aleksandrov [N. A. Durova], *Gudishki*, part 4 (St. Petersburg: V tip. Shtaba otdel korpusa, 1839), 127, 196. See Vaiskopf, *Pokryvalo Moiseia*, 105.

83. Vaiskopf, *Pokryvalo Moiseia*, 276.

84. *Russkii Invalid* 23 (1833): 177–81. Vaiskopf attributes the story to A. F. Voyeikov, the editor of *Russkii Invalid*. Vaiskopf, *Pokryvalo Moiseia*, 201.

85. Vaiskopf, *Pokryvalo Moiseia*, 219.

86. For more on Pogorelsky, see Serkov, *Russkoe masonstvo, 1731–2000*.

87. See OR RGB, f. 14, op. 781, d. 3.

88. Antonii Pogorel'skii, *Izbrannoe* (Moscow: Sovetskaia Rossia, 1985), 352. The story originally appeared in the newspaper *Babochka* 17 (February 27, 1929) and 18 (March 2, 1829). Pogorelsky called "A Magician's Visitor" "a translation from English"; most probably the story is a translation from the work with the similar title by English Romantic poet Henry Neele, published in the British almanac *Forget-me-not* (1828), 91–98, about a year before the publication of Pogorelsky's novella.

The kabbalistic and Masonic symbolism in "A Magician's Visitor" has been recently briefly analyzed in a conference presentation by M. Turian, "Posetitel' magika: k istorii odnogo perevoda," (presented at *Vtorye chteniia pamiati E. G. Etkinda* (St. Peterburg, 2002). Turian also mentions a French story by Amédée Pichot published in Russian translation as "Ocharovannoe zerkalo: Epizod iz zhizni Korneliusa Agrippy" in the newspaper *Molva* in 1833 (September 30), which was probably influenced by the same English original.

89. Pogorel'skii, *Izbrannoe*, 351.

90. Ibid., 353.

91. Faddei Bulgarin, *Sochineniia* (St. Petersburg, 1836), 1: 290. See Vaiskopf, *Pokryvalo Moiseia*, 101.

92. *Biblioteka dlia chteniia* 28 (1838): 49. Vaiskopf, *Pokryvalo Moiseia* 270–71.

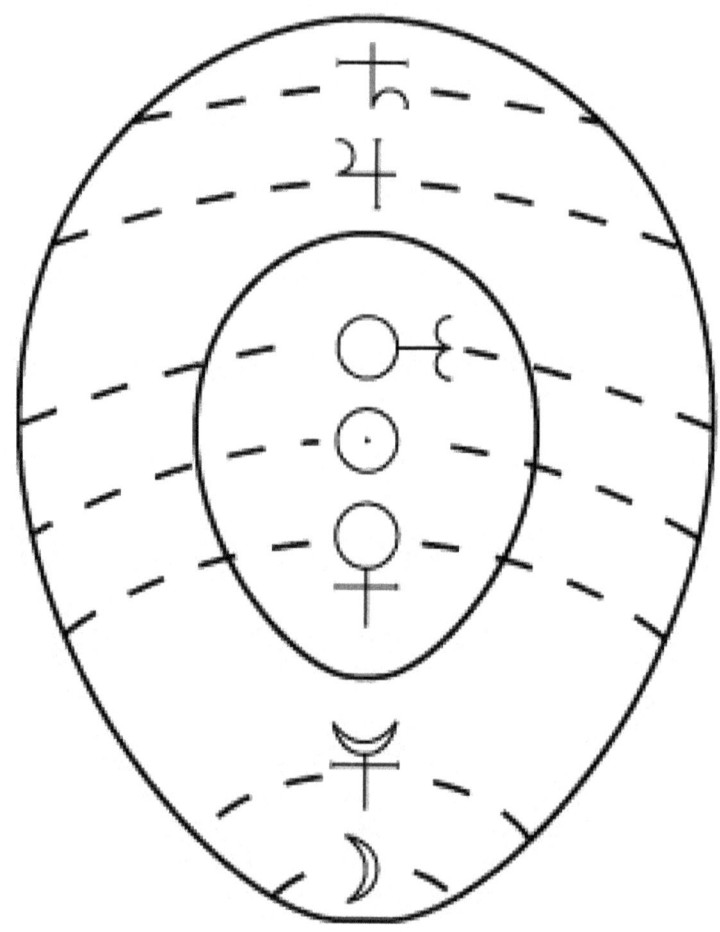

The cosmic egg
(From J. Dee, *Monas Hieroglyphica*, 1654)

Alchemic Kabbalah and Russian Romantic Literature

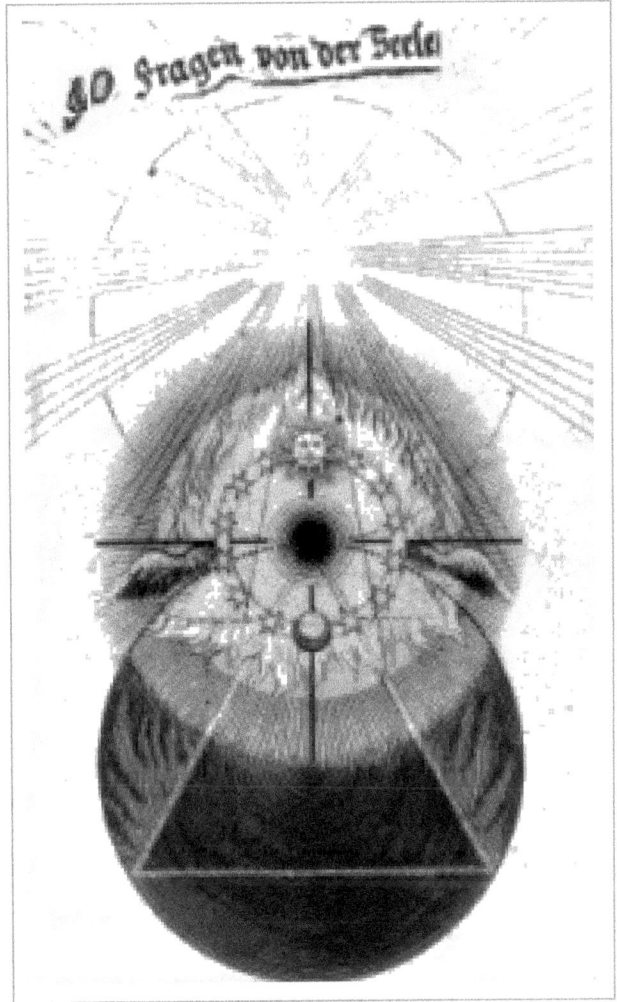

The cosmic egg

(From a Russian manuscript translation of J. Boehme,
Forty Questions of a Soul, approx. 1780s)

Knowledge Hidden in Letters

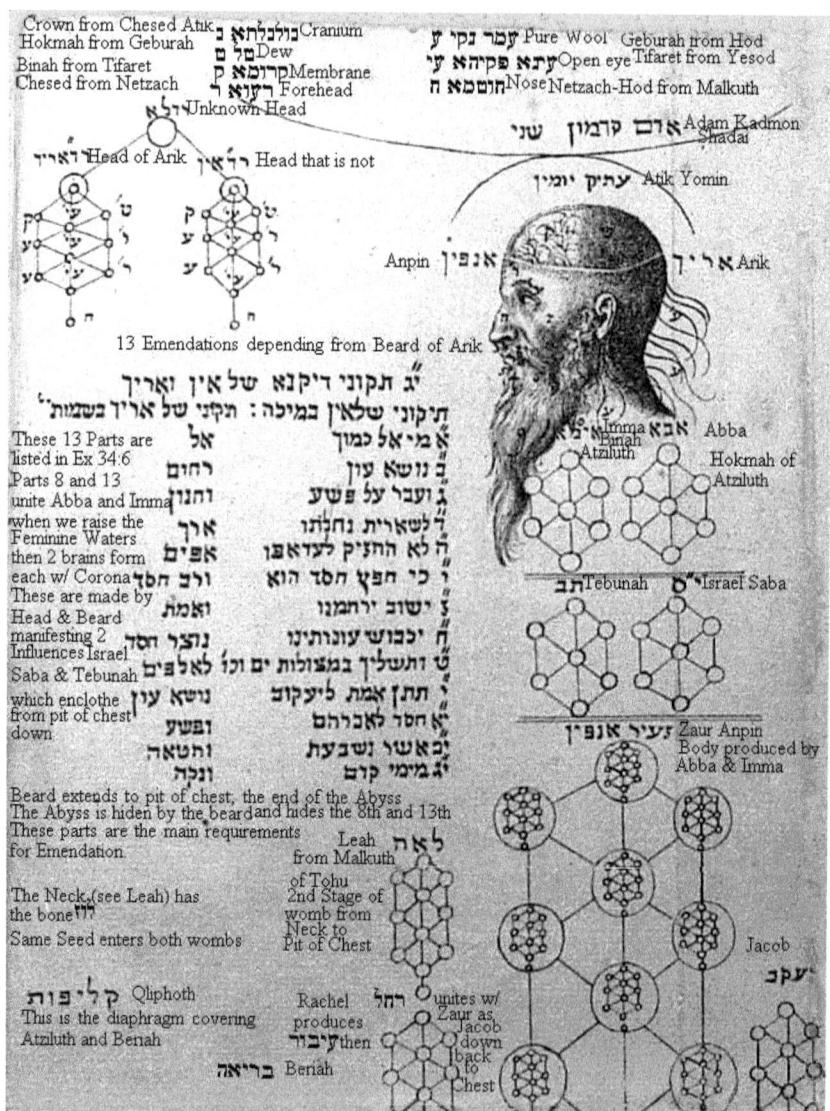

The ten Sefirot form the cosmic body of the first man, Adam Kadmon

(From C. Knorr von Rosenroth, *Kabbalah Denudata*, 1684)

Alchemic Kabbalah and Russian Romantic Literature

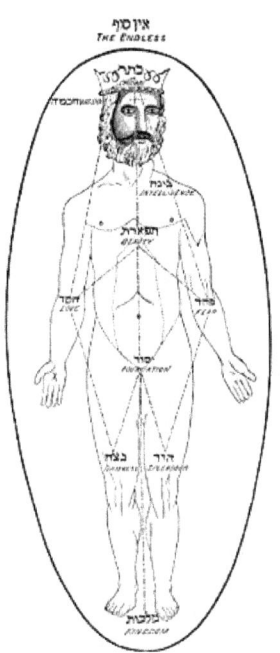

Adam Kadmon - illustrations from 17th-century manuscripts

In one of these manuscripts the author compared the human anatomy to a four-story house. The four stories correspond to the four worlds in which the entire cosmos is divided in the image of the Tree of Sephirot.

(From Tobias Cohn, *Maaseh Toviiyah*, 1707)

Knowledge Hidden in Letters

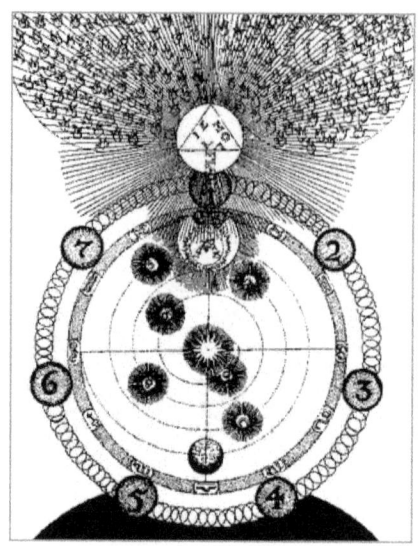

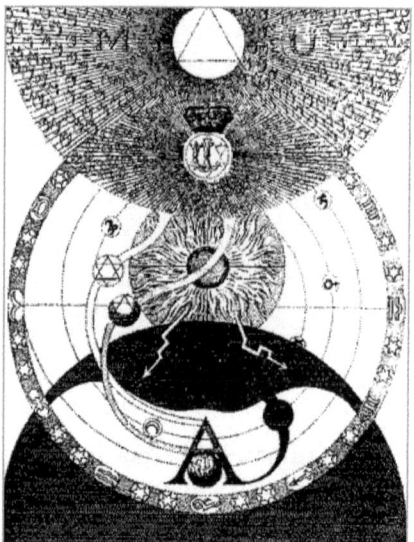

**Here a fall of Adam
is interpreted as a breakage of the divine vessels**

The seven Sefirot manifest themselves as planetary forces that form the Wheel of Universe.

(From a Russian manuscript translation
of J. Boehme *Mysterium Magnum*, approx. 1780s)

Alchemic Kabbalah and Russian Romantic Literature

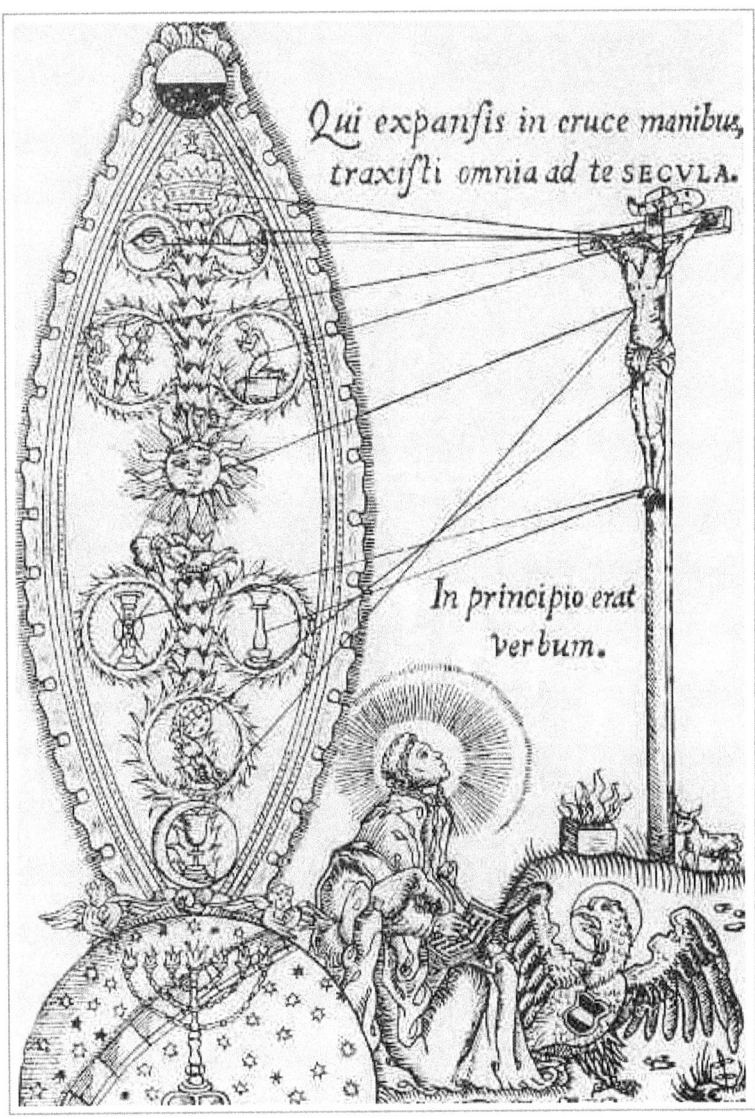

**Masonic engraving of Christ as *Adam Kadmon*
"Cosmic Christ" corresponding to the *Sephirotic* "Tree of Life"**

Note the split black and white (good & evil) *"Ayn Soph"* at the top and the seven-branched *Menorah* dominating the lower world of *Malkhut*.

(17th century)

The Temple of the Rosy Cross
(From Theophilus Schweighardt Constantiens, 1618)

In the Beginning Was the Word
Magical Kabbalah, the Occult Revival, and the Linguistic Mysticism of the Silver Age

The late nineteenth and early twentieth centuries, the period usually known as the Silver Age, witnessed a sudden and robust revival of interest in mystical and magical issues. The occult was an integral part of prerevolutionary Russian culture. Occult doctrines appealed to artists, writers, and political activists. Modernist poets and painters were intrigued by the idea of a fourth dimension. Philosophers and lay theologians explored the occult in their quest for new religious forms.[1]

An occult journal, *Rebus*, reported in 1906 that all of Petersburg was caught up in a powerful mystical movement and that a veritable maelstrom of little religions, cults, and sects was arising there: "This movement embraces both the upper and the lower levels of society. At the upper levels we find the Theosophic-Buddhist trend. Elsewhere, we see a crescendo of interest in Freemasonry, as well as a resurgence of long-silent religious movements from the last century."[2] Petersburg, Moscow, and the provinces were all caught up in this trend. They buzzed with new secret societies, demonstrations of hypnotism, and gypsy fortune-telling. Every educated reader had at least a nodding acquaintance with Theosophy and Spiritualism, Rosicrucianism, Martinism, and tarot. People were acquainted with these ideas even if their knowledge was based only on café gossip and sensational newspaper articles in popular magazines.[3]

But was the occult revival really so sudden and unexpected? Like their predecessors, the intellectuals at the end of the nineteenth century found themselves involved in a struggle between rationalist positivism and mystical idealism.[4] Like the pre-Romantic and Romantic writers, the authors of mystical publications in the late nineteenth century claimed that "the old embittered world . . . is dying, the utilitarian, materialist culture is falling apart . . . [and] the days of . . . utilitarian science are ending."[5] Nevertheless, they worried about the dangers of materialism, rationalism, and utilitarianism that still dominated society. Rudolph Steiner argued in 1911 that popular materialistic literature, widely disseminated in Russia, was more dangerous than straightforward revolutionary literature. He proclaimed that materialistic writings were like a poison for the Russian soul, for a Russian could accept the spiritual in his own soul only if he saw it in the nature that surrounded him.[6]

There was a surge in demand for many early published occult and mystical texts at the end of the nineteenth century, and most were reprinted.[7] The new era also saw a large number of original occult publications, many of which not only reinterpreted earlier ideas, but developed their own occult and mystical theories, some of which became influential.

In recent years a modest but steady flow of articles and books has captured the paradoxes that punctuate the development of occult tradition in prerevolutionary Russia. Yet the role of Kabbalah in prerevolutionary culture and literature has largely remained outside of the scope of these studies. Moreover, K. Burmistrov has argued that "the interest in Kabbalah in the symbolist literary milieu was surprisingly weak" in comparison to other mystical movements such as Theosophy or Spiritualism.[8] While touching upon kabbalistic motives and images in the literature of the Silver Age, most scholars usually do not distinguish Kabbalah from other occult theories, thus often interpreting kabbalistic symbolism as simply occult. As this chapter will show, the mystical doctrine of Kabbalah (and quasi-Kabbalah) in fact played a central role in the poetic ideology of the Silver Age, and an understanding of the role of Kabbalah in the various artistic movements and concepts of the Silver Age can shed light on many enigmatic literary puzzles characteristic of this complicated epoch.

Western Influences and the Missionaries of Occult Kabbalah

Several major sources influenced the Russian understanding of kabbalistic doctrines. A general interest in mysticism and occultism led to the partial reprint of some eighteenth-century Rosicrucian and mystical texts and these experienced at least some popularity among the authors of the Silver Age. However, these writings were mostly devoted to mystical, not occult subjects; therefore, Russian "scholars of the occult" derived much of their knowledge from nineteenth-century French sources. These modern French publications had virtually no connection with the original mystical doctrine of Kabbalah, and also misrepresented many Christian kabbalistic ideas. However, due to the lecturing activities of the French occultists, their books circulated in large numbers and became particularly popular among the French and later, the Russian artistic elite.

The first major source for the would-be adept was French occult writer Alphonse-Louis Constant (1810 — 1875), known mostly under his pseudonym Magus Eliphas Lévi. An ex-Catholic priest, excommunicated for his left-wing political writings and his interest in necromancy, Lévi made a living from his writings and by giving lessons in the occult. Lévi was an extremely well-known figure in French occult circles and influenced Charles Baudelaire, Arthur Rimbaud, Paul Verlaine, and, in England, Oscar Wilde.[9] Lévi revived and popularized the occult version of Christian Kabbalah. He did not know Hebrew or Aramaic, and his knowledge of original Jewish texts was based on Latin Christian translations. Most of his writings had no connection with Jewish originals at all, but were based on Renaissance Christian texts on practical Kabbalah and magic, and on the works of Martines de Pasqually, particularly his *Traité de la reintégration des êtres*. Lévi also combined Christian kabbalistic symbolism with seventeenth- and eighteenth-century Masonic and Rosicrucian allegory, which he knew well.[10]

The idea that magical powers derive from various numerological and alphabetical "kabbalistic" combinations became the keystone of Lévi's kabbalistic theory. Lévi also stressed the importance of sexual energies in relationship to these powers. Lévi viewed creation as the house of the Word-Creator, which was also the house of the phallus.[11] He also developed a new, linguistic, interpretation of the myth of Adam Kadmon, whom he defined as the synthesis of the word, formulated by the human figure: "When his mouth was manifested, the word passed into expression; and thus was completed the first day of creation."[12] In addition, Lévi linked the twenty-two letters of the Hebrew alphabet, attributed by *Sefer Yetzirah* to the twenty-two aspects of God, to the twenty-two cards, or Major Arcana, of the tarot.

Lévi's books became extremely popular among Russian artistic circles of the Silver Age. An anonymous writer in an occult magazine called Lévi a genius whose works were distinguished by gleaming logic and a luxuriant literary style, such that he would be able to rebuild the destroyed temple of the Wisdom of Solomon.[13] However, Lévi never visited Russia or had any direct contact with the Russian elite. By contrast, another famous French occult writer, Gérard Encausse (1865 — 1916), widely known as Papus, was introduced directly into Russian aristocratic society.

Papus revived the occult and mystical Order of the Elus Cohens (the Elected Priests) created by Martines de Pasqually in the late eighteenth century, and renamed it the Kabbalistic Order of the Rose and Cross. In 1890 he created a Martinist order, a new version of the original eighteenth-century Martinist organization.[14] Papus's goals were quite different from those of the eighteenth-century Martinists: his order concentrated on occult rather than mystical subjects and functioned as an esoteric society. It belonged to the occult wing of masonry, which was extremely unpopular in France, and, as in any occult society, it defined its goals as the acquisition of secret primordial knowledge necessary to obtain power over nature.[15] In 1889, the French magazine *L'Initiation* published an article on the Order. It explained to its readers that:

> the distinctive symbol adopted by the members of the Supreme Council of the Kabbalistic Order of the Rose Cross is the Hebrew letter Alef. Every new member of this society takes an oath of obedience to the directives of the Council, declaring that, although they are free to leave the society any time they please, they will abide by their promise to keep secret the teachings received from

the Order. They receive training in the Kabbalah and mystical subjects.[16]

In that same year, the Kabbalistic Order of the Rose Cross in Paris established its own college, which conferred three university degrees "in Kabbalah." The first degree presented the student with the title of Bachelor of Kabbalah, the second with that of Graduate of Kabbalah, and the third, conferred after an examination and the presentation of a thesis, bestowed the status of Doctor of Kabbalah.[17]

Ten years after creating the Order, Papus went to Russia in order to create a branch of his French organization. He lectured in Moscow and St. Petersburg to large audiences, which included the tsar and his court. He visited Russia again in 1905 and 1907.[18] Papus created a Russian branch of the French Martinist lodge in 1910. Although the story that Nicholas himself decided to join the lodge is no more than a legend, many people believed it and joined for that reason.[19] In 1911 Papus met the famous publisher and critic, Ivan Antoshevsky, and together they established an occult magazine, *Isida*, which was intended to serve as a rival to the major magazine of the spiritualist movement, *Rebus*. While *Rebus* was interested in spiritualist and philosophical subjects and denied the connection between mysticism and the occult, *Isida* was devoted primarily to occult publications. Between 1908 and 1912, A. V. Troianovsky translated all of Papus's major works, which were immediately published in *Isida* and subsequently in book form. *Isida* also published a wide range of materials on occult and mystical subjects, although mystical issues still remained rather marginal in Martinist publications and it seems that its publishers did not distinguish between the mystical and the occult interpretation of Kabbalah. In 1912 *Isida* published chapters from Lopukhin's *Spiritual Knight* and, simultaneously, a book on the role of numerology in Kabbalah written by Boris Leman, a poet and scholar of theosophy and a well-known figure in the occult circles of the Silver Age, who published his poetry under the pen name Boris Diks.[20] In 1910, for seven months in a row the magazine serialized the translation of the anonymous work *Sozdanie mira po kabbale* (*The Creation of the World according to Kabbalah*). In the same year Leman advertized a study group on Kabbalah that met every week "to practice the magical powers of sounds and numbers."[21] The use of the word "sounds," rather than "letters" was not accidental, but in tune with the Modernist apprehension of Kabbalah.

Papus's ideas were further developed in the works and lectures of the occult writer Grigorii Mebes, known among his followers as GOM. Nikolai Bogomolov called Mebes "an acknowledged head of Russian masonry, Martinism, and Rosicrucianism, a man of a great spiritual potential and enormous practical power."[22] A native of Riga and a graduate of the Department of Physics and Mathematics of St. Petersburg University, he was one of the major figures in the Russian Martinist order and was among the leading personages on the Russian esoteric scene until his arrest in the late 1920s.[23] In 1911 — 1912 Mebes gave an extended lecture course, called *The Encyclopedia of the Occult* (*Entsiklopedia Okkul'tizma*). The lectures were published as a separate book in St. Petersburg in 1912. In these lectures Mebes developed Papus's view of Kabbalah as an occult doctrine, "the basic Law of modern Cosmogony and a part of the primordial tradition."[24] The course was extremely popular, especially among the esoterically oriented members of the so-called Guild of Poets (*Tsekh Poetov*), the major Acmeist society. Some of the members of the society, such as Nikolai Gumilev, were eager listeners to the lectures but did not play any active role in GOM's activities. Other, more minor authors such as Aleksei Skaldin and Nina Rudnikova participated in these activities directly.

This new occult pseudo-Kabbalah of the nineteenth century was also broadly reflected in the works of Madame Helen Blavatsky. Blavatsky stands out as one of the luminaries of modern occult thought. She was born in Russia in 1831, died in England in 1891, and is best known as a founder of the Theosophical Society, which was arguably the most important avenue of "Eastern" teaching to the Western adepts of esotericism.[25]

The discussion of kabbalistic allegories played a significant role in Blavatsky's teaching, which later resulted in her being accused of "Masonic and Jewish satanic plots" by some right-wing critics.[26] She was the author of a number of articles devoted to Kabbalah, such as "Kabbalah and Kabbalists" and "Tetragrammaton."[27] Although these articles prove that Blavatsky was at least superficially familiar with Rosenroth's *Kabbalah Denudata*, her perception of Kabbalah nevertheless primarily originated from French occult sources. Blavatsky not only widely quoted Lévi and Papus, but also based much of her own argument about the existence of seven races in human history on the key idea of Papus' *Qabbalah*. The first race consisted only of primordial Adam, the second race was made up of the Patriarchs who still lived in close connection with the divine realm; the third race was the people of Atlantis, and so on.[28]

Although in general Blavatsky was a well-educated person, her works on Kabbalah were riddled with mistakes. She accepted, for example, the popular occult opinion that Kabbalah was "a secret doctrine" that originated from ancient sources. In her *Theosophical Glossary*, she defined Kabbalah as "hidden wisdom of the Hebrew Rabbis of the Middle Ages, derived from older secret doctrines concerning divine things and cosmogony which were combined into a theology following the captivity of the Jews in Babylon."[29] Yet simultaneously she claimed that these sources were Zoroastrian and Hindu rather than Jewish. In her major work, *The Secret Doctrine*, she speculated on the Gnostic influences on Kabbalah, particularly on the duality of God presented as both infinite substance and finite embodiment: *ein-sof* and *sefirot*. She used this duality to assert that Kabbalah was true Judaism, which was polytheistic rather than monotheistic. This proof was extremely important for Blavatsky's belief that "theosophy accepts all faiths and philosophies and refuses to accept only gods of the so-called monotheistic religions, gods created by man in his own image and likeness, a blasphemous and sorry caricature of the ever Unknowable."[30] In the article "Kabbalah and Kabbalists," she argued that although only Kabbalah revealed the true essence of the Bible, modern Kabbalah had little in common with original kabbalistic teaching, since it had completely changed over the last five hundred years.[31] She argued that original Kabbalistic teaching survived only in Buddhist philosophy, and she constantly searched for the parallels between the ideas of Kabbalah and those of Buddhism.

Many kabbalistic allegories received a new treatment in Blavatsky's work. She was particularly interested in the image of Adam Kadmon, whom she identified as "a trunk of the divine tree of *sefirot*" and "the synthesis of *sefirot*."³² In the *Theosophical Glossary*, she described *ein-sof* as "one principle of the religious metaphysics of the Hebrew philosophers, the Boundless or Limitless Deity emanating and extending," and *sefirot* as "the ten emanations of the Deity, of which the highest is formed by the concentration of the Limitless Light, *ein-sof*."³³

By contrast, the concept of Sophia-Wisdom played no significant role in Blavatsky's work and was rarely mentioned at all. Blavatsky repeatedly explained the allegory of the tree of *sefirot* esoterically, giving it a pagan and occult reading, and even arguing that the *Zohar* contained a parallel between the tree of *sefirot* and the Egyptian cross in "its phallic aspect."³⁴ In her interpretation, the tree of *sefirot* loses its mystical value, becoming an allegory of a ritual sexual union rather than that of a spiritual bond between God and man. Hence, the image of the tree of *sefirot* becomes an image for a "divine hermaphrodite" and a "divine phallus."

Blavatsky's separation from the mystical "kabbalistic" tradition can also be seen in her interpretation of the term *tikkun*. The image of *tikkun* as a restoration of the universal primordial utopian state through human spiritual restoration is completely missing in Blavatsky's works. She asserted, rather, that *tikkun* was just another name for primordial man. According to Blavatsky, "In Kabbalah, Adam Kadmon is the "only-begotten," an androgynous or heavenly man, who is also a universal form of every being. He is also known as *Tikkun* or *Tetragrammaton*."³⁵ Moreover, Blavatsky claimed that the allegory of Adam Kadmon originated in India and stemmed from the Hindu name *Adami*, rather than originating in Jewish sources. She tried to prove that the original word *adami* meant "father" and had its source in Chaldean and Zoroastrian mythologies. She attempted to unite the allegory of Adam Kadmon not only with Buddhist mythology but also with astrological symbolism.³⁶

Blavatsky's belief in non-Jewish sources of "authentic" Kabbalah was, in fact, characteristic of the whole generation of occult adepts of Kabbalah in the late nineteenth and early twentieth centuries. This attitude is an interesting shift from the views established in Western and later Russian Romantic circles. Romantic writers were often quite hostile to Jews in their conviction that Jews were creators and disseminators of "black" kabbalistic magic. Even those who favored occult *kabbalistika* still regarded it as a heresy that might well lead its adepts to sin and destruction. By contrast, the new generation of the adepts of the occult, such as Blavatsky, Lévi, and Papus, as well as their later Western and Russian followers, praised Kabbalah highly, yet simultaneously attempted to detach it from Judaism and Jewish tradition. Their interest in Kabbalah went hand in hand with a rather strong Judophobia. Papus genuinely believed in the ancient origin of Kabbalah as "primordial" knowledge; however, he also widely expressed an opinion that Jews distorted original kabbalistic teaching and that "true Kabbalah" had an Aryan, not a Jewish origin. Similarly, Mebes's lectures stressed that Jews had forgotten the true meaning of Kabbalah. Moreover, he accompanied his first lecture with the anti-Semitic note that "Moses had to hide the secrets of kabbalistic magic from his own nation due to the typical negative aspects of Jewish character that we all are well aware of."[37] All three authors promoted the belief that Kabbalah was not a theosophical or philosophical teaching but a "secret" and powerful ancient occult doctrine, available only to the "chosen" initiated. As a result, these authors were largely responsible for the dissemination of the modern image of Kabbalah as a secret Jewish magical doctrine that shaped Russian public opinion in the early twentieth century.

This new generation of authors borrowed from the early Christian kabbalistic tradition and adopted a concept that might be called the keystone of the modernist perception of kabbalistic doctrine — the belief in the existence of an almighty creative primordial language that contained all the secrets of creation. While for the earlier Christian kabbalists that language was Hebrew, Blavatsky, Lévi, and Papus argued for the ability of an esoteric adept to magically transform the world through the powers of creative *personal* language. They believed that the primordial language was not the established Hebrew of the Bible but a mysterious "hidden" language, which could be restored by any initiated individual, and which they considered to be the symbolic and living image of the generative idea of language. They believed that a word should bear a mystical rather a semantic meaning: every word is a mystical sign, and therefore, a writer is able to create his own words by applying the same concepts that were used in Kabbalah (those of *gematriagematria* and *notarikon*, or simply the principles of combining the letters in unconventional order).

These views largely developed from the works of Antoine Fabre d'Olivet (1767 — 1825), a French occultist who attempted an alternate interpretation of Genesis, based on what he considered to be connections between the Hebrew alphabet and hieroglyphs. D'Olivet believed that contemporary Hebrew was only a colorless simulation of the tongue of the mysteries of creation, and that if one could again find this mysterious language, it would hold the key to all cosmogonies. Drawing upon various linguistic resources, he claimed that he had restored the tongue of the mysteries. D'Olivet became the first modern propagandist of the theory that authentic Kabbalah was an Egyptian, not a Jewish doctrine, transplanted into the Jewish tradition by Moses, whom d'Olivet considered to be an Egyptian priest. D'Olivet's ideas strongly influenced the views of those who followed him, including Lévi, Papus, and Blavatsky, and the particular "kabbalistic" occult system that they promoted. His works were also well-known in Russian occult circles: parts of his book on "restored" creative Hebrew, *The Hebraic Tongue Restored*, were published in *Isida*; and the second part of the book, called *The Cosmogony of Moses*, appeared as a separate edition in 1911.[38]

The popularity of works by Blavatsky, Lévi, and Papus in the literary circles of the Silver Age influenced the development a new literary function for kabbalistic imagery. The new interpretation different significantly from that of the eighteenth-century Masons and nineteenth-century early Romantics, in that it was based on the personal occult interests of an individual rather than on linguistic mysticism oriented towards the restoration of world unity. It was also, however, different from later Romanticism in that it was interested not in simple magical numerological or literal formulas (*kabbalistika*), but in a well-developed occult theory based on linguistic mysticism, i.e., the magical "creative" powers of the primordial alphabet, and the aspiration of making individual language rule common reality. This new interpretation was quickly adopted in the esoterically oriented literary milieu. Much as had happened a hundred years earlier, these ideas, originating in philosophical or esoteric writings, soon began to penetrate contemporary belles lettres. The kabbalistic myth created by Lévi, Papus, Blavatsky, and their followers became and remained an important part of Russian literary and artistic culture.

Kabbalah and Russian Philosophical Thought of the Fin de Siècle: Vladimir Soloviev and Pavel Florensky

One of the first to revive kabbalistic allegories popular in the eighteenth century was Vladimir Soloviev (1853 — 1900), probably the only writer of this period whose deep interest in Kabbalah has already been acknowledged in criticism.[39] In 1887 the magazine *Voprosy filosofii* (*Questions of Philosophy*) published an article by the well-known Russian-Jewish historian, David Ginzburg, entitled "Kabbalah, the Mystical Philosophy of the Jews." Soloviev recommended the article for publication and wrote a preface to the Ginzburg's piece. In the preface he stressed that kabbalistic theosophy was not the worldview of an individual philosopher, nor was it the system of one particular school. He argued that the central goal of kabbalistic theosophy was "the establishment of the mystical connection between all living things," and linked it to neo-Platonic linguistic mysticism. As he stated:

> The roots of Kabbalah are hidden in the dark depths of Jewish thought, and its upper, younger branches are interwoven with neo-Platonic and Gnostic teachings. However, while neo-Platonic doctrine regards a gradual transfer from the Absolute unity through the world of minds into the world of souls negatively, Kabbalah considers this transformation to be a positive process, a completion of the universal restoration. Kabbalah believes in the existence of four worlds, where each world is an emanation of divine thought and the material man on Earth corresponds to the primordial spiritual Man in Heaven. All human elements are placed in Kabbalah at various stages of the world structure from which they ascend and descend from low to high and vice versa. This structure in Kabbalah is allegorically perceived as the biblical Jacob's ladder. This idea of Man as an absolute and veritable universal form is absolutely antithetical to the Greeks and is a true biblical Truth, granted to the Christians by the Apostle Paul.[40]

Soloviev's own theory of the divine Wisdom (*Sophia* or *Hokhmah*) had a great influence on early Russian Symbolism, and contained many references to kabbalistic theosophy. Soloviev's interpretation of Sophia as a kabbalistic concept is most evidently present in his early writings, particularly in his mystical-theosophical tractate *Sophiia*, composed in 1875 yet never completed. While presenting his doctrine to the reader, Soloviev discusses the divine characteristics revealed in the process of creation. He asserts that in the basic forms of being, God primarily correlated with his own substance. God possesses this substance inside himself, and thus the process of creation can be described as the emanation of this divine substance. God as possessor of the creative energy observes inside himself what is to be born in the future, and emanates these future living forms out of himself, for he is the Creator and the creation simultaneously.[41] This description of creation, although it certainly reflects Gnostic tradition, also parallels the Lurianic description of God as *ein-sof*, a force that uses the space inside itself to give birth to the world. Soloviev stresses this parallel in a diagram, written on one of the pages. The diagram deconstructs the word "Sophia," so that the name is read "ai-sof." Soloviev then scribbles down a parallel: "Ain-Sof-Sophia-Logos." He explains the diagram, commenting that by the term "Logos" he means the verbal pronunciation of the divine power, "ain-sof;" and adds that there is a duality in this image: "Logos as the demiurge is First Adam. Logos as Christ is Second Adam. Logos is Divine reason, Sophia — Divine spirit."[42] Soloviev also commented on the kabbalistic interpretation of the word *bereshit*, arguing for the idea that, according to mystical interpretations of the Bible, God created Heaven and Earth in the Godhead, that is, "in his Wisdom."[43] Therefore, he regarded Wisdom not only as a creative divine force but also as a power able to join the separated parts of the world into one total unity.[44]

In a recent study of Soloviev's sophiology, Judith Kornblatt has extensively commented on Soloviev's interest in Kabbalah. Transitioning from Soloviev's life to his approach to sophiology, Kornblatt traces the development of Sophia from Greek culture through its adaptation in twentieth-century literature, spending a considerable amount of time on Sophia's representation in

Magical Kabbalah and the Linguistic Mysticism of the Silver Age

kabbalistic texts. She draws explicit and implicit links between the paradoxes in Soloviev's work and the many contradictions that surround the idea of Sophia, for example, that Sophia, who takes on a feminine form in the Proverbs, was never personified in the Torah. Kornblatt discusses the role of Kabbalah in influencing the numerous contradictions in Soloviev's own sophiological attitude, for instance, the fact that Soloviev's Sophia is associated with both the divine world and the natural world; that she exists as an idea of God but is also the actualization of that idea; and that Sophia is at the same time identified as the body of God and the soul of the world. Kornblatt believes that "Soloviev found in Kabbalah confirmation of his mystical vision of an erotic yet androgynous divine ideal with the Godhead. He understood Kabbalah's *sefirot* as multiple hypostases of the one living God who acts like humans and is acted upon by mortal men and women."[45]

However, Kornblatt's argument limits Soloviev's mystical doctrine to a particular time period. While analyzing in depth the biblical, Orthodox Christian, and mystical roots of Soloviev's sophiology, Kornblatt does not link his interpretation of Sophia with previous Russian secular mystical tradition, in particular with eighteenth-century Masonic mysticism. Yet, although we do not have an exact proof that Soloviev was deeply familiar with eighteenth-century Masonic literature, his own poetic interpretation of Wisdom as *ein-sof* largely echoes the eighteenth-century Russian interpretation of kabbalistic symbolism. Consider, for instance, the image seen in Bobrov's "A Meditation on the Creation of the World":

> This is that great God who watches
> All that is yet to be born inside him.
> He draws the images of creatures not yet born
> And conceives their future motion.[46]

In this short stanza Bobrov interprets God in kabbalistic terms, regarding Him as a creature that interacts with his own creative nature. The process of creation here is similarly described as the emanation of the divine substance: God observes inside himself what is to be born in the future, and prepares to emanate these future living forms out of himself. The similarities between this eighteenth-century Masonic allegorical interpretation of Wisdom, represented by Bobrov's poetic example, and Soloviev's own allegory of Sophia can also be seen in his understanding of the role of divine Wisdom, whom Soloviev regarded as the indivisible substance of the divine Creation.[47] Moreover, similar to the eighteenth-century Masonic authors, Soloviev believed in the existence of three forces in man. He considered that "all world creatures are united into one unity by Spirit, 'ideally' are distinguished by Reason; and in reality are divided by Soul. These three realities represent one world in its unity. Between these worlds there is an ideal link."[48]

In contrast to Kornblatt's opinion, which largely argues for the uniqueness of Soloviev's theory, limits his beliefs to being a product of a particular historical period, and considers his doctrine an inclusive product of the Silver Age, thus denying any link between his writings and previous Russian modern mystical literature (such as eighteenth-century Masonic writings), I agree with Konstantin Burmistrov who supposes that Soloviev's sophiology stems from an established Russian secular mystical tradition that had been broadly influenced by Kabbalah for more than a hundred years prior to Soloviev's own findings. On the one hand, Soloviev's ideas paralleled the eighteenth-century mystical Masonic interpretation of Kabbalah. On the other, his belief in the Absolute and in Wisdom as a force to restore the original world unity that has been lost after the fall also reflected the mytho-poetic Romantic interpretation of kabbalistic teaching.

However, Soloviev developed the ideas of his predecessors further. He argued for the presence of the essence that served as a reflection of divine Wisdom in the earthly world. He called this essence the "world soul" - Anima Mundi (*mirovaia dusha*). In his explanation of the concept of the world soul he also introduced the kabbalistic name, *Malkhut*, and described it as "God's kingdom on earth that is united with *Hokhmah* through the power of the Word. Therefore, the Word is the exposed light of God, a ray that is revealed to the world in the process of creation."[49] In Lurianic kabbalistic symbolism, *Malkhut*, the last *sefirah*, is regarded as the divine presence on earth, separated from the other *sefirot* after Adam's fall. At the same time, Lurianic Kabbalah always stresses the role of language as a restorative link to the lost connection between the divine, the *Malkhut*, and the earthly substances. Soloviev's interpretation of the Word certainly echoes this theosophical concept, although it also combines it with the traditional Orthodox and Platonic belief in the power of the creative word, or *Logos*. This echo can also be seen in Soloviev's discussion of the relationship between man and divine Wisdom. In *Sophiia*, Soloviev introduces the image of Adam Kadmon (the divine prototype of a human) as the soul of the world hidden in a human soul (that of Adam haRishon, the first human). He saw Adam Kadmon as an internal link between all creatures, "a conscious center and an inner universal interrelationship;" and a metaphor for the Anima Mundi. According to his view, both God-man and Sophia originated from *ein-sof*, in the process of the divine emanation. As for St. Paul, for Soloviev the God-man means Christ. Yet by contrast to St. Paul, in this case, Soloviev does not mean the historical Jesus Christ but just the primordial man — Adam Kadmon. In the drafts to "Sophiia" Soloviev draws a diagram of the Tree of Sefirot. He comments upon the diagram, using the terms "Adam Kadmon" and "Christ" as synonyms, both referring to one of the hightest entities, whereas the historical Jesus is located at the bottom of his scheme. Another diagram in the manuscript states his belief that "Logos+Sophia=Adam Kadmon." As Burmistrov properly noted, such views directly echo the views of Russian eighteenth-century Masonic mystics, who always distinguished between the Heavenly man (Christ, Adam Kadmon) and Jesus.[50]

Soloviev's principal source of his knowledge of Kabbalah was von Rosenroth's *Kabbalah Denudata*, which Soloviev read at the British Museum during his stay in London. In his dictionary entry on Kabbalah he also mentions texts by such Christian kabbalists as Robert Fludd, Francis Mercury van Helmont, and Abraham von Franckenberg, as well as such mystical authors as Boehme and Swedenborg.[51] It seems plausible that the enormous popularity of Soloviev's doctrine of Wisdom in intellectual and artistic circles catalyzed the revival of interest in those books, as well as in other eighteenth century Russian Masonic and Rosicrucian writings. Rosicrucian mythology particularly interested early Russian Symbolists, whose views derived largely from Soloviev.[52] Soloviev's own poetic works reflect his theosophical ideas; however, they also show not only ideological but also literary parallels to earlier "kabbalistic" Russian literary texts. In presenting his Sophia to the reader, Soloviev frequently uses the word "azure": Kornblatt notes this image in her book on Soloviev, yet she neither analyzes its possible sources, nor connects it with the eighteenth-century Masonic poetic tradition. Soloviev's constant depiction of Sophia, however, as "gold dressed in white and azure," reflects both Rosicrucian imagery found in the *Chemical Wedding* and Russian eighteenth-century mystical poetic works.[53] In one of his poems, Soloviev also comments that "his empress has a lofty palace with seven pillars and a seven-pointed crown." The image of "seven pillars" in Kabbalah often serves as an allegorical representation of the seven lower *sefirot*, often referred to as "the seven pillars of wisdom," or "the seven pillars of the world," and parallels the seven days of creation. The seven-pointed crown, an image which derives from the same symbolism, is worn by a queen in the *Chemical Wedding*.

Despite the parallels shown here, Soloviev's reading of Kabbalah stays closer to the Romantic mytho-poetic interpretation than to the moral-ethical Masonic interpretation of kabbalistic doctrine. For Soloviev, language is the central component of kabbalistic mysticism, and his reading of Sophia as a force for the restoration of the Golden Age is directly connected to his belief that Wisdom is the embodiment of the divine Word. In the Symbolist literary views that emerged largely from Soloviev's philosophical theories, the aesthetic mytho-poetic interpretation of Kabbalah, advocated by German and Russian Romantics, matured into an elaborate mystical worldview, based mostly on the magical and linguistic interpretation of kabbalistic doctrine.

A similar interpretation of kabbalistic mysticism is seen in the works of Pavel Florensky (1882–1937), the Russian Orthodox theologian and philosopher, who was influenced by Soloviev's philosopical views yet simultaniously created his own, highly original, theosophical system. Florensky's theosophy incorporated various kabbalistic concepts, which he, however, often combined with images taken from Gnostic and Christian writings and ancient

Egyptian mysticism. He believed in the existence of a primary point, an ontological center from which the universe developed. He often used the term *ein-sof* while describing the endless flow of divine energy born with the Deity and gradually returning to its origin, and he broadly analyzes the images of the Tree of Life (which he regards as a "synthetic idea of Life"), and of the androgenous primordial man, whom he often refers to as Adam Kadmon.[54] In the tractate *Microcosm and Macrocosm* he quotes, although from memory and without providing a direct source, a passage "from Kabbalah" that "in accord with the structure of human body, which is composed of multiple parts, the world is composed of many creations which all symbolize one universal body."[55] He claims that when "our eyes regain their true vision to see the abyss of the world, we will see ... humanity as a united *grand d'être*, Adam Kadmon of Kabbala."[56] Florensky extensively comments on the images of Adam Kadmon and "material Adam," often using the widespread eighteenth-century term "threadbare" Adam (*vetkhii Adam*) (most probably borrowed from a Russian translation of the Apostle Paul's writings). He says, in particular, that the first Adam was the king of the world because the world was, in fact, his own body. When taken away from the spring of life, Adam killed his spiritual self, and, separated from the spiritual world by material sinful "shells," lost his androgenous unity and his power over the world.[57] The image of "shells," which Florensky calls by their Hebrew name (*qelippoth*), derives from Lurianic allegory, where the image of a "shell" stands for an allegorical obstacle that since the fall of Adam and the introduction of evil into the world has been separating *sefirot* from their source of spiritual energy, i.e., God. Burmistrov, in his analysis of Florensky's interest in Kabbalah, argued that Florensky mostly used Western occult sources in his Kabbalah study; however, Burmistrov did not comment on the strong stylistic parallel between Florensky's writings and Russian eighteenth-century Masonic texts. In fact, Florensky's style, in his presentation of the allegory of Adam Kadmon, reflects that of early Russian mystical works. In comparison with Blavatsky, for example, who primarily uses new, late nineteenth-century translations of kabbalistic terms (such as "divine hermaphrodite" as a term for

Adam Kadmon), Florensky often uses established Russian terms that derive from the older, eighteenth-century tradition. Besides "threadbare Adam," Florensky often calls the microcosm "a small replica of the whole world" (*malyi mir*) (compare to Kheraskov's "[the first-born was] a small replica of the whole world").[58] He also names Adam Kadmon "a lantern of reason" (*sviatil'nik razuma*) and "the ray of divine light" (*luch bozhestvennogo sveta*) (compare to Kheraskov's lines: "This spark of the Divine, this flame of Wisdom / The Fall has turned into the ashes of sin [*tot luch bozhestvennyi i razuma svetilo / grekhopadenie v grekhovnost' obratilo*"].[59] In addition, Florensky's most important early literary work is an incomplete poem titles "Holy Vladimir"; the title is certainly linked with Florensky's admiration for Soloviev; yet it also reminds the reader of image of Duke Vladimir as a spiritual enlightener of Russia that dominates Kheraskov's epic *Vladimir Reborn*. Soloviev in this context himself turns into the reborn, being regarded as a new incarnation of Duke Vladimir on the earth, a new spiritual father of Russia.

At the same time, Florensky often utilizes the views of German Romantics when he analyzes the concepts of creation and Adam Kadmon. He calls God by Schelling's term "Absolute," he widely quotes Novalis, and his theosophy is as much mytho-poetic as philosophical. Florensky's interest in kabbalistic teaching in centered upon the mystical nature of the divine alphabet and the doctrine of the names of God. Problems related to the nature of language and the status of names, the connection between word and reality, and the internal and the external forms of the word were basic to Florensky's philosophy of language. Florensky regarded names, and more than anything, the divine name, as a source of energy. He believed that every name is *logos spermatikos*, or the mystical center of one's personality, and that every word has a direct link with reality, with ideas that possess a hypostatical existence. In one of his most famous works, *Names* (*Imena*), Florensky turns to kabbalistic (or quasi-kabbalistic) methods of deconstructing words by writing them in the Hebrew alphabet. Florensky borrows this technique from Antoine Fabre d'Olivet's book *The Hebraic Tongue Restored*, which attempted to reconstruct humanity's proto-language through discovering basic roots of ancient Hebrew. D'Olivet claimed that the original Hebrew root should consist of two, not three letters, since according to the *Sefer Yetzirah* God created the world by combining the 22 letters of the Hebrew alphabet into two-letter binary pairs. Florensky follows d'Olivet's argument and further develops it. He also comments on the connection between letters and numbers, which he believes are essential for the divine organization of the world. He argues that number is "the form of external organization," while letter signifies the "internal essence of things": in other words, that the "number is cosmologically what the idea is ontologically."[60] This belief also reflects the ideas originating in the *Sefer Yetzirah* that numbers do not have the same attributes as letters, since numbers create space and time while letters create the world and physical objects.

Florensky's profound interest in the nature of names was also closely connected to his participation in the circle of followers of the religious doctrine of *Imiaslavie*, a movement that was condemned by the Russian Orthodox Church, and which asserted that God is present in his name. One of the main ideas in *Imiaslavie* was the belief that that knowledge of the secret name of God alone allowed one to perform miracles — a concept very similar to that of the divine name in kabbalistic mysticism.

Florensky's linguistic mysticism can be compared to the linguistic mysticism of Romantic philosophers. The connection between Florensky's mysticism and literature is evident: after explaining his theosophical argument in detail, Florensky immediately applies it to literary works, primarily to Pushkin's poem *Gypsies* (*Tsygane*). He argues that Pushkin's poem is "all about the name of the main character, Mariula." He believes that the phonetic structure of the poem mirrors that of the name Mariula, and that the letters (or, more accurately, sounds) of the name "have narrated" their poem to Pushkin.[61] Florensky claims that the only way to decipher "the metaphysics" of those sounds is "through Kabbalah." In order to do so he transcribes the name in Hebrew letters and in corresponding numbers. Then, "to be completely objective" he takes characteristics of every letter as a "metaphysical origin." In this transcription "M" serves as "the origin of metaphysical maternity," "A" as "a primary point," and "L" as "a constant movement." Florensky then analyses the two-letter syllables, arguing that, according to D'Olivet's definitions, "M-A is describing primary, primitive maternity, while L-A signifies continuous non-stop action." He concludes by stating that, "kabbalistic analysis helps us to see the name Mariula as an infinite female nature in its endless, uncontrolled movement."[62] He then adds that according to Kabbalah each letter also represents a part of a human body, and therefore readers should be aware that the name Mariula purposely contains the letter "u" that he transcribes in Hebrew as "vav." Florensky argues that "vav" in Kabbalah "metaphysically represents an ear, which stands for both the symbol for wind and as a sign for "intellectual essence." Hence, linked to the letter "a" (alef), "u" (vav) becomes "a union of freedom (wind) with intellectualism (anti-freedom) that unites being with non-being and makes Pushkin's poem a symbol of the conflict between reason and uncontrolled passion."[63] This type of analysis, which combines theosophy with occult tradition and linguistic analysis, can be regarded as a theosophical version of early Russian formalism. Florensky's ideas are also comparable to the ideas of Russian symbolists, who claimed that the metaphysics of sound create true poetry and that the actual established meanings of the words are secondary to the true mystical meaning hidden in sounds.

Florensky gained his knowledge of Kabbalah mostly from non-Jewish and largely occult sources, although Burmistrov is correct in asserting that Florensky's own approach to Kabbalah was mystical rather than occult. At the same time, Florensky evidently shared the popular belief that Kabbalah was not philosophy but a secret science, a "theosophy of the chosen," and he echoed an established Silver Age opinion that true Kabbalah did not belong to the Jews who had distorted it. In a letter to a friend he wrote that "it is repulsive to see how the stinking mob pushes into the caves of mystery and to smell the odor of garlic that poisons the sweet smell of the most delicate incense."[64] In contrast to Soloviev's attitude to Jews and Judaism that was with no doubt positive, Florensky's interest in Kabbalah went hand-in-hand with somewhat mixed attitudes to Jews that sometimes verged on hostility. For example, during the famous

Beilis case, Florensky shared most reactionary anti-Semitic views, providing an anonymous commentary that argued that Jews use Kabbalah as an ideological tool for ritual murder.[65] These evidently anti-Semitic views were generally characteristic of the intellectual atmosphere of the Silver Age. While praising Kabbalah as a mystical doctrine given (at least indirectly) to the world by Jews, Russian thinkers and writers of that time simultaneously shared a negative attitude to the Jews as a nation, argued that Jews distorted and ritualized the true essence of the kabbalistic mystical teaching, and tried to distance Kabbalah from its Jewish origins, providing it instead with a "universal" mystical essence and uniting it with other esoteric systems.

From Mystical Mytho-Poetics to Political Myth: the Case of Vasilii Rozanov

The employment of Jewish mysticism in Russian literature has been always linked to the attempt to acquire anew the primordial Wisdom that Adam lost after the fall. However, while those particular poetic goals did not change over the course of two centuries, the interpretation of kabbalistic allegory varied during different periods. From its introduction in the 1770s until the 1920s, kabbalistic allegory in Russian philosophical and literary thought developed in two directions, the mystical theosophical and the occult. The followers of both branches were interested in primordial wisdom. Yet whereas the mystical branch aimed for the salvation of humanity on the basis of Judeo-Christian moral principles, the occult branch, oriented towards obtaining primordial knowledge, collected pseudo-kabbalistic magical practices, and was regarded even by its adepts as an anti-Christian force. The popularity of this branch and its broad dissemination in the prerevolutionary years led to an extreme misrepresentation of kabbalistic doctrine, which, together with the established image of *kabbalistika*, was largely responsible for the formation of the "kabbalistic" aspect of the Judeo-Masonic myth. This myth was widely promoted by Russian nationalist media in the twentieth century, and represented Kabbalah as a secret Judeo-Masonic magical teaching.

In the Beginning Was the Word

The myth of the Judeo-Masonic conspiracy originated in the right-wing press of the late nineteenth century. The first connection between Jews and Freemasons appeared in 1806, in a text written supposedly by army officer J. B. Simonini, who attempted to draw readers' attention to "the Judaic sect which, in close alliance with Freemasons, is preparing the way for the Antichrist."[66] Although earlier authors such as Simonini asserted the link between Freemasons and magic, the connection of the Judeo-Masonic conspiracy to Kabbalah appeared for the first time only in 1869, in a text directly linking Kabbalah, Freemasonry, and Jews as sorcerers and allies of Satan. This work, entitled *Le Juif, le judaïsme, et la judaïsation des peuples chrétiens* (*The Jew, Judaism, and the Judaization of Christian Peoples*) was authored by French political writer Gougenot des Mousseaux. Mousseaux considered Kabbalah to be a secret religion, a systematic cult of evil, established by the devil at the very beginning of the world. He claimed that Kabbalah was later adopted by the Chaldeans, and in due course they passed their secret on to the Jews. Subsequently the Gnostics, the Manicheans, and the Assassins had also practiced this cult; they then handed down the diabolic folklore to the Templars, who in their turn handed it on to the Freemasons. Mousseaux claimed that the cult centered on the worship of Satan, that its chief symbols were the serpent and the phallus, and that its ritual included erotic orgies of the wildest kind. He was also certain that by murdering Christian children the Jews in particular were able to acquire magical powers.[67]

The first Russian text that dealt with the danger of the Judeo-Masonic conspiracy was *The Talmud and the Jews*, a three-volume work written by the former Catholic priest Hippolytus Lutostansky and published in Odessa in 1880.[68] Lutostansky's book was founded on the argument that the Bible had three levels of interpretation: literal, allegorical, and encoded. The encoded interpretation could be understood only by those who had been initiated into a secret sect that the author traced to the Chaldeans. This knowledge had passed from one generation of Jews to another. After centuries, the Jews hired certain initiated Gentiles such as Templars, and later Masons, who could help them to preserve this knowledge. Although *The Secret of the Jews* was based on fantasy, many of its ideas reflected those set forth in the writings of Papus and Lévi. Doubtless the hysterical fears and fantasies of the political anti-Semitic pamphleteers of late nineteenth-century Europe were influenced by the same occult notions that abounded in intellectual society.

The beginning of the twentieth century brought a wave of apocalyptic ideas. Many Russian intellectuals regarded the birth of the new century as a special and meaningful event. As Alexander Blok noted in 1911, "We felt January of 1900 to be completely different from December of 1899, which had just ended. It stood under a totally different astrological sign, and brought hundreds of new omens, mystical fears, and hidden prophecies."[69] The artistic elite regarded the Revolution of 1905 as confirmation of these feelings. Bely noted that "The revolution of 1905 woke dark forces that had slumbered until now but were suddenly released. We witnessed changes in the social and artistic canons. The old is dying, giving way to the new."[70] An article in *Novoe vremia* (*New Times*) claimed that "the beginning of the twentieth century threatens to become the beginning of a new era, a cosmopolitan era, an era of the world revolution that will be different from all other revolutions we know. It will be a true victory of the new world-order over old tradition."[71]

The Revolution of 1905 also activated strong anti-Semitic feelings. The most popular Russian anti-Semitic text, *The Protocols of the Elders of Zion*, which promoted and popularized the theory of the Judeo-Masonic conspiracy, directly reflected the mystical and revolutionary fears of the time. Although the *Protocols* did not mention Kabbalah, both Nilus in particular and anti-Semitic opinion in general soon made this connection, combining ideas from the *Protocols* with popular contemporary occult books and articles. For example, a third edition of the *Protocols*, published by Nilus in 1911, was enriched by the knowledge he gained from the occult books he had ordered from a famous Moscow store just for this purpose. On the cover of this edition Nilus placed a picture of the king from the tarot deck taken from the first page of Papus's *Quabalah* with the heading, "Here is the face of the Antichrist."[72]

In July 1911 a child named Andrei Yushchinsky was found murdered in Kiev. A Jewish inhabitant of Kiev, Mendel Beilis, was arrested and charged with his murder. Beilis' accusation revived a long-forgotten medieval anti-Semitic belief: the blood libel. The prosecutors claimed that the boy was killed in a Jewish ritual process and was an ostensible victim of religious fanaticism. A number of famous journalists and political leaders helped Beilis in his case, since his innocence was clear from the very start of the trial even to the most biased and uneducated witnesses. He was eventually released and cleared of all accusations in 1913. However, right-wing political organizations persisted in disseminating the idea that a Christian child had been killed by Jews in order to obtain his blood for the rites of the Jewish religion.

The government's case against Beilis is frequently interpreted as a politically expedient form of anti-Semitism. Most scholars, like Alexander Tager, believe that the Beilis trial was basically political, and was largely part of the tsarist effort to justify pogroms and maintain a strong sense of Russian national identity.[73] In opposition to established opinion, Leonid Katsis treats it in terms of specific kind of elite production characteristic of the culture of the Silver Age. In particular, he argues that the most important support for the ritual murder charge in the form of supposed special knowledge of secret Jewish occult practices came not from a politician, but from philosopher and writer Vasilii Rozanov, who was associated with Russian Symbolists and Decadents and who, during Beilis's trial, produced a number of articles on the case. Rozanov's collection of articles, published together under the title *The Olfactory and Tactile Relationship of Jews with Blood* (*Oboniatel'noe i osiazatel'noe otnoshenie evreev k krovi*) (1914) is still regarded as the most provocative Russian political pamphlet on Kabbalah. Although at the first glimpse the collection manifests vivid support for the most bizarre anti-Semitic ideas of the Black Hundreds, Katsis believes that Rozanov's argument on the Beilis case was not a product of political hatred, but of a thoughtful theological search. He has expressed the provocative opinion that "the theoreticians of the onomatodoxy aimed to create their own doctrine of blood sacrifice in Judaism based on the knowledge of ecstatic rituals in their own as well as in the other cults."[74] Katsis argues that Modernists, both Symbolists and Acmeists, through their pursuit of particular kind of mystical and secret Jewish knowledge, provided a context for the ritual murder charge against Beilis.

Rozanov's life-long philosophical dialogue with Judaism and Jews, and especially his understanding of Kabbalah, very much replicated that astonishing mixture of praise and fear that characterized the general attitude of Russian intellectuals of Romanticism, and then Modernism, to kabbalistic teachings. Rozanov adored Kabbalah for the very same reasons that he hated it. He sincerely believed that Kabbalah was a not a mystical or philosophical but an occult doctrine, hidden in secrecy through generations so that no Gentile could obtain true knowledge of it. He argued that this secrecy was contained not in Kabbalah as such but "in the basis of Kabbalah in particular and Judaism in general," that is "the secret language of the Jews, Hebrew."[75] Against those occultists who argued that contemporary Hebrew had lost its magical creative value, Rozanov believed that Hebrew was still "a holy alphabet," a "scrawl" that had no analogy in any other linguistic tradition and that was deliberately created in such a way that no Gentile might understand it. He attempted to prove his argument by the fact that Hebrew does not contain any vowels; therefore, "it is only Jews who can decipher the secret meaning hidden in unpronounceable consonants."[76] Rozanov's interpretation of Hebrew echoes the views of Russian experimental writers of Silver Age, who, as Harriet Murav notes, were, in 1913, "the year of Beilis trial . . . developing theories of the transrational meaning of language and writing poetry, consisting only of consonants... and painted their faces with cryptic messages and codes... to establish contact with the divinity."[77]

In the articles that continue the collection, however, particularly in the article "Ekhad [One] or The Thirteen Wounds of Yushchinsky" ("Ekhad: Trinadtsat' ran Yushchinskogo"), Rozanov attempted to prove that Beilis had been able to murder the boy because "he was driven by the power of ancient cells which had existed in Jewish bodies from the times of antiquity, when humankind practiced human sacrifice."[78] He pronounced an undeniable link between Kabbalah, ritual murder, and the Jewish attitude toward blood. Rozanov analyzed the structure of wounds on the boy's body in great detail. His conclusions, however, were extremely anti-Semitic.

He believed that the thirteen wounds found on Yushchinsky's corpse allegorically represented "in graphic form" the specific excerpt from *Zohar* that called for the destruction of Gentiles, and claimed that the wounds formed two triangles, which, being placed together, displayed a drawing of a hexagram, the "Star of Solomon." He asserted that the murder of Yushchinsky was certainly a religious ritual, performed according to the rules of kabbalistic magic, since the arrangement of wounds on the Yushchinsky's corpse was not accidental and, if interpreted kabbalistically, "when each number corresponds to a particular letter," read as follows: "Let your mighty powers destroy fallen Christianity, allegorically represented here in this sacrificed child, a sacred offering to Satan."[79] Rozanov also declared that the structure of the wounds corresponded to the tree of *sefirot* and should be interpreted as a magical formula. He concluded that "if ritual murders exist they indisputably always should be interpreted as kabbalistic 'procedures,' always aimed at a particular goal, that use the formulas hidden in Kabbalah as both the initial and the terminal points of influence."[80]

Rozanov's views, expressed in his articles on Jews, Kabbalah, and blood libel, have been linked to the similar beliefs of Pavel Florensky, who also sincerely believed in Beilis' guilt. Zinaida Gippius remembered that in a private conversation Florensky once declared: "If I were a Jew, I would certainly perform a ritual murder."[81] Florensky also wrote an anonymous comment that accompanied Rozanov's articles on the Beilis case and Kabbalah. While Rozanov's views on Judaism shifted over the years from clear admiration to pure hate, Florensky's strong views on the anti-Christian nature of Kabbalah, in spite of his deep interest in the magical powers of mystical kabbalistic teaching, had been pronounced in his writings years before the Beilis case.[82] His negative attitude toward Jews can be clearly seen in a preface to the book *Israel in the Past, Present, and Future* (*Izrail v proshlom, nastoiashchem, i budushchem*), which he composed and published anonymously. In this preface, Florensky proclaimed that the world has learned of God through the Jews, yet through the Jews the world also gained contact with Satan. He openly declared that in world history, Judaism served as the origin of "most satanic cults" that were hidden under the guise of

Freemasonry; yet at the same time he also wondered why God had chosen the Jews as "his nation" if they were so evil and corrupt. Florensky concluded that while in socio-economic and political areas Judaism was certainly corrupt and evil, its mystical, spiritual side still hid "Divine Wisdom and Love."[83]

By contrast, Rozanov wrote in his diaries that his attitude toward Jews "has undergone a strong transformation since the revolution of 1905."[84] In his exhaustive description of the magical powers of Hebrew letters in "Ekhad," Rozanov admired them as much as condemned them. He defined *sefirot* as "demonic principles," yet regarded them too as mystical religious concepts. He commented on the spiritual nature of the Hebrew alphabet, saying that it served as the primary "sign" for the world. Yet throughout his collection of articles devoted to the case of Yushchinsky's murder, Rozanov also emphasized the secrecy of kabbalistic doctrine, the chosen "secret" nature of Hebrew alphabet, and its link to "the magical mysteries of creation."

Rozanov's writings mirrored the eschatological and apocalyptic fears that were characteristic of the Russian intellectuals of the Silver Age, and thus they cannot be called a product of simple political anti-Semitism but rather of the broad cultural context of the Silver Age, and in particular of those cultural stereotypes that had been created and popularized by Russian literature, from Symbolism to avant-garde. Rozanov elaborated on that particular "numerological" occult interpretation of Kabbalah that had become widespread in the literary milieu of the early twentieth century.[85] Although he repeatedly claimed to have used Jewish sources in his analysis, he interpreted the "kabbalistic" signs on Yushchinsky's body in line with the two most popular occult books of the period: Lévi's *Dogme et Rituel* and Papus's *Quabalah*. These works were superficial, inaccurate, and often falsely presented kabbalistic symbolism, but most members of the Russian artistic and cultural elite of the early twentieth century took their ideas for granted. Kabbalah in Rozanov's compositions, just as in Florensky's philosophy and in Symbolist and Acmeist literature, was a universal theory of a symbolic "sign," the divine "poetic" semiotics that they believed to contain the secrets of nature and the primordial world. Yet while the literary elite eliminated the Jewish nature of this mystical semiotic system and stressed its occult rather than mystical character, political propaganda deliberately emphasized the Jewish roots of Kabbalah, at the same time employing the non-Jewish occult sources that were popularized in the artistic circles of the early twentieth century, and passing them off as authentic Jewish doctrine. It is difficult not to agree with Murav, who believes that Rozanov adapted avant-garde experimentation with the "magic of words" for his own purposes.[86] Whatever these purposes were, Rozanov's aim was definitely not the promotion of a pogrom. He analyzed kabbalistic "magic" not as a politician but as a literary person who wanted to believe that Yushchinsky's murder served as an amazing proof that kabbalistic rituals did indeed exist and were as powerful and almighty as he wished them to be. He sincerely and emotionally hoped for the existence of mystery in nature: the mystery that we as simple non-initiated mortals could not perceive. As Alexander Blok once said upon learning about the tragedy of the *Titanic*, "There is still Ocean."[87] However, in the political context of the right-wing ideology of the years following 1905, Rozanov's articles were not acknowledged as literary or theological experiments in kabbalistic occult theology, but as clear and harsh anti-Semitic propaganda. As Murav noted,

> Symbolist and decadent writers were themselves conscious of, and some troubled by, the possible connection between their own and Rozanov's work, and hence their connection to the ritual murder charge. They raised questions about the legal and the political consequences of cultural discourse, or, to use the language of the time, the relation between the "word" and the "deed". These writers came face to face with problems of law and literature — not as theoreticians, but as participants in a cultural discourse whose legal implications appalled them.[88]

At the 1914 meeting of the Religious and Philosophical Society, Dmitry Filosofov claimed that although Rozanov's words were not evil acts in themselves, they produced a strong effect on those who turned them into acts. Published in print and detached from his own persona and his own ambiguous and troubled relations with Judaism, Jews, and Kabbalah, Rozanov's words turned into a force that aroused hatred in the masses and encouraged them to commit acts of violence.[89] Following a quasi-trial, Rozanov was expelled from the Society and socially ostracized, which lasted until his death. However, Rozanov's works completed the vicious circle: a culture produced a particular stereotype that had been originally intended as a pure literary device, which, once it was popularized in a text, became a powerful political force, which was activated and reproduced on multiple occasions as a part of nationalist and anti-Semitic propaganda.

NOTES

1. Bernice Rosenthal, ed., The Occult in Russian and Soviet Culture (Ithaca, NY: Cornell University Press, 1997), 5.

2. Quoted in Maria Carlson, *No Religion Higher than Truth: A History of the Theosophical Movement in Russia, 1875–1922* (Princeton: Princeton University Press, 1993), 5. See also idem, "Fashionable Occultism: Spiritualism, Theosophy, Freemasonry, and Hermeticism in Fin-de-Siècle Russia," in *The Occult in Russian and Soviet Culture*, 135–52.

3. Carlson, *No Religion Higher than Truth*, 5.

4. Maria Carlson recently observed: "The appeal of a bridge [between the empiricism of modern science and the faith of religion] to a fin-de-siècle European culture cut off from God by excessive rationalism and the rise of modern science and industry, was enormous. The modern European mind had lost its faith; the traditional Church could no longer provide a direct link to God. The scientific positivism then prevalent in European culture did not offer spiritual revelation; people looked beyond traditional religion and science to meet their spiritual needs." Carlson, *No Religion Higher than Truth*, 12.

5. Ibid., 79.

6. Quoted in Gennady Obatnin, *Ivanov-mistik: Okkul'tnye motivy v poezii i proze Viacheslava Ivanova (1907–1919)* (Moscow: Novoe Literaturnoe Obozrenie, 2000), 169.

7. For the full list of these magazines, see E. Kasinec, in *The Occult in Russian and Soviet Culture*, 423.

8. Konstantin Burmistrov, "Andrei Bely i Kabbalah," in *Jews and Slavs*, ed. W. Moskovich (Jerusalem: The Hebrew University Press, 2006), 13: 265–78.

9. Carlson, *No Religion Higher than Truth*, 21.

10. Lévi's ideas were most developed in *The Dogma and Ritual of High Magic*. They were further elaborated in his two major pseudo-kabbalistic studies: *The Key of the Grand Mysteries*, and his own translation of the *Zohar*, which is called *The Book of Splendors* and differs significantly from the translated Latin, which already deviates from the original version. In *Transcendental Magic*, Lévi declared that he had received his knowledge of Kabbalah during his meditations from *Baphomet*, the black spirit, who was the God of the Templars. He also claimed that the name *Baphomet*, if decoded according to the rules of Kabbalah, should be read TEM OHP AB. He believed that TEM OHP AB was an abbreviation from the phrase *Templi omnivm hominum pacis abbas*, meaning *the father of the Temple of all people on Earth*, and argued that this line referred to the Temple of Solomon and was, therefore, an encoded symbol of the Freemasons. See Éliphas Lévi, *The History of Magic* (New York: Weiser Books, 1968), 87.

11. Ibid., 85.

12. Ibid.

13. *Isida* 9–10 (1912): 11.

14. This order is, however, generally connected with the name of Louis-Claude de Saint-Martin. See Obatnin, *Ivanov-mistik*, 169.

15. Ibid., 71.

16. The article and the program were reprinted in the Russian magazine *Isida* 1 (1909): 13–21.

17. *Isida* 1 (1909): 13.

18. In his memoirs, Maurice Paléologue, the French ambassador to Russia, related that Nicholas II, frightened by the events of 1905, asked Papus to tell his fortune using tarot cards. Papus read the cards and told the tsar that he would die at the hands of the revolutionaries. He promised the tsar, however, that he would create a magical spell that would protect the royal family, but it would work only until Papus' own death. Upon his return to France from Russia, Papus commented on his fortune-telling in the following way: "These people are mad. They believe in every stupid story you tell them. One does not need to be a fortune-teller to realize that this country is doomed." Ironically, Papus was killed at the German front just a few weeks before the February Revolution. Maurice Paléologue, *Rasputin: Vospominaniia* (Moscow: Izd. dev. Ianvaria, 1923),103.

19. Andrei Serkov, *Istoriia russkogo masonstva, 1845–1945* (St. Petersburg: Izd-vo im. N. I. Novikova, 1997), 71.

20. For more on Leman, see Nikolai Bogomolov, *Russkaia literatura nachala XX veka i okkul'tizm: Issledovaniia i materialy* (Moscow: Novoe Literaturnoe Obozrenie, 1999), 264–66.

21. Bogomolov, *Russkaia literatura*, 43.

22. For more on the influence of Mebes on the members of The Guild of Poets, see ibid., 255–63.

23. Mebes joined the Martinist Order in 1910 when he was already a middle-aged man with his own system of esoteric viewpoints. Upon entering the Order he was immediately initiated into the degree of the highest rank and was presented with a diploma of Doctor of Hermetic Sciences from the Parisian School of Hermetic Studies. Mebes was a founder of the first Martinist lodge in Russia: the Lodge of St. Apollonius in St. Petersburg, which he headed from its foundation. Ibid., 264–66.

24. GOM, *Entsiklopedia Okkul'tizma* (St. Petersburg, 1912), 11.

25. For more on Helen Blavatsky see J. Gordon Melton, Jerome Clark, and Aidan A. Kelly, eds., *New Age Almanac* (New York: Visible Ink, 1991), 16. For the influence of Blavatsky on the Russian cultural life of the Silver Age, see Carlson's *No Religion Higher than Truth*.

26. Carlson, *No Religion Higher than Truth*, 140.

27. See E. Blavatskaia [H. P. Blavatsky], *Tainye Znaniia* (Moscow: MTSF, 1994), 272–91, 408–30.

28. Papus also belonged to the General Council of Blavatsky's Theosophical Society and was an influential member of the French theosophically oriented society *Isis*. A short article describing Papus's visit to Russia in the magazine *Rebus*, the official magazine of the Theosophical Society, observed that "the ideas of Papus echo those of Theosophy," and mentioned that some members of the Society had close contacts with the French Martinist Order. *Rebus* 3 (1907)

29. H. Blavatsky, *Teosofskii slovar'* (Moscow: Sfera, 1994), 169.

30. Carlson, *No Religion Higher Than Truth*, 141.

31. E. Blavatskaia [H. P. Blavatsky], *Tainye Znaniia*.

32. Ibid.

33. Blavatsky, *Teosofskii slovar'*, 12.

34. Ibid., 38.

35. Helen Blavatsky, *The Secret Doctrine: H. P. Blavatsky Collected Writings* (Wheaton, IL: Theosophical Publishing House, 1978), 2: 422.

36. Ibid, 65. Blavatsky gave a similar esoteric interpretation to the teaching of the existence of three souls in man that played such a significant role in earlier mystical Masonic tradition. She stated that Kabbalah posited the presence of two souls in man: *nefesh* or the spirit of life, and *neshama*, a higher soul connected with the divine spirit known as *sechel* or *ruah*. However, Blavatsky tried to prove that the true elaboration of this concept was lost in Kabbalah and was retained in Buddhist doctrines.

37. GOM [Grigorii Mebes], *Entsiklopediia okkultizma* (St. Petersburg, 1912), 117.

38. Fabr D' Olive, *Kosmogonia Moiseia*, trans. V. Zapriagaev (Viaz'ma, 1911).

39. See Judith Kornblatt, *Divine Sophia: the Wisdom Writings of Vladimir Soloviev* (Ithaca: Cornell University Press, 2009); Burmistrov, "The Interpretation of Kabbalah," 157–87; Burmistrov, "Vladimir Soloviev and Russian Freemasonry: Some Kabbalistic Parallels," *Tirosh (Studies in Judaica)* 6 (2006): 35–50; Kornblatt, "Russian Religious Thought and the Jewish Kabbala"; idem, "Soloviev's Androgynous Sophia and the Jewish Kabbalah," *Slavic Review* 50 (1991): 487–96; Hamutal Bar-Yosef, "Sophiology and the Concept of Femininity in Russian Symbolism and in Modern Hebrew Poetry," *Journal of Modern Jewish Studies* 2, no. 1 (2003): 62–65. See also Daigen Uri, "Kabbalah in Russian Religious Philosophy: the Impact of Kabbalah on the Russian Sophiological Movement" (Ph.D. diss., Bar Ilan University, 2008).

40. V. Soloviev. In D. Ginzburg, "Kabbala, misticheskaia filosofiia evreev," *Voprosy filosofii i psikhologii* 33 (1896): 277–300, 277.

41. Vladimir Soloviev, *Rossia i Vselenskaia tserkov'* (Minsk, 1999), 438.

42. Ibid., 445.

43. Vladimir Soloviev, "Sophiia," in *Sochineniia* (Moscow: Nauka, 2000), vol. 2, 93.

44. Soloviev, *Rossia i Vselenskaia tserkov'*, 445.

45. Kornblatt, *Divine Sophia*, 68–69.

46. Semen Bobrov, *Rassvet Polnochi*, 3:51–52.

> Се тот великий Бог который созерцает
> Все то чему в себе родиться подобает,
> Се образ их существ несозданных чертит,
> И будущее их движенье умозрит.

47. "Sophia's main activity is the creation and the initial regulation of the Universe. She is the beginning of Creation, the internal and the external revelation of God on earth." (Soloviev, *Rossia i Vselenskaia tserkov'*, 454.)

48. Ibid., 453.

49. Soloviev, "Sophiia," 53.

50. Soloviev, "Sophiia," 57, 164, 172. See also Burmistrov "Christian Orthodoxy And Jewish Kabbalah: Russian Mystics In The Search For Perennial Wisdom." In *Polemical Encounters: Esoteric Discourse and Its Others*, 41.

51. For more on the influence of kabbalistic philosophy on Swedenborg, see Marsha Keith Schuchard, *Restoring the Temple of Vision: Cabalistic Freemasonry and Stuart Culture*. Leiden: Brill, 2002.

52. See for example, Bogomolov's article on Anna Mintslova, which describes her profound interest in both Soloviev's teaching and Rosicrucian mysticism. Bogomolov, *Russkaia literatura*, 23–113; Soloviev, *Rossia i Vselenskaia tserkov'*, 455.

53. See, for example:

>As the heavenly glory is reflected
>In the pure azure of the quieted seas
>So in the light of the free spirit's passion
>To us eternal good appears . . .
>
>And amid those flowers and in eternal summer
>Enveloped in azure silver
>How beautiful you are, and in the starry light
>How free and pure is love . . .
>
>The voice of my homeland is in your magic speech,
>In the light of your azure eyes,
>In the golden color of you marvelous curls . . .

In Kornblatt, *Divine Sophia*, 105.

54. Pavel Florensky, *Sochineniia* (Moscow: *Mysl'*, 1999), 3, 114. For a brief analysis of Florensky and Kabbalah see Burmistrov, "The Interpretation of Kabbalah."

55. Ibid., 3, 443.

56. Ibid., 3, 114.

57. Ibid., 3, 436.

58. Ibid., 3, 221; Bobrov, *Rassvet Polnochi*, 3, 6; Kheraskov, *Vladimir*, 182.

59. Ibid., 3, 173.

60. Ibid., 3, 177.

61. Ibid., 3, 179.

62. Ibid., 3, 179

63. Ibid., 3, 179

64. Quoted in Burmistrov, "The Interpretation of Kabbalah," 169. As Burmistrov observes, Florensky obviously reckoned himself among "the occultists by the grace of God," whereas the odor of garlic alludes to Jews. Ibid., 180.

65. See ibid. See also Efim Kurganov and Henrietta Mondry, *Vasilii Rozanov i evrei* (St. Petersburg: Akademicheskii proekt, 2000). See also a brief but interesting article by Felix Philipp Ingold, "Was Pavel Florensky an Anti-Semite?" *Neue Zürcher Zeitung*, November 22, 2002, available in Russian at <http://www.inosmi.ru/translation/165162.html>. Last accessed on July 27, 2009.

66. Jury Delevsky, *Protokoly Sionskikh Mudretsov* (Epokha, Berlin, 1923), 40.See also Norman Cohn, *Warrant for Genocide: The Myth of the Jewish World-Conspiracy and the Protocols of the Elders of Zion* (London: Serif, 1967), 27.

67. Norman Cohn, *Warrant for Genocide*, 27, 61–62.

68. Norman Cohn, *Warrant for Genocide*, 61–62.

69. Alexander Blok, *Dnevniki* (Moscow: Aleteia, 1997), 79.

70. Andrei Bely, "Revoliutsiia i kultura," in *Simvolizm kak miroponimanie* (Moscow: Respublika, 1994), 297.

71. *Novoe vremia*, September 18, 1911: 4.

72. *Masonstvo* (St. Petersburg, 1911), 24.

73. See Harriet Murav, "The Beilis Ritual Murder Trial and the Culture of Apocalypse," *Cardozo Studies in Law and Literature* 12, no. 2 (2000): 243–63. See also Alexander Tager, *Delo Beilisa: issledovaniia i materialy* (Jerusalem, Moscow: Gesharim, 1995).

74. Leonid Katsis, *Krovavy navet i russkaia mysl': Istoriko-teologicheskoe issledovanie dela Beilisa* (Jerusalem: Gesharim, 2006), 358.

75 Vasilii Rozanov, *Sakharna: Oboniatel'noe i osiazatel'noe otnoshenie evreev k krovi* (Moscow: Respublika, 1998), 277.

76. Ibid., 367–93.

77. See Murav, "The Beilis Ritual Murder Trial and the Culture of Apocalypse," 248.

78. Rozanov, *Sakharna: Oboniatel'noe i osiazatel'noe otnoshenie evreev k krovi*, 13.

79. Ibid.

80. Ibid., 369.

81. Zinaida Gippius, *Zhivye litsa* (Tbilisi: Merani, 1991), 2, 118.

82. See Burmistrov, "Osobennosti vospriiatiia kabbaly v russkoi religioznoi filosofii (V. Soloviev, P. Florensky, S. Bulgakov, A. Losev)," Tirosh: Moscow, 2004, 67–90.

83. See Burmistrov, "Osobennosti vospriiatiia kabbaly v russkoi religioznoi filosofii (V. Soloviev, P. Florensky, S. Bulgakov, A. Losev)."

84. See Leonid Katsis, "Iudeiskaia tainopis' i shifry russkogo avangarda," *Lechaim* 7, no. 171 (July 2006), available at <http://www.lechaim.ru/ARHIV/171/katsis.htm>. Last accessed on August 16, 2010.

85. For a detailed study of Rozanov's writings on Beilis case in the cultural context of Russian avant-garde see Murav, "The Beilis Ritual Murder Trial and the Culture of Apocalypse."

86. Murav, "The Beilis Ritual Murder Trial and the Culture of Apocalypse" 248.

87. Alexander Blok, "Diaries [April 5, 1912]," *Sobranie sochinenii* (Moscow, 1963), 7, 80.

88. Murav, "The Beilis Ritual Murder Trial and the Culture of Apocalypse," 245.

89. Murav, "The Beilis Ritual Murder Trial and the Culture of Apocalypse," 256.

MODERNISM AND KABBALAH
Linguistic Mysticism in the Literary Doctrine of the Russian Silver Age

While the volume of literary criticism dedicated to the Russian Silver Age is extremely vast, the number of studies that explore the role of kabalistic symbolism in Russian literature is rather limited. Nevertheless, in the recent years a number of studies have appeared devoted to the occult and mystical motifs in early twentieth-century Russian literature. Nikolai Bogomolov has researched the occult interests of Acmeists. Together with John Malmstad, he has also produced a substantial study of occult imagery in Kuzmin's poetry. Gennady Obatnin has commented on the mysticism of Viacheslav Ivanov, Maria Carlson has provided a detailed study of the Theosophical movement in early twentieth-century Russian literature, Lena Silard has spoken about the link between the mysticism of the Symbolists and the mystical doctrine of Novalis, and Konstantin Burmistrov has briefly analyzed the kabbalistic imagery in Andrei Bely's works. Although most of these works dealt only sketchily with the subject of Kabbalah, they created a foundation upon which it is possible to construct an argument about the importance of the literary reception of kabbalistic symbolism and its place in the artistic process of this period.

Interest in occult, Gnostic, and kabbalistic mythology was part and parcel of the general atmosphere of the Symbolist movement. Symbolist artistic ideology focused heavily on the creation of new mythologies, or *mifotvorchestvo* (myth-creation).[1] Symbolists attempted to find an amalgamation of life and creativity that could be regarded as a kind of alchemical "philosopher's stone" for art, and hence were subconsciously drawn to occult activity in their creative processes.[2]

The Symbolists developed not only the conception of *mifotvorchestvo*, but also that of *mirotvorchestvo* (world-creation) — the perception of language as a tool for the creation of a new personal world through the writer's own language. Andrei Bely's description of these views reflected the Romantic poetic concept of the lost Golden Age when he argued that "poetry and human apprehension of nature were united [during the Golden Age], and, therefore, human speech was Magic, and humans were able to communicate directly with God." Bely claimed that "ancient myths in various forms allude to the existence of a primordial magical language, whose words could conquer and subdue nature. Most myths show an unconscious eagerness to symbolize the magical power of the Word."[3]

In contradistinction to many Romantics, who considered themselves prophets, or voices of the divine able to restore our understanding of the divine speech, the Symbolists regarded poets as demiurgic figures, the masters of their own linguistic world. The Symbolists believed that through their artistic capabilities poets could create their literary and personal worlds as the Deity created the actual world.[4] They regarded poetry as occult knowledge and the poet as a theurgist, a professor of occult knowledge.[5] Fyodor Sologub claimed in his early poem "Poet": "I am the God of a mysterious world / I myself am the Creator and the created." Similar views appear in a poem by Valery Briusov: "The Gods have granted me an agonizing gift / having been made a Creator at the mysterious precipice." Aage Hansen-Löve notes that:

> The Symbolists made the poet a participant in a cosmic theurgic game, which consisted of an endless, cyclical, diabolic process of Creation in the center of which was the demiurgic poet. He was a Creator of his own universe based on his own metaphoric and mystical worldviews, in which he was perceived as God. Thus, the composing of poetry in the Symbolist literary ideology turns into an occult activity, a process that started as early as during the Renaissance, and through Faust and Werther led to German philosophical idealism.[6]

Such poetic ideology clearly presupposed a significant growth of interest in linguistic mysticism. The last two decades of the nineteenth century witnessed the formation of a vast body of pseudo-kabbalistic literature that included translations of earlier Christian kabbalistic books as well as many contemporary works by French occultists such as Papus, Lévi, and others.

In his poem "Vowels," written in the mid-1880s, French Symbolist Arthur Rimbaud explored the idea that sounds can express emotions just as words do, and that they can have colors, as well. Therefore, letters and sounds — linguistic units that had previously been denied semantic meaning — were now said to possess this meaning. Almost simultaneously, a similar idea appeared in an article by Blavatsky. She claimed to know a linguist who always saw vowels in colors: "A looked red to him, E was white, and O had a yellow color."[7] Blavatsky went on to stress the inability of modern scientists to understand such phenomena. However, in the Middle Ages and the Renaissance, visualizing letters in color was a popular practice during kabbalistic meditation. Part of visualizing *sefirot* as a way for the meditating aspirant to unite himself with the Deity was to see the *sefirot* in color. For example, Moshe Cordovero, a Safed kabbalist of the sixteenth century, explained how this visualization should take place. He advised the adept to "imagine water flowing through vessels of different colors: white, red, green, and so forth . . . as the water spreads through those vessels, it appears to change into the colors of the vessels, although the water is devoid of any color. So it is with the *sefirot*."[8] Blavatsky actually knew about these practices, although she gave them a magical rather than a mystical purpose. In one of her theosophical works she noted that one of the necessary components of success in a kabbalistic prayer was the adept's ability to see the letters in color.[9] Similarly, Papus claimed that Kabbalah was a kind of magic that was revealed to us by the sixth form of movement, that is, sound.[10]

The concept that the semantic meaning of the word was not as important as the secret mystical essence of letters and sounds became the keystone of the Symbolist "occult" approach to poetry. For this kind of literary doctrine, the central ideas of the *Sefer*

Yetzirah, that "the world-process is essentially a linguistic one, based on unlimited combinations of the letters by which heaven and earth are created," were extremely fruitful.[11] Symbolists also strongly believed that the Creation had been an act of divine pronounciation, a process in which the sounds played that sematically meaningful role that in everyday human language has been given to words. Valery Briusov, among others, claimed in one of his most famous poems, "Tvorchestvo" ("Creative Work") that sounds (just as letters) can be scribbled on a wall. The excessive focus on sound in Symbolist literature was not accidental, but esoterically motivated. The Symbolists believed in the magical potency of sounds. Like Rimbaud and many occult writers, the Russian Symbolists longed for a "vowel language." For example, Sologub once expressed a wish to have been born on an exotic island where everyone spoke a language full of the vowel "a":

> If I were born in Madagascar
> I would speak in a dialect with many "a's,"
> There I would compose verses about the fire of Love,
> About the naked beauties of the island of Samoa.[12]

Thus, while the Symbolist approach to language was linked with occult theories in general, Symbolist ideology particularly distinguished and favored kabbalistic linguistic mysticism. Russian critic Grigori Nefediev even believes that the name of one of the first Symbolist groups, the Argonauts, derives from the Renaissance hermetic interpretation of an ancient Greek myth rather than from the myth itself. He argues that

> The esoteric meaning of the image of Golden Fleece corresponds with hermetic symbolism in which language plays a key role. The members of the group of the seekers of the Golden Fleece are united by their mutual understanding of the secret language, the kabbalistic speech, the mysterious language of creation, different from the everyday language of humans. In other words, the ship that carries those who look for Golden Fleece is the kabbalistic Ark that contains only those initiates who are in charge of the hermetic navigation, performed exclusively by secret linguistic means that have been lost and forgotten by modern mankind.[13]

The Symbolists were followed by a younger generation of poets, the Acmeists. The Acmeists opposed themselves to the Symbolists by concentrating on objectivist aesthetics rather than on subjectivism and creative spontaneity. Acmeism demoted the poet from oracle to craftsman and made a fetish of his raw material, that is, his employment of words.[14] However, the Acmeists inherited from their predecessors the concept of the creative, "divine" role of a primordial language of meaningful letters and sounds, as opposed to modern language, in which these units had lost their semantic meaning. The spiritual leader of the Acmeists, Nikolai Gumilev (1886–1921), who translated Rimbaud's sonnet "Vowels" into Russian, expressed this belief in his own poem "Na Venere, akh, na Venere" ("On the Planet Venus"):

> On Venus, ah, on the planet of Venus,
> There are no offensive or despotic words.
> And the angels on the planet of Venus
> Speak a language of vowels only.
>
> If they say to you "ea" and "ai"
> This is a happy promise.
> And the "uo" and "ao" are a golden reminder
> Of an ancient paradise. [15]

The same ideas appear in Gumilev's poem "Slovo" ("Word"), which is often referred to as the poetic manifesto of Acmeism, and in which number and sound are seen as the high and the low sides of primordial language:

> In olden days, when above the new world
> God inclined his face, then
> The sun was halted with a word,
> Cities were destroyed with a word.
>
> And the eagle did not flap its wings,
> The terrified stars would cling to the moon
> If, like a pink flame,
> The word floated in the heavens.
>
> And for lowly life there were numbers,
> Like domestic, yoked cattle,

> Because an intelligent number expresses
> Every shade of meaning.
>
> The graying Patriarch, who bent
> Good and evil to his will,
> Daring not to turn to sound,
> Drew a number in the sand with his cane.[16]

In the first variant of the poem "Poema Nachala" ("The Poem of the Beginning") Gumilev also stated his belief that the primordial creative language, the result of the emanation of the divine light, was simultaneously word and number. As he proclaimed: "Between the word and the number there was neither word nor number / but the divine light that became flesh."[17] In the poem "Estestvo" ("Nature"), Gumilev expressed a belief in the parallel between the work of kabbalists and that of poets in order to reconstruct the primordial creative language. He declared that "primordial words are the pledge of immortality for mortals." He also proclaimed poets to be the only humans able to comprehend this "almighty language which the sphinxes spoke in the circle of the Dragon's masters."[18] Nikolai Bogomolov comments on "Nature": "The definition of the word in this poem completely corresponds to the characteristic of God as *Logos*, a word that became flesh. Thus, the pronunciation of the word becomes part of a magical ritual in which the poet corresponds to the possessor of secret knowledge and the poetic word coincides with a magical spell."[19] In his commentary on the poem Bogomolov identifies the origin of Gumilev's interpretation of the divine power of "Word" in the image of *Logos* as it is seen in the Gospel of St. John. However, Gumilev's reading of Logos differs from a traditional Christian interpretation. He opposes "word" to "number," i.e. to an abstract symbol. Such an opposition is not accidental. For Gumilev the divine word *Logos* signifies a word not as a linguistic sign in its common semiotic sense but as a divine abstract sign, a mystical combination of letters and sounds that possesses a creative power and is incomprehensible to humans.

These examples suggest why linguistic mysticism, and together with it, various magical and pseudo-kabalistic speculations, gained such wide acceptance in the artistic circles of the Silver Age. It became so popular because of their occult significance, which was directly linked to contemporary artistic and literary beliefs. Similarly to Pavel Florensky, Russian poets of the early twentieth century regarded Kabbalah as a mytho-poetic occult science. They borrowed kabbalistic images mostly from such indirect sources as Papus's or Blavatsky's works, rather than from Jewish or Christian kabbalistic literature. Yet they moved one step further in their apprehension of Kabbalah as a universal, "Aryan" esotericism by gradually replacing the creative role of Hebrew with that of an individual poetic language. While Florensky, like D'Olivet, aimed to recreate the original divine Hebrew proto-language, Symbolists and later Acmeists declared any poetic language a proto-language, thus diminishing the importance of a "Jewish" language, so important for early occult kabbalistic tradition, and basically depriving Kabbalah of its Jewish origin. Both movements widely used the mystical allegories of divine creation, *sefirot*, and Adam Kadmon; yet their understanding of those concepts differed greatly from the previously established reading.

The Allegories of Divine Creation, SEFIROT, and Adam Kadmon in Russian Poetry, 1900–1920s

While in eighteenth-century Russian literature kabbalistic allegory was used primarily in poetry and Romantic writers mostly employed it in fiction, in Russian Modernism kabbalistic imagery was broadly used in both genres. The image of Sophia as Universal Love, which was a primal force for divine Creation, was central for the mystical poetics of the Russian Symbolists. In their description of creation the Symbolists often employed such allegorical terms as "night," "creative love-wisdom," "universal fire," "worlds" (used as a synonym for "universe"), and "mixture," that originated in eighteenth-century Masonic mystical poetics. For example, in Viacheslav Ivanov's poem "Spirit" ("Dukh"), the creative spirit manipulates the universe ("worlds") by the "helm" of love: "above the abyss of night the fiery Spirit / Led worlds by the helm of Love." [20] The poet's spiritual meditation allows his own spirit to join with divine love in the "fire of worlds," and see his own reflection in her image.

In Symbolist poems the biblical image of primordial chaos as eternal darkness is often opposed by that of divine light (usually described as 'divine rays') and Word-*Logos*. For example, Ivanov characterizes creation as a process of constant emanation and constant movement.[21] Ivanov also uses the image of the Tree of Life as a symbol for the universe. He calls it "a great trunk," a universal soul that contains the whole universe:

> Thus a secret Tree grows as one soul
> From deep, moist Eternity
> Clothed in the all-sensing spring of worlds,
>   in universal, starry-eyed leaves
> This is the Tree of Life that blossoms as one soul.
>
> Its forces rise into the glimmering canopy
> From the abundant bosom of Eternity
>
> And roots give light to branches and
> The branches give dreams to roots,
> And all is held by the almighty trunk,
> And one soul burns with the soul of all flame.[22]

In Kabbalah the "divine tree," the tree of *sefirot*, or as Papus and Blavatsky usually call it, the Tree of Life, is often allegorically presented as "the divine trunk" and represents Adam Kadmon.[23] The speaker's description also contains multiple sexual connotations that are characteristic of kabbalistic symbolism. Ivanov describes the primordial point as "the abundant womb of Eternity." He calls Eternity "moist," which suggests fecundity. He also proclaims that the Tree of Life grows from "the seed of divine light." In the poem "Darkness" ("Tem'") he says that the seed (*semia* — a term that can be translated as both "seed" and "semen") of the sun will illuminate the souls of the "fallen generation" and show people the face of a mysterious "Mother" who "conceived from the seed of the divine spirit."[24] By contrast with other numerous mythological representations of Earth-Mothers, there is an evident parallel between Ivanov's image of "Mother," "conceived from the seed of the divine spirit," and the kabbalistic symbol of fertility, the supernal mother *Binah*, who has been conceived from the seed of the divine and is usually represented as a root of the divine tree that was "watered" by the divine phallus, *Hokhmah*. Following this parallel, it becomes clear why Ivanov calls the roots of the divine tree "the light of the branches" and why "the branches are the dream of the roots." According to Scholem, "*Binah* is often compared to the roots of the tree of [life] that are watered by *Hokhmah* and branch out into seven *sefirot*."[25] Kabbalah proclaims that the lower seven *sefirot* are separated from the upper three after Adam's fall; therefore, *Binah* and *Hokhmah*, the "divine roots" of the tree in Ivanov's poem "dream about their branches" because they are now separated from their lower "sisters."[26]

Ivanov's interpretation of the allegory of the Tree of Life most probably derives from his knowledge of Rosicrucian symbolism, which influenced the mystical semiotics of his poetry. Being an active participant in Russian theosophical circles, Ivanov was familiar with Blavatsky's works, and these most probably served as a direct source of his kabbalistic imagery. At the same time, his close friendship with Pavel Florensky and his deep interest in Florensky's doctrine of names may also have contributed to his knowledge of quasi-kabbalistic symbolism.[27]

The image of *sefirot* also appears quite often in the Symbolist poetic imagery. In his book *Symbolism*, Andrei Bely discusses the creative, emanating power of "divine rays," which he calls "zefirot."[28] Later Bely writes in *Glassololia*: "I know. The lands of Light have descended to Earth as the *zefirot* rays of the ancient sun. ("Sepher Iezira" calls the rays of Wisdom *zefirot*). Where is she now, Zefirea? She has disappeared."[29] Burmistrov points out that Zefirea, whom Bely identifies as "the queen of the land of sun," undoubtedly bears the same significance as Soloviev's Sophia-Wisdom and the "Divine Mother" of Ivanov's poem. Burmistrov does not comment on the fact that in the writing of the Symbolists the image of *sefirot* had a completely different meaning than in traditional kabbalistic literature: they were not regarded as primal divine elements or principles of creation but rather, as seen in Ivanov and Bely, as divine rays that descend from a primordial beautiful land of sun that has been lost to humans. This interpretation was characteristic of occult kabbalistic tradition. Blavatsky, for example, called *sefirot* "the rays of the land of Sun," and Bely's quotes from either the *Sefer Yetzirah* or the *Zohar* derive mostly from Blavatsky's interpretation of these books in her *Secret Doctrine*. Both Ivanov and Bely also combine kabbalistic symbolism with other esoteric images, either Hindu, Greek, or Egyptian. In Ivanov's poem "Darkness," the lost primordial land is referred to as "the land of Titans," and Bely repeatedly mentions "Egyptian wisdom" while discussing kabbalistic imagery.

The numerological formula of the tree of *Sefirot*, 1-3-7=10=1, was widespread in Symbolist works and usually linked to occult knowledge. For example, Nikodim, the protagonist of the unfinished fantasy novel *The Life and Adventures of Nikodim the Eldest* (*Zhizn' i prikliucheniia Nikodima Starshego*) written by Symbolist poet Aleksei Skaldin, received a strange request from a friend of his, a "well-known philosopher," to guard *one* closet that contained *three* shelves. When Nikodim arrived at his friend's house, however, he found *ten* closets, each containing *three* shelves. He also found a strange note saying that both shelves and closets are "principles."[30] The mystical subtext of Nikodim's discovery is clearly pronounced: ten and one are the same, i.e., ten principles, divided into three groups, represent one God. Later Nikodim finds a mysterious stairway with seven stairs. He comments on his discovery:

> The seven stairs are the seven colors of the rainbow. If we pass one stair after another what will we see? Each stair is a new glimpse of the world. When you step on the first stair, the world will be red, then orange, then yellow ... and only at the end the world will it be white, just as it should be. Then you can triumph — you will have learned the secret.[31]

Attributing the seven colors of the rainbow to the seven inferior *sefirot* was a well-known kabbalistic technique.[32] Yet Skaldin's novel reflects a poetic quest as well as a mystical one. The Symbolist belief that vowels have colors is certainly reflected in this passage. The power of language becomes for the Symbolist a magical stairway that can help him to see the world differently each time and eventually help him to learn the mysterious secret of being that is the eventual goal of Nikodim's search. Ivanov similarly mentions the mystical stairway, which he calls "a road to great mysteries, known to us as the stairway of Jacob, where spirits meet each other on their way to earth from heaven."[33] In Skaldin's novel, Nikodim's discovery of the stairway in a forest near his own house is the first stage in his demonic initiation, which finally comes to an end in Palestine.

In Symbolist mystical semiotics the allegory of the Tree of Life and *sefirot* frequently represent the figure of Adam Kadmon. This image is vital for the Symbolists' system of values and clearly reflects their interpretation of reality. In the article "The Emblem of Meaning" ("Problematika smysla"), which can be considered one of the most important manifestos of Russian Symbolism, Andrei Bely asserts that Symbolist perception allows man to return to "his motherland," "the land of Adam Kadmon," and transform back into the primordial state of humanity, "united, free, and almighty." Bely calls the creative poetic process "a human journey from a worthless grain of sand to the glorious state of Adam Kadmon, where mother, father, and son are one, and man and universe are one."[34]

The image of primordial Adam as a symbol, a divine vessel that contains the whole world, is essential for Maksimilian Voloshin's long poem "Space" ("Kosmos"):

> A star-studded countenance arose over chaos,
> Its shadowy reflection thrown over the abyss
> of lower waters.
> Two eyes, shut by the night, unlocked.
> And there was light.
> Two fiery rays traversed the water
> and formed a hexagram.
> Mute lips unsealed,
> and word emerged from the silent chasm.
> The first breath of the universe set ablaze
> a host of spirits.
> The right hand brought up the continents,
> and the left distributed the waters.
> From the loins, came earthly creatures,
> and plants emerged from sinews,
> and bone begat the rocks. And the doubles,
> the earthly and the heavenly, touched each other's
> moist feet, thus coming into contact.

> God's breath flew in the face of Hell,
> thus the lower werewolf became Adam.
> Adam was the world, and the world was Adam.
> He thought through sky, and pondered
>   through the clouds,
> became flesh through clay, and grew through plants.
> He hardened through the rocks, felt passion
>   though the beasts.
> He saw through the sun, dreamt through the moon,
> inhaled with the wind and murmured with the planets.
> And all — above, below — was proportion-driven,
> full of divine harmony.
> And everything around was a sign
> Of eternal mysteries inscribed in heaven.
>
> The world was built to the size of man, and man
> served as the measure of all things.[35]

It is interesting to note that in Voloshin's interpretation the creation was finally manifested when "divine rays" formed the Jewish mystical symbol of the hexagram. In kabbalistic symbolism the hexagram — two triangles placed upon each other — allegorically symbolize *sefirot*. In occult Kabbalah this image is regarded as a primary Jewish symbol and has often served as a magical sign. As a symbolic representation of *sefirot* it is widespread in the writings of Papus and Lévi. Voloshin also uses kabbalistic terminology while interpreting the image of "waters" from the first lines of Genesis as "lower waters" — a term often used in Kabbalah to symbolize the last *sefirah Malkhut* and the material world. The two "doubles," the "heavenly" and the "earthly," are certainly the heavenly and earthly Adams. Voloshin stresses that in the primordial state man was "the measure of all things, a microcosm that contained the macrocosm." For Voloshin, just as for Bely and Ivanov, the most important allegory of the divine creation is the allegory of the creative power of the Word. Bely regards Adam Kadmon as the primary *Logos*, the primordial almighty creative Word. Similarly, Voloshin declares that the world has been created by the Word that "exited from the abyss of muteness" and that the primordial universe was a reflection of "eternal mysteries inscribed in heaven."

Symbolist poetry widely employs the image of the primordial Adam as a crystal vessel filled with divine light. In the poem "Diamond" ("Almaz"), Ivanov proclaims that man — presently dark and black as a coal — will be reborn as a clear crystal diamond when he has been healed by "a white ray of seven-eyed transparency" that he also calls "the ray of the divine sun." Ivanov concludes that this spiritual transformation will allow man to become a God-like figure — "O Light, in the narrow facets we will be You."[36]

Russian Symbolists, strongly influenced by Rosicrucian mystical semiotics, borrowed the Rosicrucian imagery that reflected such established "kabbalistic" images as those presented above. Bely and Ivanov most probably gained their knowledge of kabbalistic symbolism from such recent sources as Blavatsky and Papus. Voloshin had more extensive knowledge of Christian Kabbalah through his friend Boris Leman, a true devotee of kabbalistic occult tradition, who in the fall of 1909 regularly met with Voloshin's wife, Margarita Sabashnikov, to teach her "the mysteries of numbers and letters as explained in Kabbalah."[37] Leman shared with Voloshin his knowledge of Christian Kabbalah and asked him to review his manuscripts on Pico and Agrippa. He also presented Voloshin with d'Olivet's book on the mysteries of Hebrew and advised him a few times to translate it. Lastly, Skaldin was a good friend of Grigorii Mebes and participated in the activities of Russian Martinist Order that promoted occult Kabbalah. Clearly, the images chosen by these Symbolist poets were drawn from Kabbalah.

The image of the primordial Adam also became central for the poetics of the Acmeist movement that followed the Symbolists. The image of Love-Wisdom played a less important role in Acmeism than in Symbolism. Acmeists instead emphasized the importance of the creative almighty *Logos* and claimed that Symbolist poetics deprived the Word of its original divine meaning while wrapping it in a thick veil of confusing symbols. Acmeists always defined primordial language as the language used by Adam before the fall. They interpreted the figure of Adam as "the inventor of names," and used him as a metaphor for the poet, which resulted in an alternative title for the Acmeist movement, Adamism.[38] Although the concept of Adamism has been broadly discussed in secondary literature, the kabbalistic origins of this image have not yet been researched. The Acmeist interpretation of the image of Adam Kadmon echoes the eighteenth century mystical allegory of "external" and "internal" Adams. This symbolism is clearly present in Gumilev's poems devoted to the image of Adam, such as the poem "Two Adams" ("Dva Adama"):

> How strange is the expression 'I, myself'
> I have external and internal Adam-selves.
>
> While the internal one writes poems on immortal love,
> The external half lusts for earthly ladies
>
> But the internal spies on it with hateful spite,
> Governed constantly by evil hate.
>
> And if the first, with his artful talk,
> Tender smile, and passionate looks
>
> Can charm the woman, then the second
> Cries that he will never let it happen,
>
> For skies are blue and angelic paths are wide
> And there your heavenly bride awaits you.[39]

Gumilev was deeply interested in Masonic and Rosicrucian symbolism. Although there is no documentary evidence that Gumilev belonged to any Masonic lodge, his early writings present a number of Masonic allegories and images and his connections with mystically oriented Masonry, and especially with the Martinist Order, have been widely discussed in secondary literature.[40] He was also deeply interested in Papus' and Blavatsky's works. Akhmatova remembers how Gumilev came to visit her in her estate "and for the whole visit talked about ... Blavatsky and theosophical occultism."[41] However, the allegory of the two Adams in Gumilev's poetry derives from Russian Masonic mysticism rather than from that particular "occult" interpretation of kabbalistic allegory that was popular in Symbolist circles, and was influenced by Blavatsky's theosophy. Through the image of two Adams, Gumilev stresses the ethical duality of human nature. However, Gumilev's interpretation of the image of the two Adams is much more personal than the eighteenth-century reading of this kabbalistic image. "Two Adams" became the vehicle for the poet's personal expression. The poem clearly demonstrates Gumilev's characteristic Acmeist style in which the primordial Adam is presented as a complex and dualistic character. It becomes an expression of a poetic personality, transformed by imagery, dramatic structure, the complex narrative voice, its colloquial tone, and a tendency toward third-person neutrality.[42]

Such eighteenth-century writers as Lopukhin believed that one's moral duty was to follow the voice of the inner Adam and cleanse oneself of the material shell of the passions. By contrast, Gumilev presented the conflict between the internal and external Adams as one that would never end. Moreover, in the tradition of the Silver Age, he compared the duality between the two Adams to an eternal argument between two major characters from commedia dell'arte, Pierrot and Harlequin. This technique had the effect of altering the conflict from a moral mystical exemplum to the evocation of an endless human argument.

Yet, in spite of his attempt to stress the moral, ethical nature of the Adamic conflict in his approach to the image of the two Adams, Gumilev also positioned himself closer to the alchemical reading of this image than did his eighteenth-century predecessors. The alchemical kabbalistic tradition regarded the first Adam as an androgynous creature. The fall of Adam drew him from an original, inner unity into the external world of opposites. The allegorical spiritual marriage — the reunification of Adam with his heavenly bride Sophia — was perceived in this tradition as Adam's restoration to his lost androgynous state, which would purify humanity of Adam's sin and hasten the return of the Golden Age.[43] The Masonic works that borrowed this image from alchemical kabbalistic symbolism portrayed this reunion as a purely spiritual, mystical experience. By contrast, the occult tradition of the nineteenth century stressed its sexual and alchemical interpretation. This interpretation, present in the works of Blavatsky and Papus, is clearly reflected in Gumilev's poem, "Androgyne" ("Androgin"). Here Gumilev describes the androgynous man as a God-like figure whose mystical resurrection would come only as the result of a sexual act:

> We will never stop praying to you,
> Miraculous divine essence,
> We know you will reveal yourself to us.
> We believe, we believe in your mighty triumph...
>
> O, hasten, my friend. Like naked spirits,
> We must perform the ancient ritual,
> Whisper breathlessly a forgotten name,
> And start at hearing the desired answer.
>
> I see that you are slow. Do not be embarrassed,
> Let two die so that the one can be born.
> Strange and radiant, from the couch of madness,
> Like a phoenix from the flames, the Androgyne will rise.[44]

On the one hand, this poem shows the influence of the alchemical kabbalistic tradition in its nineteenth-century occult interpretation. However, Gumilev's poem also evidences a strong mystical subtext. The ideas of "Androgyne" are certainly linked to those conveyed in "Two Adams." Both poems reveal the androgynous theme of Gumilev's poems, with his interpretation of the concept of the two Adams as the connection between body and soul. The alchemical transformation in "Androgyne" is a metaphor for the personal mystical transformation of a poet through the creative process, which the narrator regards as an occult and mystical activity. Nikolai Bogomolov noted that "the poem "Androgyne" was written under the influence of Papus' theory, according to which *androgynes* symbolized the primordial race of mankind characterized by its original spiritual and material unity."[45] However, Bogomolov linked the image of Adam and androgynous man directly to Papus and Blavatsky's writings, without mentioning the previous use of this image in earlier Russian mystical texts. Nevertheless, the image of the androgynous Adam clearly reflects the Silver Age interpretation of the earlier Russian Masonic kabbalistic tradition, which, although refracted through the works of the nineteenth-century French occult writers, had not lost its original mystical alchemical and kabbalistic significance.[46]

Gumilev's use of alchemical and kabbalistic symbolism stems from his knowledge of Masonic mysticism and occultism. In the case of other Acmeist author, Mikhail Kuzmin, the kabbalistic allegory of Adam Kadmon might derive from his interest in Gnostic teachings, yet again combined with the images borrowed from nineteenth-century esoteric authors. Such genealogy is evident in Mikhail Kuzmin's poem "First Adam" ("Pervy Adam"):

> O doves of Ioni, O depths of Ioni,
> O John of the streams of Jordan,
> O myrtles of Cypria, O cedars of Cybele,
> O Milky Mother, O Margarethe of the seas.
>
> I left the Gates, silent to the Will,
> And let a moist wave be my cradle,
> Shore and Wind to me! What else do I need?
> Golden intoxication to the middle-heart.
>
> Growth to the upper Sowing!
> Remembrance to the lower waters
> Smoke is bewitching the maiden of Delphi.
> O divine tree! O eternal Adam![47]

Nikolai Bogomolov and John Malmstad have recently attempted to analyze the poem's symbolism. Bogomolov noted that the origin of the image of the first Adam in Kuzmin could be found in the kabbalistic concept of Adam Kadmon, "a metaphor for the primordial union of the material and the spiritual egos in man."[48] He believed that the central image of the poem, the divine trunk (*stvol bogonosnyi*), served as an allegory for a phallus. Without doubt the image of the divine tree in Kuzmin's poetic semiotics can be interpreted as a divine phallus. However, Bogomolov failed to connect this image with the sexual interpretation of the tree of *sefirot*, represented by the figure of Adam Kadmon as an allegorical structure for the world.

The parallel between the "divine trunk" and the primordial Adam concludes Kuzmin's poem, inasmuch as the last line reads: "The divine trunk is the Eternal Adam!" This parallel suggests that Kuzmin has coded the complete structure of the divine tree in the lines of "First Adam." If so, the poem should be considered a parable, an allegory of the structure of the divine tree that reveals itself to the reader through the figure of the first Adam (Adam Kadmon). Just as in kabbalistic symbolism, the first lines of the last stanza of Kuzmin's poem clearly divide the divine tree into two parts: the "upper sowing" (*verkhnii sev*) and the "lower waters" (*nizhnie vody*). The image of "lower waters" was also used in Voloshin's poem. Kuzmin, however, elaborates on this image, placing it into a well-structured semiotic allegory. The first stanza conceals the images of the three highest *sefirot*: *Keter, Hokhmah*, and *Binah*. The Creation is represented as a sexual act in which the divine seeds of the "higher sowing" are cast by the divine power of *Ioni* into a divine womb: the *sefirah* of *Hokhmah*, allegorically called the womb of *Ioni* (*ioniny nedra*).

Bogomolov believes that the name *Ioni* (*ioni-golubki*) most probably came to Kuzmin's poem from Blavatsky's works, in which *Ioni* is described as a Hindu term for the divine creative power.[49] Interestingly enough, the word *Ionati* also means "my dove" in Hebrew — a detail which explains why Kuzmin calls *Ioni* "female doves" (*golubki*). In the *Secret Doctrine*, Blavatsky drew a direct parallel between *Ioni* and the *sefirah* of *Keter*, which she called "the divine creative energy of Kabbalah." She also called the *sefirah* of *Hokhmah* "the end of the divine phallus through which God releases his semen into the higher world."[50] From Ioni's womb the seeds flow further through the rivers (*strui*) of the middle *sefirot* into the endless sea of the last *sefirah*. Kuzmin then introduces the image of a mysterious tree, through the images of the Cybelian cedars and Cyprian roots that reflect the Greek Goddess of love, Aphrodite, called by one of her names, Cypria, and the goddess of fertility Cybele, known also as Earth-Mother (*korni Kipridy, Kibeliny kedry*), which are watered by Ioni's womb (*ioniny nedra*). Therefore, the images of the "Milky Mother" and "Margarethe of the seas" that conclude the stanza are probably an allegory for the *sefirah* of *Binah*, which begins the journey of the divine rivers (*iordanskie strui*) into the lower waters.

In kabbalistic symbolism, Adam's sin resulted in the total separation of the lower and higher realms, in the process of which Adam allegorically left the divine world through the symbolic gates that separate the border between the inferior and the superior *sefirot*. This allegorical withdrawal is codified in the line "Not responding to the Will, he exited through the Gates," which refers to Adam's exit from the higher world into the lower. Malmstad noted that according to hermetic tradition, "Will is the first God and the father of Reason."[51] This interpretation is characteristic not only of general hermetic symbolism, but also of Kabbalah. However, kabbalistic tradition always characterized Adam's sin as a breach of the divine will. A similar interpretation can be seen in eighteenth-century Russian mystical Masonic texts. For example, Lopukhin states in *The Spiritual Knight* that, "the divine spirit reigned in the soul of Adam and covered him with majestic garments. Adam's disobedience to the divine will extinguished the light of the divine Wisdom in Adam's soul and cast him down into the world of mortals."[52] Behind the gates there lies the middle heart of *sefirot*, the *sefirah* of *Tiferet*, known also as the heart of Adam Kadmon, and called "the middle heart" in Kuzmin's poem. In kabbalistic astrology *Tiferet* represents the sun. Papus also claimed that that "in astrology Tipareth corresponds with the sun and therefore is a key to the vitality we seek throughout our sojourns."[53] In Christian alchemy, where every *sefirah* was associated with a particular chemical element, the tree of *sefirot* was regarded as a mixture, which combined the four major elements: fire (or sun), water, air, and earth.[54] All four of these elements are present in the second, or middle stanza. It unites sun (*solnechnyi khmel'*), earth (*bereg*), air (*veter*), and water (*voda*). Therefore, the second stanza describes the middle *sefirah*, *Tiferet*, which at the same time represents the heart of the speaker, that is, of the first Adam.

The alchemical interpretation of the kabbalistic allegory was certainly known by Kuzmin from at least one source. In his letters he mentioned the novel *Der Engel vom westlichen Fenster* (*Angel of the West Window*) by Gustav Meyrinck as among his favorite books and called it "a great novel that significantly influenced my poems."[55] The novel depicts the life and activities of John Dee, alchemist and Christian Kabbalist. Meyrinck describes many alchemical processes quite precisely and gives a detailed description of various alchemical metaphors, such as the alchemical interpretation of the kabbalistic allegory of "the divine trunk" and of "First Adam."[56]

The last stanza summarizes the two worlds: the higher and the lower, but it also describes the lowest sefirah, *Malkhut* (*Shekhinah*). Kuzmin again uses Greek mythology as an allegory for *sefirot*: *Malkhut* is represented by the image of the priestess of Delphi. Kuzmin used the image of the female oracle of Delphi, whose task was to interpret the unwritten divine will, to symbolize the *Shekhinah*. In some kabbalistic texts the starting point of creation was envisaged as flames, while *Shekhinah* was regarded as the smoke produced by these flames. Kabbalistic texts taught that "ashes cannot be separated from the fire and the smoke always returns to its origin, that is, the flames."[57] This allegory is understood to mean that it is *Shekhinah* that contains the remembrance of the whole of creation, which allows the divine emanation to always return to its beginning in a cyclical process. Therefore, it is endless (*ein-sof*). The image of the smoke of a sacrifice, which is brought to the oracle of Delphi, reminds us allegorically of the last *sefirah*, *Shekhinah*.

Nikolai Bogomolov, in his discussion of the last stanza of the poem, admits that he does not understand the following lines: "growth to the upper sowing / remembrance to the inferior waters." He asserts that, "we cannot comprehensively explain what is meant by either inferior waters or upper sowing, and why they are characterized by either growth or remembrance."[58] However, in kabbalistic allegory the terms "seed" and "semen" are interchangeable and the term "seed" often stands as an allegory for divine "semen., i.e. his creative energy." Therefore, these lines should be understood in the context of the poem's title, that is, of the image of Adam Kadmon, its significance for the Silver Age occult revival and its role in Kuzmin's work. Clearly, Kuzmin interprets the process of creation as a kabbalistic allegory. Similarly to Kabbalistic teaching, Kuzmin regards Creation as *ein-sof*, an infinite perpetual action in which human deeds influence those of the Deity and vise versa. Adam, represented by the image of lower waters and separated from the divine world of higher *sefirot*, symbolizes the human world that after his fall is linked to his previous divine life only by remembrance. The more he attempts to remember and recollect the higher realm, the sooner he will be able to return to his creative divine origin, that is, his divine seed, or as Kuzmin phrases it, "upper sowing". The image of Adam becomes an allegory for a poet, an artist, who, by the power of his creativity, will be able to unite the broken halves of the world and mend it, thus returning to his prior state of eternity and becoming again "the divine trunk" of the universe.

Kuzmin's interest in the kabbalistic interpretation of creation is evident from his biography. In his letters he compared the period when he was under the influence of Gnostic and kabbalistic teachings to the time of first love, when every breath was a breath of love and spiritual purification.[59] Like Voloshin, he was a good friend of Boris Leman. A few months before he wrote the poem "The First Adam," Kuzmin began a short story, "Cagliostro," in which Boehme and Swedenborg were among the central characters. Bogomolov mentions Kuzmin's interest in eighteenth-century alchemical texts from a Masonic collection, published shortly after 1910.[60]

Again, it is extremely hard to distinguish between the occult, Gnostic, and kabbalistic sources in Kuzmin's mystical symbolism, since they are fused and cannot be separated. For example, in his poem "Basilid" (1916), Kuzmin mentioned the Gnostic term *Abrosaks*, and explained in an interview to the newspaper *Poslednie novosti* (*The Latest News*) that "in Kabbalah this term means 365, the unity of all creative forces."[61] However, "First Adam" shows a clear kabbalistic, not Gnostic, symbolism, and is a strong example of the use of the kabbalistic allegory of Adam Kadmon in the poetry of this period.

Kuzmin draws a straightforward parallel between the first Adam as the prototype of the world, and the lyrical "I" of the poet. The speaker in Kuzmin's poem wants to be not only the primordial Man, but also a kabbalist who possesses the linguistic ability to conceal the allegory of Adam Kadmon in his writing in order to create his own mystical parable of the tree of *sefirot*. He wants to convey to the reader that he is simultaneously the primordial Adam, containing all ten divine aspects, and the creator of these aspects: God and creation at the same time.[62] Kuzmin regards Adam Kadmon as an allegorical representation of *Logos*, thus rendering the poet as a divine linguistic vessel that stimulates creation. The poem concludes wth the parallel of the tree of life-*Logos*-Adam, with a clear anagram hidden in the last lines, revealing that the image of the divine trunk corresponds to that of the first Adam (stvoL bOGOnoSny — pervy **ADAM**).[63]

Evidently all of the poems presented above share analogous images, combined with a corresponding interpretation of those images. The allegories of "inferior waters," "divine trunk," "watered roots," "remembrance," "fiery creation," "God-Man," and "two Adams" can be seen in both Symbolist and Acmeist authors. These images are clearly not isolated and unrelated examples of the use of quasi-kabbalistic symbolism in the literature of Silver Age, but rather the elements of one mystical semiotic system, which was characteristic of the whole generation.

Kabbalah and the Mythopoetic Ideology of the Silver Age

From the last decade of the nineteenth century up to the Revolution, kabbalistic symbolism reclaimed the interest of Russian writers. Like the Romantics, Silver Age writers stressed the alchemical and linguistic side of Kabbalah, and were especially interested in the concept of the primordial language that bore the original powers of creation. However, the Romantic belief in Kabbalah as a universal science, able to unite both the artistic and the scientific sides of life and to reestablish the harmony destroyed by the Enlightenment, was missing in the literature of the Silver Age. While Romantics attempted to restore the original primordial "poetic" language, Modernists believed in their own individual ability to re-create it anew: they drew a direct parallel between the lost primordial speech and modern poetic language.[64] They further elaborated the Romantic ideas of creative linguistic powers by stressing the role of an individual's divine power, obtained through a personal poetic language, which eliminated the importance of collective universal restoration. The mytho-poetic process, *mifotvorchestvo*, was part of a more general attempt by the artistic world of the Silver Age to create new personal myths on the basis of ancient ones, new languages on the basis of existing ones, and eventually to create new personal worlds. The Kabbalah of Papus, Lévi, and Blavatsky demonstrated the practical results of this attempt in their occult doctrines. Soloviev and Florensky used kabbalistic theosophy to create their own philosophical mytho-poetics. The mystical poems analyzed above exemplify the literary embodiment of the same effort.

The development of kabbalistic allegory in the literature of the Silver Age is not dissimilar to that in Romantic literature. As in later Romantic writings, in many later works of the Silver Age kabbalistic knowledge was linked to an interest in demonolgy, the incarnations of spirits or demons, or the creation of artificial life forms, such as the homunculus or androgynous man. While in earlier Modernist works, primarily influenced by Soloviev, the mystical interpretation of Kabbalah was paramount, it gradually diminished in the later writings where world-creation (*mirotvorchestvo*) was transformed from a mystical experience into an artistic performance, which often mixed life, art, and occult activity.[65] This connection was common for both Symbolists and Acmeists. For example, Symbolist Valery Briusov used the protagonist of his novel *A Fiery Angel* (*Ognennyi angel*) to explain that:

> To summon a demon you need to know his kabbalistic name and character. To research this name you should combine the letters of the Hebrew alphabet and the corresponding astrological sign. This name, which should certainly be written in Hebrew, constitutes the primary power of your spell, and the magical power of this divine name lies in the correct kabbalistic combination of letters and numbers.[66]

Likewise, in one of Gumilev's poems the author depicted himself sitting in an infernal restaurant and summoning the owner of the restaurant by the name Asmodeus, the king of demons in kabbalistic demonology, to bring him a check at the end of his meal.[67] Akhmatova remembered that Gumilev often brought Lévi's books with him when he came to her estate; and a contemporary, Lev Gornung, noted that "Gumilev not only read Lévi but tried to practice his kabbalistic recommendations."[68] The painter Della Vos-Kardovskaia, Gumilev's neighbor in Tsarskoe Selo, related how he and a group of his fellow students had endeavored to see the Devil while at university in Paris between 1906 and 1908:

they had to undergo a series of trials — read Kabbalistic texts, fast for several days, and on the appointed evening to drink some sort of potion. After this the Devil was to have appeared, and it should have been possible to enter into conversation with him. Gumilev's friends quickly abandoned the project, and only Gumilev persisted to the very end, and indeed saw a vague figure in a semi-darkened room.[69]

Gumilev's search for occult powers was ultimately for the purpose of recreating the magical primordial language. In January 1907 Gumilev quoted a passage from Papus's *Practical Magic*: "Magic is the only way to develop the divine powers hidden in man, and language is the only force that can help us to animate these powers."[70] However, in *Practical Magic* the passage continues as follows: "This magical power of language is revealed to us through the science of Kabbalah."[71]

In Russian literary circles of the Silver Age, this interest in kabbalistic linguistic mysticism did not reflect any interest in Jewish mystical tradition per se. As a result, Russian mystical philosophers' interest in Hebrew was not widely shared in literary circles, and by contrast with eighteenth-century Russian mystical authors, most of Russian writers of that time perceived Kabbalah as "ancient secret knowledge," often of Egyptian or Zoroastrian origin, rather than as a Jewish mystical teaching. The attitude toward Jews in Russian literary milieus of that period was probably more negative than positive. Besides, in most authors of the Silver Age, the interest in mystical masonry went hand in hand with a genuine fear of a powerful Judeo-Masonic conspiracy. In his memoirs, Bely wrote that "now [he understands] that the plans of the revolution of 1905 were organized in a Masonic 'kitchen.'"[72] Skaldin's protagonist Nikodim was met on his spiritual quest to Palestine by a Jew called Yankel who explained to him that he was now in charge of "a small anonymous company, mostly never heard of, which serves the governmental powers of the whole world and holds in its hands the threads to all governmental and banking secrets."[73] Both Yankel and his partner Laser Vekselman (a name that most probably derives from the Russian word for bill, *veksel*) turn out to be demons.

Silver Age literary mysticism constitutes the third and the last stage in the history of Russian philosophical and literary attempts to find the way back to the primordial state of man and the lost Golden Age with the help of Kabbalah. Silver Age writers and philosophers used magical kabbalistic symbolism as a tool in their attempts to reconstruct the world prior to Adam's fall, when language was still used to create and not to describe reality. The philosophical and literary examples analyzed in this chapter not only help us to understand more clearly the implicit kabbalistic subtext of the works presented above, but most of all to show the significance of this subtext in the overall artistic process that dominated the texts of the Silver Age.

NOTES

1. For the detailed classification of symbolist mythology see Aage Hansen-Löve, *Der Russische Symbolismus: System und Enfaltung der poetischen Motive* (Wien: Verlag der Österreichischen Akademie der Wissenschaften, 1989). Quoted in Russian translation: Hansen-Löve, *Russkii simvolizm* (St. Petersburg: Akademicheskii proekt, 1999.)

2. G. V. Nefediev, "Russkii simvolizm i rozenkreitserstvo," *Novoe Literaturnoe Obozrenie* 51 (2002): 68.

3. Bely, *Simvolizm kak miroponimanie*, 133.

4. Ibid.

5. Carlson, *No Religion Higher than Truth*, 200. See also Valery Briusov, *Stikhi* (Moscow: Sovremennik, 1972), 102; Fyodor Sologub in Mikhail Gasparov, ed., *Russkaia poeziia serebriannogo veka: 1890–1917* (Moscow: Nauka, 1993), 76.

6. Hansen-Löve, *Russkii simvolizm*, 54.

7. Helen Blavatsky, *Skrizhali astral'nogo sveta* (Moscow: Eksmo, 2001), 442.

8. See, for example, Moses Cordovero, *Sefer Pardes Rimonim* (Jerusalem: Hebrew University Press, 1962), 4:4, 17d–18a. Scholem also speaks about the importance of visualizing the color attributed to letters during meditation. See *Kabbalah*, 97.

9. Helen Blavatsky, *Skrizhali astral'nogo sveta*, 443.

10. Papus [Gérard Encausse], *Principes de physique occulte* (Paris: Bibliothèque Chacornac, 1903), 68.

11. Scholem, *Kabbalah*, 25.

12. U. Schimid, "A Symbolist Under Soviet Rule: Sologub's Late Poetry," *Slavic and East European Journal* 43, no. 4 (1999): 636–49.

> Родился я на Мадагаскаре.
> Говорил бы наречием где много «а»
> Слагал бы стихи о любовном пожаре,
> О нагих красавицах на острове Самоа.

13. Nefediev, "Russkii simvolizm i rozenkreitserstvo," 71.

14. Yelena Rusinko, "The Two Adams: Gumilev's Creative Personality," in *Nikolaj Gumilev 1886–1986: Papers from the Gumilev Centenary Symposium*, ed. Sheelagh Duffin Graham (Oakland: Berkeley Slavic Specialties, 1987), 239–47.

15. Nikolai Gumilev, *Izbrannoe* (Moscow: Veche, 2001), 307.

> На Венере, ах, на Венере
> Нету слов, обидных и властных,
> Говорят ангелы на Венере
> Языком из одних только гласных.
>
> Если скажут еа и аи,
> Это радостное обещанье.
> Уо, ао — о древнем рае
> Золотое напоминанье.

16. Ibid., 331.

> В оный день, когда над миром новым
> Бог склонял лицо свое, тогда
> Солнце останавливали словом,
> Словом разрушали города.
>
> И орел не взмахивал крылами,
> Звезды жались в ужасе к луне,
> Если, точно розовое пламя,
> Слово проплывало в вышине.
>
> А для низкой жизни были числа,
> Как домашний подъяремный скот,
> Потому что все оттенки смысла
> Умное число передает.

> Патриарх седой, себе под руку,
> Покоривший и добро и зло,
> Не решаясь обратиться к звуку,
> Тростью на песке чертил число ...

17. Ibid., 419.

18. Ibid., 377.

19. Bogomolov, *Russkaia literatura*, 128.

20. Viacheslav Ivanov, *Sobranie sochinenii* (Brussels: Foyer Oriental Chrétien, 1971–1987), 1, 518.

21. Ibid, 742.

22. Ibid, 746–747.

> Так Древо тайное растет душой одной
> Из влажной Вечности глубокой,
> Одетое миров всечувственной весной,
> Вселенской листвой звездноокой:
> Се, Древо Жизни так цветет душой одной.
>
> Восходят силы в нем в мерцающую сень
> Из лона Вечности обильной...
> И корни — свет ветвей, и ветви — сон корней,
> И все одержит ствол великий, —
> Одна душа горит душами всех огней.

23. It is worth noticing that although the Tree of Life is an ancient symbol that can be found in many folkloric traditions, both Papus and Blavatsky identify the Tree of Life in their writings as a kabbalistic symbol. Blavatsky, however, compares the kabbalistic allegory of the Tree of Sefirot with a similar allegory found in Buddhist and Hindu cults.

24. Ivanov, *Sobranie sochinenii*, 1, 376

> Но Небом был зачат
> Наш темный род — Титанов падших племя.
> И Солнца семя,
> Прозябнув в нас, осветит
> Твой лик, о Мать!.. Ах, если Свет, что светит,
> В себе распят,—
> Пусть Дух распнет нас, кем твой свет зачáт.

25. Scholem, *Kabbalah*, 109.

26. Ivanov, *Sobranie sochinenii*, 746.

27. For more on mystical interests of Ivanov, see Gennady Obatnin, *Ivanov-mistik*.
28. Andrei Bely, *Simvilizm: kniga statei* (Moscow: Musaget, 1910), 623.
29. Andrei Bely, *Glassololia* (Berlin, 1922), 68.
30. Aleksei Skaldin, "Stranstviia i prikluchenia Nikodima Starshego" in *Stikhi, proza, stat'i, materialy k biografii* (Izd-vo Ivana Limbaha, 2004), 126.
31. Ibid., 200.
32. See, for example, Scholem, *Kabbalah*, 97.
33. Ivanov, *Sobranie sochinenii*, 2, 127.
34. Bely, *Simvolizm*, 494–95.
35. Maximilian Voloshin, *Stikhi* (Moscow: Sovetskii pisatel', 1987), 78.

>   Созвездьями мерцавшее чело,
>   Над хаосом поднявшись, отразилось
>   Обратной тенью в безднах нижних вод.
>   Разверзлись два смеженных ночью глаза —
>   И брызнул свет. Два огненных луча,
>   Скрестясь в воде, сложились в гексаграмму.
>   Немотные раздвинулись уста,
>   И поднялось из недр молчанья слово.
>   И сонмы духов вспыхнули окрест
>   От первого вселенского дыханья.
>   Десница подняла материки,
>   А левая распределила воды,
>   От чресл размножилась земная тварь,
>   От жил — растения, от кости — камень,
>   И двойники — небесный и земной —
>   Соприкоснулись влажными ступнями.
>   Господь дохнул на преисподний лик,
>   И нижний оборотень стал Адамом.
>   Адам был миром, мир же был Адам.
>   Он мыслил небом, думал облаками,
>   Он глиной плотствовал, растеньем рос.
>   Камнями костенел, зверел страстями,
>   Он видел солнцем, грезил сны луной,
>   Гудел планетами, дышал ветрами,
>   И было все — вверху, как и внизу —
>   Исполнено высоких соответствий.
>   Все в преходящем было только знак
>   Извечных тайн, начертанных на небе.
>
>   Мир отвечал размерам человека,
>   И человек был мерой всех вещей.

36. Ivanov, *Sobranie sochinenii*, 1, 782.
> Когда, сердца пронзив. Прозрачность
> Исполнит солнцем темных нас,
> Мы возблестим, как угля мрачность,
> Преображенная в алмаз.
> Взыграв игрою встреч небесных,
> Ответный крик твоих лучей,
> О Свет, мы будем в гранях тесных.
> Ты сам — и цель твоих мечей!

37. Margarita Voloshina, *Zelenaia Zmeia: istoriia odnoi zhizni* (Moscow: Enigma, 1993), 146.

38. Rusinko, "Adamism and Acmeist Primitivism," *Slavic and East European Journal* 32, no. 1 (1988): 84–97.

39. Gumilev, *Izbrannoe*, 393.
> Мне странно сочетанье слов «я сам»,
> Есть внешний, есть и внутренний Адам.
>
> Стихи слагая о любви нездешней,
> За женщиной ухаживает внешний.
>
> А внутренний, как враг, следит за ним,
> Унылой злобою всегда томим.
>
> И если внешний хитрыми речами,
> Улыбкой нежной, страстными глазами
>
> Сумеет женщину приворожить,
> То внутренний кричит: «Тому не быть,
>
> Не знаешь разве ты, как небо сине,
> Как веселы широкие пустыни,
>
> И что другая, дивно полюбя,
> На ангельских тропинках ждет тебя».

40. Akhmatova remembers how Gumilev came to visit her in her estate "and for the whole visit talked about . . . Blavatsky, and theosophical occultism." (Quoted in Pavel Luknitsky, *Acumania: Vstrechi s Annoi Akhmatovoi* (Paris, 1991), 49. For more on the relations between Gumilev and Masonry and the influence of Masonic and Rosicrucian symbolism on Gumilev's works see Yelena Rusinko, "The Two Adams: Gumilev's Creative Personality." (In *Nikolaj Gumilev 1886–1986: Papers from the*

Gumilev Centenary Symposium, ed. Sheelagh Duffin Graham, 239–47. Oakland: Berkeley Slavic Specialties.) See also Nikolai Bogomolov, *Russkaia literatura nachala XX veka i okkul'tizm: issledovaniia i materialy*. (Moscow: Novoe Literaturnoe Obozrenie, 1999) and Miroslav Jovanovich, "Nikolai Gumilev i masonskoe uchenie" (in *Materialy nauchnoi konferentsii 17–19 oktiabria 1991 goda*. St. Petersburg, 1992)

41. The semantic structure of Gumilev's poems contains numerous references to various esoteric symbols as well as the hidden use of Masonic symbolism. Gumilev broadly discussed the symbolism of various types of Freemasonry in his poems, and while in the later poems he often abandoned occult symbolism for Orthodox mystical religious allegories, his early poems display Masonic symbolism as a personally experienced semiotic system.

42. See Rusinko, "The Two Adams," 254. In another poem, entitled "Adam's Dream," the reader follows the history of Adam from his primordial creation through his fall to his final transformation back to the primordial state. The whole history of humanity is seen in the poem as a long nightmare at the end of which the protagonist, "thrown into abyss by the painful light," is finally resurrected.

43. Roob, *The Hermetic Museum*, 165.

44. Gumilev, *Izbrannoe*, 93.

> Тебе никогда не устанем молиться
> Немыслимо дивное Бог-Существо,
> Мы знаем, Ты здесь, Ты готов проявиться,
> Мы верим, мы верим в Твое торжество.
>
> Спеши же, подруга. Как духи, нагими,
> Должны мы исполнить старинный обет,
> Шепнуть, задыхаясь, забытое имя.
> И вздрогнув, услышать желанный ответ.
>
> Я вижу, ты медлишь, смущаешься…Что же?!
> Пусть двое погибнут, чтоб ожил один,
> Чтоб странный и светлый, с безумного ложа,
> Как феникс из пламени, встал Андрогин.

45. Bogomolov, *Russkaia literatura*, 141.

46. For more on the androgynous symbolism in Gumilev, see Marina Aptekman, "Androginnaia allegoriia serebriannogo veka v tekstakh Nikolaia Gumileva i Mikhaila Kuzmina," *Die Welt der Slaven* 2 (2005), 303–22.

47. Mikhail Kuzmin, *Izbrannye proizvedeniia* (Leningrad, 1990), 544.

> Йони голубки, Ионины недра,
> О, Иоанн Иорданских струй.
> Корни Киприды, Кибелины кедры,
> Млечная мать, Маргарита морей.
>
> Вышел вратами, немотствуя воле,
> Влажную вывел волной колыбель.
> Берег и ветер мне! Что еще боле?
> Сердцу срединному солнечный хмель.
>
> Произрастание верхнему севу!
> Воспоминание нижним водам
> Дымы колдуют Дельфийскую деву.
> Ствол богоносный Вечный Адам.

48. Bogomolov, *Russkaia literatura*, 161.
49. Blavatsky, *The Secret Doctrine*, 2, 131. The Sanskrit word *yoni* means the female genitals. *The Secret Doctrine* describes it as meaning "female principles." Compare with Rufus. C. Camphausen, *The Yoni: Sacred Symbol of Female Creative Power* (Rochester, VT: Inner Traditions, 1996).
50. Blavatsky, *The Secret Doctrine*, 2, 131.
51. Nikolai Bogomolov and John Malmstad, *Mikhail Kuzmin: iskusstvo, zhizn', epokha* (Moscow: Novoe Literaturnoe Obozrenie, 1996).
52. Lopukhin, *Masonskie trudy*, 170.
53. Roob, *The Hermetic Museum*, 321; Papus, *Principes de physique occulte*, 41.
54. Roob, *The Hermetic Museum*, 322.
55. G. Sheron. "*Forel' razbivaet led*: The Austrian Connection," *Wiener Slawistisher Almanach* 12 (1983): 108.
56. See Gustav Meyrinck, *Angel zapadnogo okna* (Moscow: ACT, 2002), 112–13.
57. See Isaiah Tishby, *Perush ha-aggadot le-rabi Azriel: me-rishonei ha-mekubalim be-Gerona; yotsei al-pi katav-yad yaḥid* (Jerusalem: Magnes Press, 1982), 49.
58. Bogomolov and Malmstad, *Mikhail Kuzmin*, 97.
59. Ibid., 98.
60. Ibid., 101.

61. Ibid.,112. One should note, however, that the term *Abrosaks* belongs to the Gnostic, not the Jewish tradition, and equals 365 in Greek, not in Hebrew. Therefore, Kuzmin either confuses or is indifferent to the differences between the kabbalistic and Gnostic numerological symbolism.

62. This sort of attempt can be seen not only in this poem but also in other of Kuzmin's texts, for example in the poem "Adam," in which Kuzmin interprets an old alchemical text about artificially created people (*filosofskie chelovechki* in Masonic terminology). Bogomolov comments on the poem "Adam" as follows: "With the help of alchemical conjunction, Kuzmin not also performs a magical action but, first of all, becomes a demiurgic figure, a creator of humans." (Bogomolov, *Russkaia literatura*, 118.) For the original of the Masonic text see Pypin, *Masonstvo v Rossii*, 120–131.

63. Bogomolov also speaks about of the possibility of an anagram in the last line of the poem. He, however, tries to prove that the word hidden in the line is a Hindu word, *lingam*, taken from Blavatsky, and therefore claims that the allegory of Adam Kadmon comes from Blavatsky's theory of Adam/Adami and the Buddhist origin of Adam Kadmon. Bogomolov's argument proves to be far-fetched. First of all, the last line does not have the letter "i" (и), necessary for the word *lingam*. Also, Bogomolov does not explain how the Hindu word and the image of Adam are connected in Blavatsky's interpretation. Kuzmin's anagram is reminiscent of the eighteenth-century Masonic quasi-kabbalistic anagram coded in the title of Kheraskov's novel *Kadm i Garmonia*, which can be decoded as a metaphor for Adam Kadmon: KADM i GarMONiA. (Bogomolov, 162).

64. For example, Blavatsky called the primordial kabbalistic "the language of the Mysteries" and said that: "the Hebrew language helps us to understand the secret key to the universal language of the great mysteries, that we now call Symbolism." Blavatsky, *The Secret Doctrine*, 1, 345–346.

65. See Adam Weiner, "The Demonomania of Sorcerers: Satanism in the Russian Symbolist Novel" and Michael Basker, "Symbolist Devils and Acmeist Transformation," in *Russian Literature and its Demons*, ed. Pamela Davidson (New York: Berghahn Books, 2000).

66. Valery Briusov, *Ognennyi angel* (Moscow: ACT, 1995), 317. For the development of the same trend in Russian futurism see Leonid Katsis, "Iudeiskaia tainopis' i shifry russkogo avangarda," *Lechaim* 7, no. 171 (July 2006), available at <http://www.lechaim.ru/ARHIV/171/katsis.htm>. Last accessed on August 16, 2010.

67. Gumilev, *Izbrannoe*, 114. For the role of Asmodeus in kabbalistic demonology see Scholem, *Kabbalah*, 323. For the role of Asmodeus in kabbalistic magic see Henricus Cornelius Agrippa, *Die Cabbala des H. C. Agrippa . . . Vollständig aus dessen Werke "De occulta Philosophia" und mit der Ansicht eines alten Esoterikers über Schöpfung durch Zahlen und Worte als Vorwort versehen durch Friedrich Barth* (Stuttgart, 1855), 512.

68. Lev Gornung, "Neizvestnyi portret Gumileva, iz vospominanii," in *Panorama iskusstv* (Moscow, 1988), 184.

69. Quoted in Basker, "Symbolist Devils," 402.

70. Gornung, *Neizvestnyi portret*, 71.

71. Quoted in Papus, *Prakticheskaia magiia*, trans. A. V. Troyanovsky (St. Petersburg: Luch, 1913), 37.

72. Quoted in Nikitin, *Mistiki, rozenkreitsery i tampliery v sovetskoi Rossii: Issledovaniia i materialy* (Moscow: Agraf 2000), 101.

73. Aleksei Skaldin, *Stikhi, proza, stat'i, materialy k biografii* (St. Petersburg: Izd-vo Ivana Limbaha, 2004), 207.

Linguistic Mysticism in the Silver Age Literary Doctrine

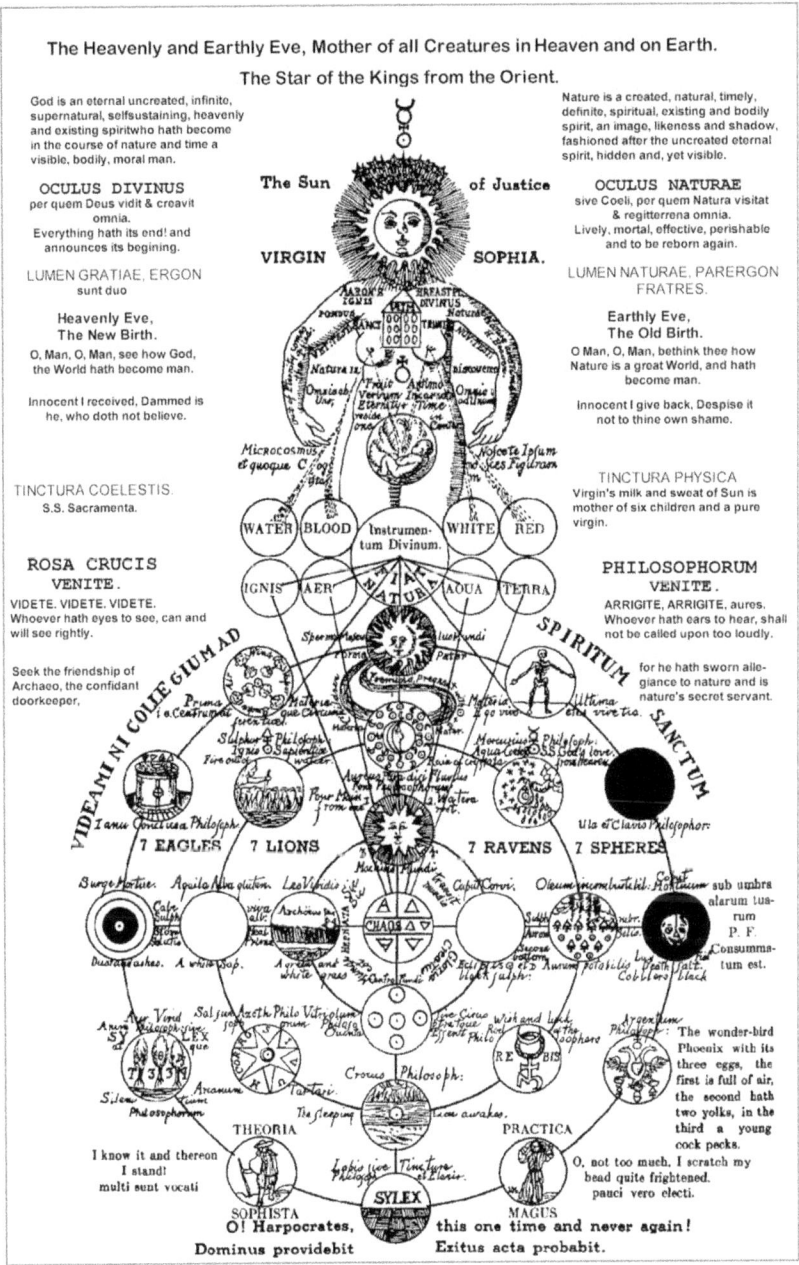

A mystical depiction of Sophia
From *Geheime Figuren der Rosenkreuzer* (Altona, 1785)

Modernism and Kabbalah

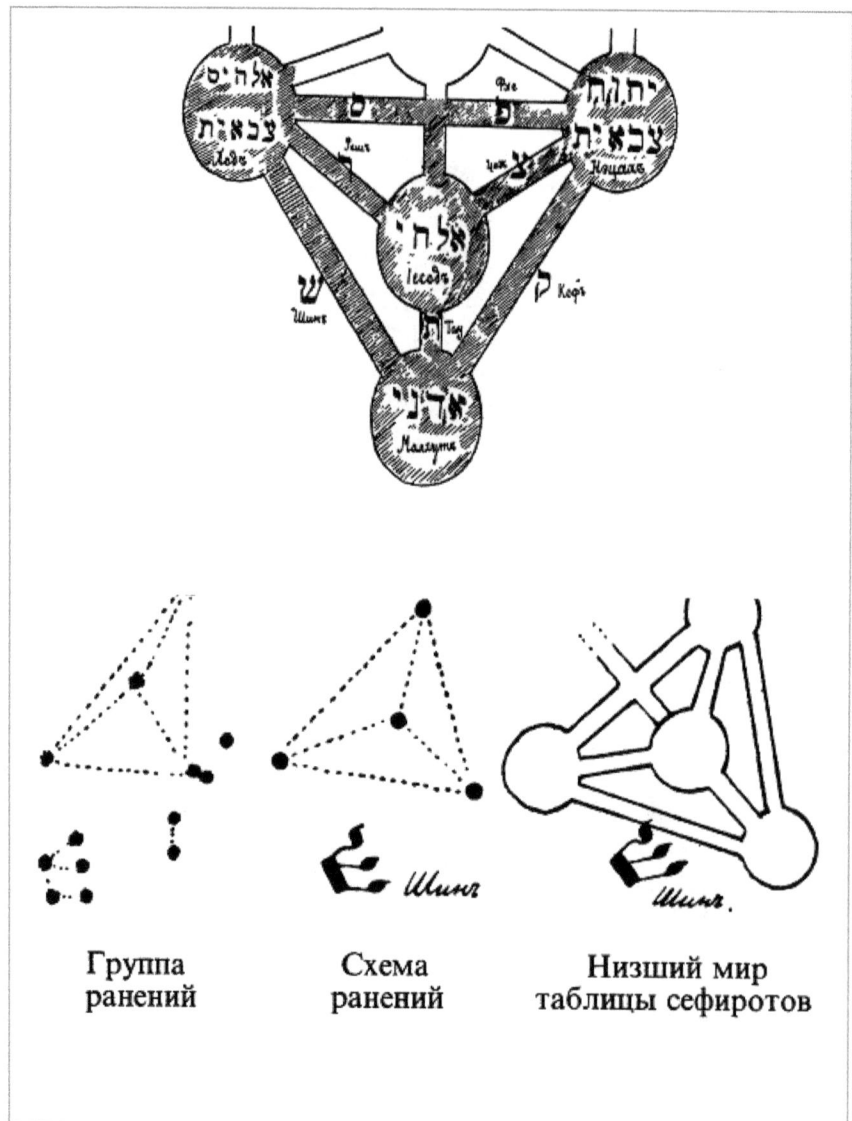

The structure of wounds on the body of Andrei Yuschinsky and its presumed correspondence to the structure of the Tree of Sefirot

(V. Rozanov, *Olfactory and Tactile Attitude of Jews to Blood*)

Linguistic Mysticism in the Silver Age Literary Doctrine

> Сопоставление отдельных уколов с литерами, имеющимися в черже низшего мира сефиротов, дает нижеследующие результаты:
>
> 1) Левая нижняя группа — литера *Шин*
>
> 2) Верхняя левая рана — литера *Реш*
>
> 3) Центральная группа из четырех ран — литера *Алеф*,
>
> (Вышеупомянутая Scriptura Coelestis каббалистов дает начертание Алеф:
>
>
>
> тогда как центральная группа ранений расположена таким образом:
>
>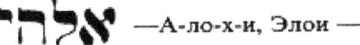
>
> Наконец, каббалистический принцип слова (шемот)
>
>  —А-ло-х-и, Элои —
>
> заключается в начальной его букве алеф,
>
> а слово это находится в центре чертежа низшего мира сефиротов и совпадает с центральной группой ран).
>
> 4) Группа из двух уколов, вправо от *Шин* — литера *Тау* —
>
> 5) Верхняя правая рана — литера *Фхе*.
>
> Сообразно с сим, каббалистическая формула на правом виске убито- получает такое начертание:

An illustration From V. Rozanov, *Olfactory and Tactile Attitude of Jews to Blood* (1914), representing the structure of wounds on the body of Andrei Yushchinsky and its presumed correspondence to the structure of the Tree of Sefirot

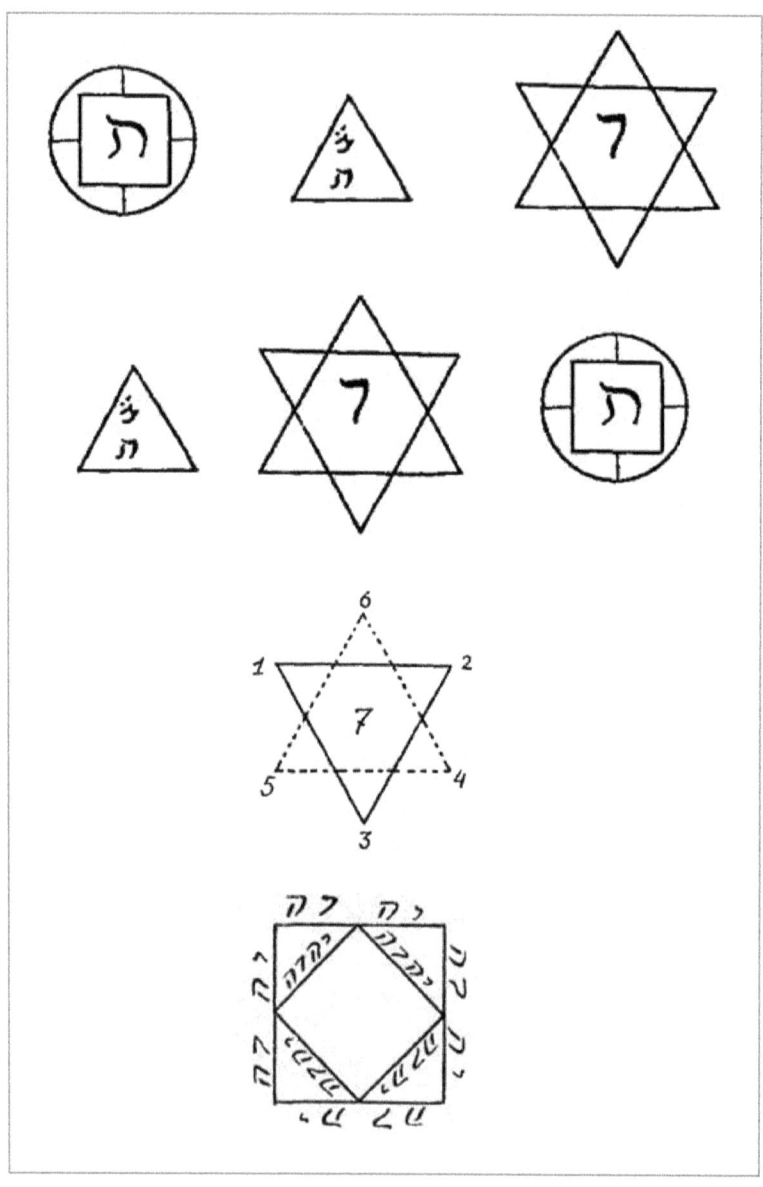

The symbols of "kabbalistic" wisdom: the star of Solomon, the numerological Chariot and the eye of Jehova

Linguistic Mysticism in the Silver Age Literary Doctrine

The title page of *The Encyclopedia of the Occult*

Conclusion

For eighteenth-century Russian Rosicrucian writers, the kabbalistic allegory of the *tikkun-ha-olam* — the reconstruction of the utopian primordial balance — was indivisible from their belief in the necessity of moral and spiritual enlightenment. Nineteenth-century Russian Romantic ideology proclaimed that mankind's ability to return to this primordial unity depended upon the powers of poetic language and universal kabbalistic "artistic science." However, for both the Rosicrucians and the Romantics, the writer's own individual efforts were always linked to a collective ideology founded on the need for social reformation. The salvation of mankind, in their view, was inseparable from the spiritual recovery of the whole universe. By contrast, in late Romantic works, the goals of the scholar of Kabbalah were primarily depicted as completely individualistic. The characters in Russian romantic works of the 1830s were not interested in reconstructing the universal primordial balance, but rather in obtaining primordial "occult" knowledge. These three approaches represent the first three stages in the development of kabbalistic allegory in Russian literature. The literary ideology of the Silver Age combined all these approaches, hence constituting the fourth and the last stage in the evolution of Kabbalah in the Russian literary imagination. The poets and philosophers of the early twentieth century believed that the linguistic mysticism of Kabbalah would teach them strategies to obtain perennial linguistic powers which would enable them to create a new personal world through a new personal language — a world that would be as balanced and complete as the primordial paradise. The two prior Russian interpretations of Kabbalah, magical and mystical, merged

Conclusion

together in the poetry of the Silver Age in an attempt to create a new artistic ideology formed on occult creative principles and humanistic mystical goals. While the means employed by writers in each of these four stages were quite different, their aims remained similar: to recover the primordial Golden Age — that utopian era when mankind had not yet lost its great secret knowledge, when man was eternal, possessed the divine secrets, and stood closest to the God who had created him.

K. Burmistrov notes that, "the main models of understanding Jewish mysticism significantly differed from each other, depending on what branch — classical or occult — a particular thinker inclined towards."[1] Nevertheless, a particular pattern existed, which characterized the development of the image of Kabbalah over the whole course of Russian thought from the mid-eighteenth century to the early twentieth century. The mystical interpretation of Kabbalah usually dominated the end of a century (1780s — 1790s, 1880s — 1890s); then was gradually replaced by the dominance of the occult interpretation (1810s — 1830s, 1910s — 1920s). This pattern may be explained by the fact that the mystical utopianism of Russian intellectuals that brought them to Kabbalah in the first place was strongly connected with the general messianic feelings that usually characterized the turn of the century. As centuries progressed, these feelings gradually receded, and the mystical images and allegories that has once dominated gradually became literary stereotypes void of their true meaning. These stereotypes have, over the course of time, assumed more and more fantastic and distorted form, and finally developed into the image of Kabbalah as evil magic based on "scientific" numerological and linguistic principles — the image that is widespread in Russia even today. Moreover, this occult interpretation provided the grounds for these particular clichés and stereotypes that gradually led to the formation of that particular image of Kabbalah as an "occult force" behind the Judeo-Masonic conspiracy that has been dominating in the anti-Semitic media since early twentieth century up to the present.

Like Theosophy, Gnosticism, and other esoteric movements, the interest of Russian religious thinkers in Kabbalah, and its subsequent reflection in Russian literature, was called into existence

Conclusion

because of the need for an alternative to materialistic positivism. Yet in Russia, as well as in Europe, the main concept of Kabbalah — the image of creation as a linguistic, "literary" process — appealed to the literary world more than any other esoteric idea. Kabbalistic allegory has never occupied a central place in Russian literature. However, the main goal of this work is to show that during certain historical epochs, the linguistic mysticism of Kabbalah, while often fused with other esoteric systems, had a significant impact on both the intellectual climate of the era and the literary imagination of its authors. The understanding of the development of the role that kabbalistic allegory played in Russian literature can help the scholar and the reader alike to clarify many puzzling images in Russian literary works of the last two centuries, to break the established stereotypes and to establish the true place of Kabbalah in Russian literary history.

NOTE

1. Burmistrov, "The Interpretation of Kabbalah," 158.

Selected Bibliography

ARCHIVES:

Rossiiskii Gosudarstvennyi Arkhiv Drevnykh Aktov (RGADA)
 (Russian State Archive of Ancient Acts)
 f. 8 — name of fond

RGA

OR RGB

RSAAA

GRA

RGADA

PERIODICALS:

Isida. 1911–1912.

Magazin svobodno-kamenshchicheskii. 1784.

Pokoiashchiisia trudoliubets. 1785.

Rebus. 1907–1911.

Vecherniaia zaria. 1782.

WORKS OF LITERATURE

Alexandrov [Durova, N. A.]. *Gudishki*. St. Petersburg: V tip. Shtaba otdel korpusa, 1839.

Baratynsky, Evgenii, "Persten'." In *Russkaia goticheskaia proza*, 17–54. Moscow: Terra, 1999.

Bobrov, Semen. *Rassvet Polnochi*. St Peterburg: Tip. Iv. Glazunova, 1804.

Briusov, Valery. *Ognennyi angel*. Moscow: AST, 1995.

Bulgarin, Faddei. *Sochineniia*. St. Petersburg, 1836.

Selected Bibliography

Grech, Nikolai. *Chernaia zhenshchina*. St. Petersburg, 1838.

Gumilev, Nikolai. *Izbrannoe*. Moscow: Veche, 2001.

Ivanov, Viacheslav. *Sobranie sochinenii*. Brussels: Foyer Oriental Chrétien, 1971–1987.

Hoffman, E.T.A. "Tsarskaia nevesta." In *Serapionovy Brat'ia*, part 8, 190-321. Tip. Stepanova, 1824.

Kheraskov, Mikhail. *Vladimir Vozrozhdennyi: epicheskaia poema*. Moscow, 1785.

Kuzmin, Mikhail, *Izbrannye proizvedeniia*. Leningrad, 1990.

Meyrinck, Gustav. *Angel zapadnogo okna*. Moscow: AST, 2002.

Odoevsky, Vladimir. *Povesti i rasskazy*. Moscow: Khudozhestvennaia literatura, 1988.

———. *Russkie Nochi*. Leningrad: Sovetskii pisatel', 1968.

Pogorel'skii, Antonii. *Izbrannoe*. Moscow: Sovetskaia Rossia, 1985.

Polevoi, Nikolai, "Blazhenstvo bezumiia." In *Russkaia goticheskaia proza*, ed. Natal'ia Budur, 253–66. Moscow: Terra-Knizhnyi klub, 1999.

Pushkin, Alexander. *The Queen of Spades and Other Stories*. London: Penguin Books, 1978.

Rozanov, Vasilii. *Sakharna: Oboniatel'noe i osiazatel'noe otnoshenie evreev k krovi*. Moscow: Respublika, 1998.

Skaldin, Aleksei. *Stikhi, proza, stat'i, materialy k biografii*. St. Petersburg: Izd-vo Ivana Limbaha, 2004.

Tolstoy, L. N. *War and Peace*. New York: Random House, 1995.

Voloshin, Maximilian. *Stikhi*. Moscow: Sovetskii pisatel', 1987.

SECONDARY SOURCES

Abrams, M. H. *The Mirror and the Lamp: Romantic Theory and the Critical Tradition*. New York: Oxford Univeristy Press, 1953.

Agrippa, Henricus Cornelius. *Die Cabbala des H. C. Agrippa . . . Vollständig aus dessen Werke "De occulta Philosophia" und mit der Ansicht eines alten Esoterikers über Schöpfung durch Zahlen und Worte als Vorwort versehen durch Friedrich Barth*. Stuttgart, 1855.

Selected Bibliography

Al'tshuller, Mark. "S. S. Bobrov i Russkaia poeziia kontsa 18–nachala 19 veka." In *Russkaia literatura XVIII veka: epokha klassitsizma*, ed. Pavel N. Berkov and Il'ia Z. Serman. Leningrad: Nauka, 1964, pp. 224-246.

Aptekman, Marina. "Androginnaia allegoriia serebriannogo veka v tekstakh Nikolaia Gumileva i Mikhaila Kuzmina." *Die Welt der Slaven* 2 (2005): 303–22.

———. "The Problem of Language and Reality in Russian Modernism: The Conception of *mirotvorchestvo* in A. Remizov's *Rossiya v pismenakh*." *Sign Systems Studies* 31 (2004): 465–82.

———."The Origins of Kabbalistic Symbolism in the Poetry of Semeon Bobrov." *Study Group on Eighteenth-century Russia Newsletter*, 2003.

———. "Kabbalah, Judeo-Masonic Conspiracy, and Post-Soviet Literary Discourse: From Political Tool to Virtual Reality." *Russian Review* 65, no. 4 (2006): 657–81.

Baehr, Stephen. *The Paradise Myth in Eighteenth-Century Russia: Utopian Patterns in Early Secular Russian Literature and Culture.* Stanford: Stanford University Press, 1992.

———. "The Masonic Component in Eighteenth-Century Russian Literature." In *Russian Literature in the Age of Catherine the Great: A Collection of Essays*, ed. A. G. Cross. Oxford: Meeuws, 1976.

Bar-Yosef, Hamutal. "Sophiology and the Concept of Femininity in Russian Symbolism and in Modern Hebrew Poetry." *Journal of Modern Jewish Studies* 2, no. 1 (2003): 62–65.

Barskov, Ia. L. *Perepiska moskovskikh masonov XVIII veka, 1780–1792.* Petrograd: Izd. Otdeleniia russkago iazyka i slovesnosti Imperatorskoi Akademii Nauk, 1915.

Berberova, Nina. *Liudi i Lozhi: russkie masony XX stoletiia.* Moscow: Progress-Traditsiia, 1997.

Blavatsky, Helen. *The Secret Doctrine: H. P. Blavatsky Collected Writings.* Wheaton, IL: Theosophical Publishing House, 1978.

———. *Skrizhali astral'nogo sveta.* Moscow: Eksmo, 2001.

———. *Teosofskii slovar'.* Moscow: Sfera, 1994.

Bely, Andrei. *Simvolizm kak miroponimanie.* Moscow: Respublika, 1994.

Billington James. *The Icon and the Axe: An Interpretative History of Russian Culture.* London: Weidenfeld and Nicolson, 1966.

Selected Bibliography

Bloom, Harold. *Kabbalah and Criticism*. New York: Seabury Press, 1975.

Bogomolov, Nikolai. *Russkaia literatura nachala XX veka i okkul'tizm: issledovaniia i materialy*. Moscow: Novoe Literaturnoe Obozrenie, 1999.

Bogomolov, Nikolai, and John Malmstad. *Mikhail Kuzmin: iskusstvo, zhizn', epokha*. Moscow, Novoe Literaturnoe Obozrenie, 1996.

Buber, Martin. *Hasidism*. New York: Philosophical Library, 1948.

Budur, Natal'ia, ed. *Russkaia goticheskaia proza*. Moscow: Terra-Knizhnyi klub, 1999.

Burmistrov Konstantin. "Christian Orthodoxy and Jewish Kabbalah: Russian Mystics in the Search for Perennial Wisdom." In *Polemical Encounters: Esoteric Discourse and Its Others*, edited Olav. Hammer and C.K.M. Von Stuckrad, 25–55. Leiden: Brill, 2007.

———."Gershom Scholem und das Okkulte." *Gnostika: Zeitschrift für Wissenschaft und Esoterik* 33 (2006): 23–34.

———. "The Interpretation of Kabbalah in Early Twentieth-Century Russian Philosophy." *East European Jewish Affairs* 37, no. 2 (August 2007): 157–87.

———. "Kabbalisticheskaia ekzegetika i khristianskaia dogmatika: evreiskaia mistika v uchenii russkikh masonov kontsa XVIII veka." *Solnechnoe spletenie* 18–19 (2002): 150–57.

———. Khristianskaia kabbala i problemy vospriiatiia evreiskoi mistiki." *Tirosh: Studies in Judaica* 2 (1998): 31–44.

———. "Zametki o kabbalisticheskoi alkhimii." *Solnechnoe spletenie* 12 –13 (2000), available at <http://www.plexus.org.il/texts/burmist_zametky.htm>.

Burmistrov, Konstantin and Maria Endel. "Kabbalah and Russian Freemasons," *Aries* 4, no. 1 (2004): 28–68.

———. "Kabbalah in Russian Freemasonry: Some Priliminary Observations." *Kabbalah: Journal for the Study of Jewish Mystical Texts* 4 (1999): 9–59.

———. "*Sefer Yezirah* v evreiskoi i khristianskoi traditsii." In *Judaica Rossica*. Vol. 2, 49–80. Moscow: RGGU, 2002.

———. "Vladimir Soloviev i Kabbalah: K postanovke problemy." In *Issledovaniia po istorii russkoi mysli, Ezhegodnik za 1998 god*, ed. M. Kolerov. Moscow: OGI, 1998, 104–7.

Selected Bibliography

Carlson, Maria. "Fashionable Occultism: Spiritualism, Theosophy, Freemasonry, and Hermeticism in Fin-de-Siècle Russia." In *The Occult in Russian and Soviet Culture*, ed. Bernice Rosenthal, Ithaca: Cornell University Press, 1997, 135–53.

———. *No Religion Higher than Truth: A History of the Theosophical Movement in Russia 1875–1922*. Princeton: Princeton University Press, 1993.

Cordovero, Moses. *Sefer Pardes Rimonim*. Jerusalem: Hebrew University of Jerusalem, 1962.

Cornwell, Neil. *V. F. Odoyevsky: His Life, Times, and Milieu*. Athens, OH: Ohio University Press, 1986.

———. *Vladimir Odoevsky and Romantic Poetics: Collected Essays*. Providence, RI: Berghahn Books, 1998.

Coudert, Allison, ed. *Die Sprache Adams*. Wiesbaden: Harrassowitz Verlag, 1999.

———. *The Impact of the Kabbalah in the Seventeenth Century: The Life and Thought of Francis Mercury van Helmont (1614–1698)*. Leiden: Brill, 1999.

———. *Leibniz and the Kabbalah*. Cambridge: Harvard University Press, 1995.

Dan, Joseph. *The Early Kabbalah*. New York: Paulist Press, 1986.

———. *Jewish Mystical Books and their Christian Interpreters: A Symposium*. Cambridge: Harvard College Library, 1997.

Danilov, Andrei. *Iwan Lopuchin: Erneuerer der russischen Freimaurerei: seine Lehre von der Inneren Kirche als eigenständiger Beitrag zum Lehrgebäude der freimaurerischen Mystik*. Dettelbach: J. H. Röll, 2000.

Daigen Uri, "Kabbalah in Russian Religious Philosophy: the Impact of Kabbalah on the Russian Sophiological Movement." Ph.D. Dissertation, Bar Ilan University, 2008.

Davydov, Sergei. "The Ace in the *Queen of Spades*." *Slavic Review* 58, no. 2 (1999): 309–28.

De Pasqually, Martinès. *Traité de la réintégration des êtres: dans leurs premières propriétés, vertus et puissances spirituelles et divines*. Paris, 1932.

Faivre, Antoine. *Access to Western Esotericism*. Albany: State University of New York Press, 1994.

———. *The Golden Fleece and Alchemy*. Albany: State University of New York Press, 1993.

Fateev, V. A. *V. V. Rozanov—pro et contra: lichnost i tvorchestvo Vasiliia Rozanova v otsenke russkikh myslitelei i issledovatelei; antologiia*. St. Petersburg: RHGI, 1995.

Fine, Lawrence, ed. *Essential Papers on Kabbalah*. New York: New York University Press, 1995.

Fiene, Donald. "What is the Appearance of Divine Sophia?" *Slavic Review* 48, no. 3 (1989): 449–76.

Fishbane, Michael. *The Exegetical Imagination: On Jewish Thought and Theology*. Cambridge: Harvard University Press, 1998.

———. *The Kiss of God: Spiritual and Mystical Death in Judaism*. Seattle: University of Washington Press, 1993.

Florensky, Pavel. *Sobranie sochinenii v dvadtsati tomakh*. Paris: YMCA Press, 1985–1989.

Florovsky, Georgii. *Puti russkogo bogosloviia*. Paris, 1937.

Garrard, John, ed. *The Eighteenth Century in Russia*. Oxford: Claredon Press, 1973.

Gerrit, Bos. "Hayyim Vital's 'Practical Kabbalah and Alchemy': A Seventeenth-Century Book of Secrets." *The Journal of Jewish Thought and Philosophy* 4 (1994): 55–112.

Ginzburg, David. "Kabbala, misticheskaia filosofiia evreev." *Voprosy filosofii i psikhologii* 33 (1896): 277–300.

Goodman-Thau, E. and G. Mattenklott, eds. *Kabbala und die Literatur der Romantik: Zwischen Magie und Trope*. Tübingen: M. Niemeyer, 1999.

GOM [Mebes, Grigorii]. *Entsiklopediia okkultizma*. St. Petersburg, 1912.

Gordin, Iakov. *Mistiki i okhraniteli: delo o masonskom zagovore*. St. Petersburg: Pushkinskii fond, 1999.

Gornung, Lev. *Neizvestny portret Gumileva: Iz vospominanii*. In *Panorama iskusstv*. Moscow, 1988.

Graham, S. D., ed. *Nikolaj Gumilev 1886–1986: Papers from the Gumilev Centenary Symposium Held at Ross Priory, University of Strathclyde, 1986*. Oakland, CA: Berkeley Slavic Specialties, 1987.

Green, Abraham Yitzhak. "Shekhina, the Virgin Mary, and the Song of Songs: Reflections on a Kabbalistic Symbol in its Christian Context." *Amercan Jewish Society Review* 1, no. 26 (2002): 1–52.

Selected Bibliography

Green, Deborah and Laura Suzanne Lieber. *Scriptural Exegesis: The Shapes of Culture and the Religious Imagination; Essays in Honour of Michael Fishbane*. Oxford: Oxford University Press, 2009.

Grozinger, Karl. "Reuchlin and die Kabbala." In *Die Kabbala und Juden*, ed. Herzig Arno, 175–87. Sigmaringen: Trorbecke, 1993.

Hansen-Löve, Aage. *Der Russische Symbolismus: System und Entfaltung der poetischen Motive*. Wien: Verlag der Österreichischen Akademie der Wissenschaften, 1989.

Hundert, Gershon. *Essential Papers on Hasidism: Origins to Present*. New York: New York University Press, 1991.

Hames, Harvey J. *The Art of Conversion: Christianity and Kabbalah in the Thirteenth Century*. Boston: Brill, 2000.

Hellner-Eshed, Melila. *Ve-nahar yotse me-Eden: al sefat ha-ḥavayah ha-misṭit ba-Zohar*. Tel Aviv: Alma: Am Oved, 2005.

Idel, Moshe. *Abraham Abulafia: An Ecstatic Kabbalist*. Lancaster, CA: Labyrinthos, 2002.

———. *Absorbing Perfections: Kabbalah and Interpretation*. New Haven: Yale University Press, 2002.

———. *Enchanted Chains: Techniques and Rituals in Jewish Mysticism*. Los Angeles: Cherub Press, 2005.

———. *Language, Torah, and Hermeneutics in Abraham Abulafia*. Albany: State University of New York Press, 1989.

———. *Kabbalah and Eros*. New Haven: Yale University Press, 2005.

———. *Kabbalah: New Perspectives*. New Haven: Yale University Press, 1998.

———, ed. *Neoplatonism and Jewish Thought*. Albany: State University of New York Press, 1992.

———. "The Origin of Alchemy According to Zosimos and a Hebrew Parallel." *Revue des Etudes Juives* 145, nos. 1–2 (1986): 117–24.

Isupov, K.G. *P. A. Florenskii—pro et contra: lichnost i tvorchestvo Pavla Florenskogo v otsenke russkikh myslitelei i issledovatelei*. St. Petersburg: RHGI, 1996.

Jacobs, Louis. *Hasidic Thought*. New York: Behrman House, 1976.

———. *Jewish Mystical Testimonies*. New York: Schocken Books, 1976.

Jonas, Hans. *Gnosticism*. St. Petersburg: Lan', 1998

Selected Bibliography

Jones, W. Gareth. *Nikolay Novikov: Enlightener of Russia.* Cambridge: Cambridge University Press, 1984.

Steven T. Katz,ed. *Mysticism and Language,* Oxford: Oxford University Press, 1992

Katsis, L. F. *Krovavyi navet i russkaia mysl': istoriko-teologicheskoe issledovanie dela Beilisa.* Jerusalem: Gesharim, 2006.

———. *Russkaia eskhatologiia i russkaia literatura.* Moscow: OGI, 2000.

Kilcher, Andreas. "Der Sprachmythos der Kabbala und die Asthetiche Moderne." *Poetica* 25, nos. 3–4 (1993): 237–61.

Kornblatt, Judith. *Divine Sophia: The Wisdom Writings of Vladimir Soloviev.* Ithaca: Cornell University Press, 2009.

———. "Russian Religious Thought and Jewish Kabbalah." In *The Occult in Russian and Soviet Culture,* ed. Bernice Rosenthal, 75–98. Ithaca: Cornell University Press, 1997.

———. "Soloviev's Androgynous Sophia and the Jewish Kabbalah." *Slavic Review* 50 (1991): 487–96.

Kraushar, Alexander. *Jacob Frank: The End to the Sabbataian Heresy.* Translated by Herbert Levy. Lanham: University Press of America, 2001.

Kilcher, A. B. *Die Sprachtheorie der Kabbala als ästhetisches Paradigma: Die Konstruktion einer ästhetischen Kabbala seit der Frühen Neuzeit.* Stuttgart: Weimar Metzler, 1998.

Klein Joachim, ed., *Reflections on Russia in the Eighteenth Century.* Wien: Böhlau Verlag, 2001.

Kravchenko, Viktoriia. *Vladimir Solov'ev i Sofiia.* Moscow: Agraf, 2006.

Kurganov, Efim and Henrietta Mondry. *Vasilii Rozanov i evrei.* St. Petersburg: Akademicheskii proekt, 2000.

Leighton, Lauren G. *The Esoteric Tradition in Russian Romantic Literature: Decembrism and Freemasonry.* University Park: Pennsylvania State University Press, 1994.

———. "Gematria in the 'The Queen of Spades': A Decembrist Puzzle." *Slavic and East European Journal* 21 (1976): 455–69.

———. "Numbers and Numerology in 'The Queen of Spades'." *Canadian Slavonic Papers* 19, no. 4 (1977): 417–43.

Lesses, Rebecca. *Ritual Practices to Gain Power: Angels, Incantations, and Revelation in Early Jewish Mysticism.* Cambridge: Harvard University Press, 1998.

Selected Bibliography

Liebes, Yehuda. *Studies in the Zohar*. Albany: State University of New York Press, 1993

Lévi, Éliphas. *Dogme et Rituel de la Haute Magie*. T. 1, *Dogme*. Paris: Félix Alcan, 1903.

———. *The History of Magic*. New York: Weiser Books, 1968.

———. *Iskusstvo vysshei magii*. Moscow: Mir, 1997.

Liebes, Yehuda. *Studies in Jewish Myth and Jewish Messianism*. Albany: State University of New York Press, 1993.

———. *Studies in the* Zohar. Albany: State University of New York Press, 1993.

———. "Zohar-ve-eros." *Alpayim* 9 (1994): 67–119.

Longinov, Mikhail. *Novikov i moskovskie martinisty*. St. Petersburg: Lan', 2000.

Lopukhin, Ivan. *Masonskie trudy: Dykhovnyi rytsar', neoktorye cherty o vnutrennei tserkvi*. Moscow: Aleteia. 1997.

Luknitsky, Pavel. *Acumania: Vstrechi s Annoi Akhmatovoi*. Paris, 1991.

Marshall, Peter. *The Philosopher's Stone: A Quest for the Secrets of Alchemy*. London: Macmillan, 2000.

McIntosh, Christopher. *The Rose Cross and the Age of Reason: Eighteenth-Century Rosicrucianism in Central Europe and Its Relationship to the Enlightenment*. Leiden: Brill, 1992.

———. *The Rosicrucians: The History, Mythology, and Rituals of an Esoteric Order*. York Beach, ME: S.Weiser, 1998.

Mandel, Arthur. *The Militant Messiah or, The Flight from the Ghetto: The Story of Jacob Frank and the Frankist Movement*. Atlantic Highlands, NJ: Humanities Press, 1979.

Malia, Martin. *Alexander Herzen and the Birth of Russian Socialism, 1812–1855*. Cambridge: Harvard University Press, 1961

Mandelker, Amy, ed. *The Supernatural in Slavic and Baltic Literatures: Essays in Honor of Victor Terras*. Columbus, OH: Slavica Publishers, 1988.

Melgunov, S. P. and N. P. Sidorov, eds. *Masonstvo v ego proshlom i nastoiashchem*. Moscow: Zadruga, 1914.

Murav, Harriet. "The Beilis Ritual Murder Trial and the Culture of Apocalypse." *Cardozo Studies in Law and Literature* 12, no. 2 (2000): 243–63.

Selected Bibliography

Newman, William R. and Anthony Grafton, eds. *Secrets of Nature: Astrology and Alchemy in Early Modern Europe*. Cambridge: MIT Press, 2000.

Obatnin, Gennady. *Ivanov-mistik: Okkul'tnye motivy v poezii i proze Viacheslava Ivanova (1907–1919)*. Moscow: Novoe Literaturnoe Obozrenie, 2000.

Paléologue, Maurice. *Rasputin: Vospominaniia*. Moscow: Izd. dev. ianvaria, 1923.

Papus [Gérard Encausse]. *Kabbala, ili Nauka o Boge, Vselennoy, i Cheloveke*. Moscow: V. L. Bogushevskii, 1910.

──────. *Prakticheskaia magiia*. Translated by A. V. Troyanovsky. St. Petersburg: Luch, 1913.

──────. *Principes de physique occulte*. Paris: Bibliothèque Chacornac, 1903.

Parchevsky, Georgii. *Karty i kartezhniki*. St. Petersburg: Pushkinskii Fond, 1998.

Patai, Raphael. *The Jewish Alchemists: A History and Source Book*. Princeton: Princeton University Press, 1994.

Pekarskii, Petr. *Dopolneniia k istorii masonstva v Rossii XVIII stoletiia*. St. Petersburg: Tip. Imp. akademii nauk, 1869

Porus, Viktor. *Germetizm i magiia: Naturfilosofiia v evropeiskoi kulture XIII–XIX vv*. Moscow, 1997.

Prokofiev, Sergei. *Vechnaia individual'nost': Ocherk karmicheskoi biografii Novalisa*. Moscow: Enigma, 2000.

Pratt, Sarah. *Russian Metaphysical Romanticism: the Poetry of Tiutchev and Boratynskii*. Stanford: Stanford University Press, 1984.

Pustarnakov, V.F., ed. *Fridrikh Shelling — pro et contra Tvorchestvo Fridrikha Shellinga v otsenke russkikh myslitelei i issledovatelei; antologiia*. St. Petersburg: RHGI, 2001.

Pypin, Aleksandr, *Masonstvo v Rossii: XVIII i pervaia chetvert' XIX v.* Moscow, 1999.

──────. *Religioznye dvizhenia pri Aleksandre I*. St. Petersburg: Akademicheskii proekt, 2000.

Rabinovich, V. L. *Alkhimiia kak fenomen srednevekovoi kul'tury*. Moscow: Nauka, 1979.

Reuchlin, Johannes. *On the Art of the Kabbalah — De Arte Cabbalistica*. Lincoln: University of Nebraska Press, 1993.

Selected Bibliography

Ritman, J. R. ed. *500 Years of Gnosis in Europe: Exhibition of Printed Books and Manuscripts from the Gnostic Tradition.* Amsterdam, 1993.

Roob, Alexander. *The Hermetic Museum: Alchemy and Mysticism.* Köln: Taschen, 2001.

Rozenberg, Yehuda Yudl. *The Golem and the Wondrous Deeds of the Maharal of Prague.* Translated by Curt Leviant. New Haven: Yale University Press, 2007.

Rosencreutz, Christian, *The Chemical Wedding of Christian Rosenkreutz.* Grand Rapids, MI: Phanes Press, 1991.

Rowland, Ingrid. *Giordano Bruno, Philosopher/Heretic.* New York: Farrar, Straus, and Giroux, 2008.

Ruderman, David, ed. *Essential Papers on Jewish Culture in Renaissance and Baroque Italy.* New York: New York University Press, 1992

⸺. *Jewish Thought and Scientific Discovery in Early Modern Europe.* New Haven: Yale University Press, 1995

Rummel, Erika. *The Case Against Johann Reuchlin: Social and Religious Controversy in Sixteenth-Century Germany.* Toronto: University of Toronto Press, 2002.

Rusinko, Yelena. "The Two Adams: Gumilev's Creative Personality." In *Nikolaj Gumilev 1886–1986: Papers from the Gumilev Centenary Symposium*, ed. Sheelagh Duffin Graham, 239–47. Oakland: Berkeley Slavic Specialties.

Sakharov, Vsevolod. *Ieroglify vol'nykh kamenshchikov: Masonstvo i russkaia literatura XVIII–nachala XIX veka.* Moscow: Zhiraf, 2000.

Sakulin, P. *Iz istorii russkogo idealizma: Kniaz' V. F. Odoevskii, myslitel', posatel'.* Moscow: Izd. M. i S. Sabashnikovykh, 1913.

Schimid, U. "A Symbolist Under Soviet Rule: Sologub's Late Poetry." *Slavic and East European Journal* 43, no. 4 (1999): 636–49.

Scholem, Gershom. *Bibliographia Kabbalistica: Verzeichnis der gedruckten die jüdische mystik (Gnosis, Kabbala, Sabbatianismus, Frankismus, Chassidismus) behandelnden bücher und aufsätze von Reuchlin bis zur gegenwart.* Leipzig: W. Drugulin, 1927.

⸺. *Briefe.* Vol. 1, 1914–1947. Munich: C. H. Beck, 1994.

⸺. *Die Erforschung der Kabbala von Reuchlin bis zur Gegenwart.* Pforzheim: Selbstverlag der Stadt, 1969.

⸺. *Kabbalah.* New York: Meridian Books, 1978.

Selected Bibliography

———. *Major Trends in Jewish Mysticism.* New York: Schocken, 1995.

———. "The Name of God and the Linguistic Theory of the Kabbala." *Diogenes* 79 (1972): 59–80.

———. *On the Kabbalah and its Symbolism.* New York: Schocken, 1965.

———. *On the Mystical Shape of the Godhead: Basic Concepts in the Kabbalah.* New York: Schocken, 1991.

———. *Origins of the Kabbalah.* Princeton: Princeton University Press, 1987.

———. *Von Berlin nach Jerusalem: Jugenderinnerungen.* Frankfurt am Main: Suhrkamp, 1977.

———. "Zur Geschichte der Anfänge der Christlichen Kabbala." In *Essays Presented to Leo Baeck on the Occasion of his Eightieth Birthday.* London: East and West Library, 1954.

Schuchard, Marsha Keith. *Restoring the Temple of Vision: Cabalistic Freemasonry and Stuart Culture.* Leiden: Brill, 2002

Schulze, W. A. "Jacob Boehme und die Kabbala." *Judaica* 11 (1955): 12–29.

Senderovich, Savelii. *Aesthetics of German Romanticism: Two Lectures.* Ithaca: Cornell University Press, 1991.

Sergeev, Viktor. *Pavel I.* Moscow: Amfora, 1999.

Serkov, Andrei. *Istoriia russkogo masonstva XIX veka.* St. Petersburg: Izd-vo im. N. I. Novikova, 2000.

———. *Istoriia russkogo masonstva, 1845–1945.* St. Petersburg: Izd-vo im. N. I. Novikova, 1997.

———. *Russkoe masonstvo, 1731–2000: Entsiklopedicheskii Slovar'.* Moscow: Rosspen, 2001.

Serman, I. Z., G. P. Makagonenko, eds. *Literaturnoe delo Karamzina.* Moscow: RGGU, 2005.

———. *Poety XVIII veka.* Leningrad: Sovetskii Pisatel', 1972.

Sheron, G. "*Forel' razbivaet led*: The Austrian Connection." *Wiener Slawistisher Almanach* 12 (1983): 107–11.

Silard, Yelena. *Germetizm i Germenevtika.* St. Petersburg: Izd-vo Ivana Limbaha, 2002.

Smith, Douglas. *Working the Rough Stone: Freemasonry and Society in Eighteenth-Century Russia.* DeKalb: Northern Illinois University Press, 1999.

Selected Bibliography

Sokolovskaia, Tatiana. *Kapitul Feniksa: Vysshee tainoe masonskoe pravlenie v Rossii, 1778–1822 gg.* Moscow: Gos. publichnaia istoricheskaia biblioteka Rossii, 2000.

Soloviev, S. M. *Vladimir Soloviov, ego zhizn' i dukhovnaya evolutsiia.* Brussels: Zhizn's Bogom, 1977.

Soloviev, Vladimir. "Introduction to David Günzburg's paper 'Kabbalah, misticheskaia filosofiia evreev.'" *Journal of Philosophy and Psychology (Voprosi filosofii i psikhologii)* 33 (1896): 277–79.

———. *Rossia i Vselenskaia tserkov'.* Minsk, 1999.

———. *Sobranie sochinenii.* 9 vols. St. Petersburg: Obshchestvennaya pol'za, 1902–07.

Thieberger, Friedrich. *The Great Rabbi Loew of Prague: His Life and Work and the Legend of the Golem.* London, 1967.

Van der Poel, Marc. *Cornelius Agrippa: The Humanist Theologian and His Declamations.* Leiden: Brill, 1997.

Vatsuro, Vadim. "Sofiia: zametki na poliakh 'Kosmoramy' Odoevskogo." *Novoe Literaturnoe Obozreniie* 42 (2000): 1–9.

Vernadsky George. *Russkoe masonstvo v tsarstvovanie Ekateriny II.* St. Petersburg: Izd-vo im. N. I. Novikova, 1999.

Vital, Hayyim ben Joseph, *Hechal Adam Kadmon.* Jerusalem: Hebrew University Press, 1973

Von Stuckrad, Kochu, and Hammer Olav, eds. *Polemical Encounters: Esoteric Discourse and Its Others.* Leiden: Brill, 2007.

Vurm, Bohumil. *Rudolph II and his Prague: Mysteries and Curiosities of Rudolphine Prague.* Prague: Robert Vurm, 1997.

Vaiskopf, Mikhail. *Pokryvalo Moiseiia: Evreiskaia tema v epokhu romantizma.* Moscow: Gesharim, 2008.

———. *Siuzhet Gogolia.* Moskva: Radiks, 1993.

Wolfson, Elliot. *Along the Path: Studies in Kabbalistic Myth, Symbolism, and Hermeneutics.* Albany: State University of New York Press, 1995.

Wolsky, Nathan. "Mystical Poetics: Narrative, Time, and Exegesis in the Zohar."*Prooftexts*, no. 28 (2008): 101–28.

Yates, Frances. *Giordano Bruno and the Hermetic Tradition.* New York: Routledge, 1999.

———. *The Rosicrucian Enlightenment.* London: Routledge, 2002.

Selected Bibliography

Zaiontz, Liudmila. "Ot emblemy k metafore: Fenomen S. Bobrova." In *Novye Bezdelki*, ed. S. Panov, 50–76. Moscow, 1995.

Zdenek, David. "The Influence of Jacob Boehme on Russian Religious Thought." *Slavic Review* 1 (1962): 43–64.

Zhirmunskii, Viktor. *Nemetskii romantizm i sovremennaia mistika*. St. Petersburg: Axioma, 1996.

Index

Agrippa von Nettesheim (Cornelius Agrippa) 26, 114, 136, 137, 200
— *De Occulta Philosophia* (*On the Occult Philosophy*) 26
Akhmatova, Anna 201, 210, 216n40
Al'tshuller, Mark 64, 68
Alexander I 106, 107, 109, 116–118, 129
Andreae, Johann Valentin 29, 120
Antoshevsky, Ivan 157
Arndt, Johann 49
Azriel of Gerona 23
— *Explanation of the Ten Sefirot* 23
Bacon, Francis 119
— *New Atlantis* 119
Baehr, Stephen 41, 72
Baratynsky, Evgenii 131
— *Persten'* (*The Ring*) 131
Baudelaire, Charles 155
Beaufort, duke 83n3
Beilis, Mendel 173, 175–178, 186n85
Bellarmino 95n114,
— *Lestvitsa umstvennogo voskhozhdeniia k Bogu po stepeniam sozdannykh veshchei* 95n114

Belobotsky, Andrei 122
Bely, Andrei 175, 188, 189, 196–200, 211
— *Glassololia* 196
— "Problematika smysla" ("The Emblem of Meaning") 198
— *Symbolism* 196
Ben Yohai, Shimon 22
Blake, William 35n17
Blavatsky, Helen 158, 159, 161–163, 183n25, 183n28, 184n36, 190, 194–197, 200–203, 205, 214n23, 219n63, 219n64
— "Kabbalah and Kabbalists" 158
— *Secret Doctrine* 159, 197, 205
— "Tetragrammaton" 158
— *Theosophical Glossary* 159, 160
Blok, Alexander 175, 180
Bobrov, Semyon 42, 63–65, 67–69, 74–76, 78–81, 96n128, 111, 115, 118, 165, 166
— *Drevniaia noch' vselennoi ili stranstvuiushchii slepets* (*The Ancient Night of*

the Universe or the Blind Wanderer) 79, 81
— "Liubov' ili tsarstvo vseobshchei liubvi" ("Love or the Kingdom of Universal Love") 67
— *The Mysterious Blind* 115
— "Noch'" ("Night") 76, 78
— "Progulka v sumerki ili vechernee nastavlenie Zoramu" ("A Walk in the Twilight or An Evening Admonition to Zoram") 74–75
— "Razmyshlenie o sozdanii mira, pocherpnutoe iz pervoi glavy bytiia" ("A Meditation on the Creation of the World, drawn from the First Chapter of Genesis") 64–66, 76, 118, 165
— "Sud'ba drevnego mira ili vsemirny potop" ("The Fate of the Ancient World or The Great Flood") 74
— *Tvorenie mira* (*The Creation of the World*) 65–67, 118
Boehme, Jacob 27, 32, 35n17, 49, 55, 85n25, 87n43, 90n60, 108, 120, 147, 150, 167, 208
— *Forty Questions of a Soul* 147
— *Mysterium Magnum* 32, 49, 150
Bogomolov, Nikolai 13, 158, 185n52, 188, 193, 203–205, 207, 208, 219n62, 219n63

Briusov, Valery 189, 210
— *Ognennyi angel* (*A Fiery Angel*) 210
— "Tvorchestvo" ("Creative Work") 191
Brucker, Jacob 50
— *A Short Version of Kabbalistic Teaching* 50
Bruno, Giordano 121
Bulgakov, Nikolai 90n60
Bulgarin, Faddei 137, 138
— *Kabbalistik* 137, 138
Burmistrov, Konstantin 13, 16, 18, 37n36, 41, 46, 69, 71, 81, 154, 166, 167, 169, 172, 186n64, 188, 196, 227
Byron, G. G. N. 129
Campanella, Tomasso 120
Carlson, Maria 181n4, 188
Catherine the Great 42, 44, 57, 63, 80, 83n3, 84n21, 106
"Chelovek" ("Man") 72
Chemical Wedding 29–32, 57, 60, 62, 77, 120, 168
Chubais, Anatolii 12
Cohn, Tobias 149
— *Maaseh Toviiyah* 149
Cordovero, Moshe 36n23, 38n42, 190
— *Pardes Rimonim* (*Pomegranate Garden*) 38n42
Coudert, Allison 12
— *The Impact of the Kabbalah in the Seventeenth Century: the Life and Thought of Francis Mercury van Helmont (1614–1698)*

Index

Cudworth, Ralph 32
Davydov, Sergei 134
Dee, John 27, 44, 113, 140n21, 146, 206
— *Monas Hieroglyphica (Hieroglyphic Monad)* 27, 146
Delakrut, Mattityahu 50
Della Vos-Kardovskaia 210
Derzhavin, Gavrila 42, 96n127
— "Felitsa" 96n127
Diks, Boris 157
Dmitriev-Mamonov, Alexander 107
Donald, Fiene 61
Duke Vladimir 60–63
Durova, Nadezhda 135
— *Gudishki* 135
Eckartshausen, Karl von 98
— *Aufschlusse zur Magie* 98
Elagin, Ivan 44, 45, 47, 51, 83n3, 83n14
— *Explanations of the Mysterious Meaning of the Creation of the Universe in Holy Scripture, which is a key for understanding of the Book of Truth and Errors* 45–46
Eli, Stanislaus Pines 45, 55, 83n9
— *Bratskie uveshchaniia k nekotorym bratiiam svobodnym kamenshchikam (Fraternal Admonitions to Some Bretheren Freemasons)* 45
Ellenberger, Johann Wilhelm (Johann Wilhelm von Zinnendorf) 47
Endel, Maria 13, 16, 41, 81

Fichtuld, Hermann 44, 45
— *Cabala Mystica Naturae* 44
Filosofov, Dmitry 180
Fishbane, Michael 18
Florensky, Pavel 13, 168–172, 178, 179, 185n54, 194, 196, 210
— *Imena (Names)* 170
— *Izrail v proshlom, nastoiashchem, i budushchem (Israel in the Past, Present, and Future)* 13, 178
— "Holy Vladimir" 170
— *Microcosm and Macrocosm* 169
Fludd, Robert 27, 44, 45, 97, 102, 103, 113, 122, 167
— *Philosophia Sacra* 102
— *Utriusque Cosmi* 97, 103
Ibn Fodelia, Samuel 36n23
Franckenberg, Abraham von 27, 32, 37n34, 55, 80, 115, 167
— *Raphael, Oder Artzt-Engel (Raphael: the Angelic Physician)* 32, 55, 80, 115
Gagarin, Ivan 87n43
Gamalea, Semyon 48, 49, 73, 93n98, 95n116, 96n124
Gikatilla, Joseph 38n42, 50, 104
— *Shaar'e Orah (The Gates of Light)* 38n42, 50, 104
Ginzburg, David 163
Gippius, Zinaida 178
Golitsyn, Alexander 108, 109, 139n7
Gordin, Yakov 107
Gornung, Lev 210
Gougenot des Mousseaux 174

— *Le Juif, le judaïsme, et la judaïsation des peuples chrétiens* (*The Jew, Judaism, and the Judaization of Christian Peoples*) 174
Grech, Nikolai 134
— *Chernaia zhenshchina* (*A Black Woman*) 134
Gumilev, Nikolai 158, 192, 201–204, 210, 211, 216n40, 217n41, 217n46
— "Adam's Dream," 217n41
— "Androgin" ("Androgyne") 202, 203
— "Dva Adama" ("Two Adams") 201–203
— "Estestvo" ("Nature") 193
— "Na Venere, akh, na Venere" ("On the Planet Venus") 192
— "Poema Nachala" ("The Poem of the Beginning") 193
— "Slovo" ("Word") 192
Hansen-Löve, Aage 189
Haugwitz, Christian August Heinrich von 70
— *Hirten-Brief an die wahren und ächten Freimaurer alten Systems* 70
Helmont, Francis Mercury van 27, 33, 37n35, 38n43, 167
Hermes Trismegistus 86n28
Herrera, Abraham Cohen de 38n42
— *Sha'ar ha-Shamayim* 38n42
Hoffman, Ernst Theodor Amadeus 127, 128, 143n61

— *Die Königsbraut* (*The King's Bride; Tsarskaia nevesta*) 127, 144n62
— *Die Serapionsbrüder* (*Serapion's Brothers*) 127
Idel, Moshe 18, 35n15
Ivanov, Viacheslav 188, 191, 194–197, 199, 200, 215n27
— "Almaz" ("Diamond") 200
— "Dukh" ("Spirit") 194
— "Tem'" ("Darkness") 195, 197
Karamzin, Nikolai 48
Katsis, Leonid 176
Kheraskov, Mikhail 42, 48, 59–63, 69, 74, 76–79, 170, 219n63
— *Vladimir Vozrozhdennyi* (*The Duke Vladimir Reborn*) 59, 62, 64, 66, 72, 77, 79, 170
— *Kadm i Garmonia* (*Cadmus and Harmony*) 72, 219n63
Kircher, Athanasius 50, 100, 122
— *Magneticum Naturae Regnum* 100
Kliucharev, Fedor 42, 56–59, 61, 62, 64, 68, 88n55
— "Masonic ode" 56, 64
— "Voploshchenie Messii" ("The Embodiment of the Messiah") 58, 88n55
Kornblatt, Judith 164–166, 168
Kriegesman, Wilhelm 50
— *The True and Right Kabbalah* 50
Kuhlman, Quirin 85n25
Kukol'nik, Nestor 135

Index

— *Prince Kholmsky* 135
Kuzmin, Mikhail 188, 204–208, 219n61, 219n62, 219n63
— "Adam" 219n62
— "Basilid" 208
— "Cagliostro" 208
— "Pervy Adam" ("First Adam") 204, 207, 208
Labzin, Aleksandr 117
Lazhechnikov, Ivan 135
— *Basurmane* (*The Pagans* or *Non-Christians*) 135
Leibniz, Gottfried Wilhelm 120, 124, 143n54
Leman, Boris 157, 200, 208
Lévi, Magus Eliphas (real name Alphonse-Louis Constant) 155, 156, 159, 161–163, 175, 179, 182n10, 190, 199, 210
— *Dogme et Rituel* (*The Dogma and Ritual of High Magic*) 179, 182n10
— *Transcendental Magic* 182n10
Levitsky, Alexander 120
Liebes, Yehuda 18
Lomonosov, Mikhail 42
Longinov, M. 41, 43
Lopukhin, Ivan 5, 48, 56, 74, 76, 84n22, 126, 127
— *Dukhovnyi Rytsar'* (*The Spiritual Knight*) 56, 66, 70, 84n23, 157, 206
Lotman, Yury 43
Lull, Raimond 44, 121–123
— *Arbor scientiae* 122
— *Ars Magna* 122

— *Velikaia i predivnaia nauka kabbalisticheskaia* (*The Great and Wonderful Science of Kabbalah*) 122
Luria, Isaac 24–26, 28, 29, 36n23, 38n42, 52, 65, 79
Lutostansky, Hippolytus 174
— *The Talmud and the Jews* 174
Luzzato, Moses Hayyim 36n24
Ma'amar Adam de Azilut 52
Maayan Hokhmah 34n11
Madonna 11
Malmstad, John 188, 204, 205
Martines de Pasqually 33, 52, 66, 108, 111, 114, 121, 155, 156
— *Traité sur la reintégration des êtres* 111, 155
Mason, John 95n122
Mebes, Grigorii 158, 161, 183n23, 200
— *Entsiklopedia Okkul'tizma* (*The Encyclopedia of the Occult*) 158, 225
Mesmer, Franz Anton 134
Meyrinck, Gustav 206
— *Der Engel vom westlichen Fenster* (*Angel of the West Window*) 206
Michelspacher, Stephan 101, 105
— *Cabala* 101, 105
Mintslova, Anna 185n52
Montgolfier, Joseph-Michel 134
Moore, Demi 11
More, Thomas 120
Murav, Harriet 177, 180
Napoleon 107, 128

— 247 —

Neele, Henry 145n88
Nefediev, Grigori 191
Nicholas II 157, 182n18
Nilus 175
Norov, Abraham 121, 143n47
Notes on Kabbalah 70
Novalis (real name G. P. F. von Hardenberg) 106, 108, 109, 111, 114–117, 119, 121, 124, 127, 170, 188
— *Die Lehrlinge zu Sais* (*The Apprentices of Sais*) 114
Novikov, Nikolai 46–53, 56, 58, 69, 70, 72, 75, 78, 81, 82, 84n18, 84n21, 84n22, 85n25, 89n56
"O mire, ego nachale i drevnikh vremenakh" ("On the World, its Beginning and Ancient Times") 67
Ob istorii Moiseevoi, tvorenii mira, i zhizni liudei do potopa (*On the History of Moses, the Creation of the World, and the Life of people before the Biblical Flood*) 66, 67
Obatnin, Gennady 188
Odoevsky, Alexander 129
Odoevsky, Vladimir 119, 120, 121, 124–127, 129, 133, 142n44
— *Kosmorama* 126, 127,
— *Letters from Petersburg: 4338* 119, 127
— *Russian Nights* 125, 142n44
— *Segeliel* 133
— "The Last Suicide" 142n44

— "The Nameless City" 142n44
Olivet, Antoine Fabre d' 162, 170–172, 194, 200
— *The Cosmogony of Moses* 162
— *The Hebraic Tongue Restored* 162, 170
An Oration of the Man of Eziless 52
Ossian 64
Paléologue, Maurice 182n18
Papus (real name Gérard Encausse) 156–159, 161–163, 175, 179, 182n18, 183n28, 190, 194, 195, 199–203, 206, 211, 214n23
— *Practical Magic* 211
— *Qabbalah* 161, 175, 179
Paracelsus 27, 67, 86n28, 114
— *Platonovo kol'tso* (*Plato's Ring*) 86n28
Partridge, John 32
Paul I 80, 84n22, 107
Peter the Great 57
Pichot, Amédée 145n88
— "Ocharovannoe zerkalo: Epizod iz zhizni Korneliusa Aggripy" 145n88
Pico della Mirandola 50, 122, 200
Plato 120
— *Republic* 120
Pogorelsky, Antonii (Alexei Perovsky) 136, 137, 145n88
— "Posetitel' magika" ("A Magician's Visitor") 136, 145n88
Polevoi, Nikolai 125

— *Blazhenstvo bezumiia* (*The Bliss of Madness*) 125
Pordage, John 49, 95n122
Pozdeev, Osip 49
Protocols of the Elders of Zion 175
Pushkin, Alexander 130, 133, 134, 137, 171, 172
— *Gypsies* (*Tsygane*) 171
— *Pikovaia Dama* (*The Queen of Spades*) 133, 134
Pushkin, Vasilii 130
Pypin, Alexander 41, 45, 82n2, 83n2, 83n6, 86n28
— "Masonic bibliography" 86n28
Radishchev, Alexander 48, 60
— *Journey from Petersburg to Moscow* 60
Raimonda Lulliia Kabbalistika (*The Kabbalistika of Raimond Lull*) 122
Reuchlin, Johannes George von 26, 47, 50
— *De Arte Kabbalistica* (*On the Art of Kabbalah*) 26
Riasanovsky, Nikolai 117
Rimbaud, Arthur 155, 190–192
— "Vowels" 192
Ritman, Joseph R. 122
Roob, Alexander 35n17
Rose, Pastor 83n6
Rosenkreutz, Christian 30
Rosenroth, C. Knorr von 27, 32, 37n34, 38n42, 44, 148, 159, 167
— *Kabbalah Denudata* 32, 38n42, 148, 159, 167

Rostopchina, Evdokiia 125, 130
Rozanov, Vasilii 13, 173, 176–181, 186n85, 222
— *Ekhad or Thirteen Wounds of Yushchinsky*
— *The Olfactory and Tactile Attitude of Jews to Blood* 176, 222, 223
Rudnikova, Nina 158
Sabashnikov, Margarita 200
Saint-Martin, Louis-Claude de 33, 46, 52, 55, 66, 108, 114, 120, 121, 141n35, 182n14
— *Des erreurs et de la vérité* 46, 66, 141n35
Sakharov, Vsevolod 64
Schelling, Friedrich 113, 114, 118, 121, 128, 170
Schlegel, Friedrich 110, 111, 114, 124, 128
Scholem, Gershom 18, 24, 52, 196, 212n8
Schott, Gaspar 50
— *The Jewish Kabbalah* 50
Schwartz, Johann Georg 54–56, 64, 66, 78–81, 87n43, 89n56, 117, 119
The Secret of the Jews 174
Sefer ha Zohar 50
Sefer Yetzirah (*The Book of Creation*) 19, 20, 34n11, 50, 171, 190, 191, 197
Silard, Lena 188
Simonini, J. B. 174
Skabichevsky, Aleksander 123
Skaldin, Aleksei 158, 197, 198, 200, 211

Index

— *Zhizn' I prikliucheniia Nikodima Starshego* (*The Life and Adventures of Nikodim the Eldest*) 197
Smith, Douglas 41
Sokolovsky, V. 118
— *Mirozdanie* (*The Universe*) 118
Sologub, Fyodor 189, 191
Soloviev, Vladimir 13, 90n60, 163–168, 170, 172, 185n52, 196, 210
Sozdanie mira po kabbale (*The Creation of the World according to Kabbalah*) 157
Spinoza, Baruch 120, 124
Sterne, Laurence 60
— *Sentimental Journey* 60
Swedenborg, Emanuel 134, 167, 185n51, 208
Tager, Alexander 176
Teophilus 152
— *Schweighardt Constantiens* 152
Tolstoy, Leo 128
— *War and Peace* 128
Troianovsky, Alexander 157
Trubetskoi, Nikolai 48, 96n124, 107
Turian, M. 145n88
Tycho Brahe 140n21
Ushakov, Vladimir 136
— "Gustave Gatzfield" 136
Vaiskopf, Michail 13, 14, 96n128, 118, 133, 145n84
Vatsuro, Vadim 119, 126
Vekselman, Laser 211
Verlaine, Paul 155
Vernadsky, George 41, 43, 55, 64, 83n2
Viazemsky, Pyotr 81
Vital, Chaim 35n18
Voloshin, Maksimilian 198–200, 205, 208
— "Kosmos" ("Space") 198
Voltaire 43, 44, 82n2, 83n2, 106
Voyeikov, Alexander 145n84
Wachter, Johann G. 51, 123, 124, 143n54
— *An Exposition of the Kabbalah or the Secret Philosophy of the Hebrews* 51, 123
Welling, Georg von 55, 86n28
— *Opus Mago-Cabbalisticum et Theosophicum* 55, 86n28
Wilde, Oscar 155
Wolfson, Elliot 20, 34n11
Wollner, Johann Christoph van 54, 84n19
— *The Compass of Wisemen* 84n19
Wolsky, Nathan 18, 19
Yates, Francis 12
— *Giordano Bruno and the Hermetic Tradition* 12
Yeltsin, Boris 12
Yushchinsky, Andrei 175, 178–180, 222, 223
Zohar (*The Divine Light*) 19, 21, 22, 24, 30, 38n42, 60, 160, 178, 197

www.ingramcontent.com/pod-product-compliance
Ingram Content Group UK Ltd.
Pitfield, Milton Keynes, MK11 3LW, UK
UKHW021848140426
5217IPUK00022B/1654